THE FRINGES OF CITIZENSHIP

Manchester University Press

THEORY FOR A GLOBAL AGE

Series Editor: Gurminder K. Bhambra, Professor of Postcolonial and Decolonial Studies in the School of Global Studies, University of Sussex

Globalization is widely viewed as a current condition of the world, but there is little engagement with how this changes the way we understand it. The Theory for a Global Age series addresses the impact of globalization on the social sciences and humanities. Each title will focus on a particular theoretical issue or topic of empirical controversy and debate, addressing theory in a more global and interconnected manner. With contributions from scholars across the globe, the series will explore different perspectives to examine globalization from a global viewpoint. True to its global character, the Theory for a Global Age series will be available for online access worldwide via Creative Commons licensing, aiming to stimulate wide debate within academia and beyond.

THE FRINGES
OF CITIZENSHIP

ROMANI MINORITIES IN EUROPE AND CIVIC MARGINALISATION

JULIJA SARDELIĆ

MANCHESTER UNIVERSITY PRESS

Published by Manchester University Press
Oxford Road, Manchester M13 9PL

www.manchesteruniversitypress.co.uk

British Library Cataloguing-in-Publication Data
A catalogue record for this book is available from the British Library

ISBN 978 1 5261 4314 3 hardback
ISBN 978 1 5261 7463 5 paperback

First published 2021
Paperback published 2023

The publisher has no responsibility for the persistence or accuracy of URLs for any external or third-party internet websites referred to in this book, and does not guarantee that any content on such websites is, or will remain, accurate or appropriate.

Typeset
by New Best-set Typesetters Ltd

For mama & ati
and
the Romani community of Kamenci

Contents

Series editor's foreword

The crisis around the movement of people at Europe's borders is matched by similar contestations, albeit less visible, around the position and movement of minorities within Europe; specifically, Romani minorities. While Romani minorities have not come from 'anywhere else', they have, nonetheless, often been considered strangers among citizens. This is the central argument of Julija Sardelić's stunning new book, *The fringes of citizenship: Romani minorities in Europe and civic marginalisation*. Essentially, Sardelić is concerned to find out why rights, formally guaranteed by institutions at the European Union level and nationally, both fail to protect Roma and fail to address their social and political marginalisation.

Sardelić argues that the processes by way of which the marginalisation of Roma occur are not exceptional; rather, similar policies are in use globally in relation to other minorities. Consequently, she deftly locates the treatment of Roma as marginalised citizens within a broader, global perspective. This is done through the concept of the 'invisible edges of citizenship' where, as she argues, 'marginalised minorities are manifestly included as a special group but yet latently marginalised as citizens'. This distinctive formulation enables her to examine a diversity of experiences within a common framework. More significantly, it points to the ways in which difference is not simply excluded, and also sheds light on how it is constructed as a justification of the exclusion.

In *The fringes of citizenship: Romani minorities in Europe and civic marginalisation*, Sardelić superbly mobilises her analysis of the civic marginalisation of Roma to investigate the concept of citizenship itself. In this way, she addresses one of the key concerns of the Theory for a Global Age series, of which this book is part, namely, to rethink the concepts and categories central to disciplinary understandings from the experiences of those who are rarely made central to such processes. This book is a powerful illustration of the urgency and efficacy of undertaking such a task and the new avenues – political and scholarly – that open up in the process. It is compelling analysis that has the potential to reshape our understandings of citizenship.

Gurminder K. Bhambra
University of Sussex

Acknowledgements

While finishing the book and writing these acknowledgements, I have felt both relieved and uneasy. The journey towards the completion of this book was long and colourful, and it has had its ups and downs. Now, at this stage, I am left wondering if I will be able to properly express my gratitude to everyone who walked alongside me through the different parts of this journey. Whilst I have that famous proverb 'it takes a village' echoing in my head, it seems to me that the journey with this book took me around the world: from that little place in rural north-east Slovenia where I grew up, all the way to New Zealand where I live now. On that journey I encountered many people who will forever be dear to me no matter how close or far away they are.

This book was very much shaped by the fact that I have spent a large proportion of my twenties in the Romani communities of Central and South East Europe, but especially in the Romani community of Kamenci in the region where I grew up. My time spent there has overwhelmingly shaped many of the perspectives I still hold today. I would particularly like to thank Ludvik and Nada Levačić as well as Adrijana Horvat from Kamenci, who I now consider to be family.

This book would not have seen the light of day if it were not for my Marie Skłodowska-Curie Fellowship project, 'Invisible edges of citizenship: readdressing the position of Romani minorities in Europe' (acronym: InviCitRom), at the University of Leuven, led by Peter Vermeersch. I therefore gladly confirm that this book is part of a project that has received funding from the European Union's Horizon 2020 Research and Innovation Programme under the Marie Skłodowska-Curie grant agreement (no. 705768). The book would also not have seen the light of day if it were not for the fantastic team behind the Theory for a Global Age series at Manchester University Press, especially the series editor, Gurminder Bhambra, as well as Caroline Wintersgill, Thomas Dark and Alun Richards.

It has indeed been a long and varied journey getting to the position of Marie Skłodowska-Curie Fellow in Leuven from my days spent in Kamenci. I started thinking about what the position of Romani minorities tells us about our society as a postgraduate. I finished my MA degree in Nationalism Studies at the Central European University (CEU) in Budapest. I would particularly like to thank my MA thesis supervisors, Júlia Szalai and Will Kymlicka, who guided the early development of my own academic voice and who continue to be supportive of my work. The CEU has also brought many friends who have remained with me way past our time spent in Budapest: Nora Wagner-Várady, Emin Eminagić, Alexander Karadjov, Eszter Weinberger, Anja Šter, Ivan Matić, Marina Vasić and, particularly, Karolis Butkevičius. I completed my PhD at the University of Ljubljana under the supervision of Ksenija Vidmar Horvat. During my PhD studies, which focused on how the position of Roma changed after the disintegration of Yugoslavia, I have particularly benefited from conversations and friendship with Miro Samardžija.

My specific interest in what the position of Romani minorities tells us about citizenship was ignited in my first academic position at the University of Edinburgh as a Research Fellow on the CITSEE research project ('The Europeanization of Citizenship in the Successor States for the Former Yugoslavia', funded by the European Research Council), led by Jo Shaw. Besides being an impressive academic, Jo has also been one of the most supportive mentors I have had on my scholarly path. She taught me how to take my first steps into international academia, and I am immensely grateful for that. I am also thankful for the exceptional team she put together when I was at CITSEE, many of whom have remained friends, especially Dejan Stjepanović, Gëzim Krasniqi, Ljubica Spaskovska, Lamin Khadar, Chiara Bonfiglioli, Katja Kahlina, Jared Philippi, Annie McGeechan and, of course, Igor Štiks (who was responsible for introducing me to Peter Vermeersch). And also I must not forget to thank Mr Alph Thomas for making the CITSEE days wittier.

The first concrete idea for this book on the invisible edges of citizenship as well as the proposal for the Marie Skłodowska-Curie (MSC) project came about during my next academic post as a Max Weber Fellow at the European University Institute (EUI). I would like to especially thank my Max Weber mentor Rainer Bauböck for his comments on the earliest drafts of the invisible edges of citizenship idea, among other things. I have learned an incredible amount from him. I am also extremely grateful to Jelena Džankić, with whom I have been connected via both CITSEE and the EUI. She has been a great colleague and a friend. I have benefited from her insightful advice on many occasions, but in particular from her comments on my MSC proposal. I am also particularly indebted to Halit M. Tagma, Adriana Bunea, Eileen Keller and Alyson Price for their comments on my MSC proposal. I have been fortunate to have many collegial and friendly conversations with the Max Weber team (especially Richard Bellamy, who was the Max Weber Director, and Ognjen Aleksić, Coordinator at the Max Weber programme) and have created many friendships and further academic collaborations with other Max Weber fellows, in particular Julia McClure, Zsófia Lóránd, Katharina Lenner (and Cameron Thibos), Fran Meissner, Aitana Guia, Juliana Bidadanure, Sofiya Grachova, Magdalena Malecka, Michael Kozakowski, Peter Szigeti, Guy Aitchinson, Diane Fromage and Diana Georgescu. I have also benefited from conversations with Lilla Farkas at the EUI. One the most amazing things that happened at the EUI was that I met Trajche Panov, who has been my best friend ever since; again, I now consider him family, as he has been an incredible support through the many struggles I have had along the way.

Some of the ideas in this book were also developed during my visiting fellowship at the University of Rijeka, where I discussed some of the analyses (especially Chapter 5) with Sanja Bojanić, Aleksandra Djurasović, Giulia Carabelli, Piro Rexhepi and Jeremy Walton. I had moved away from the book when I started another project as a postdoctoral researcher at the University of Liverpool, working in particular with Helen Stalford and Eleanor Drywood as my mentors. I would also like to thank the members of the EU Law Unit for their comments on earlier chapter drafts. In particular, Stephanie Khoury, Narzanin Massoumi and Nuno Ferreira provided useful discussions about the book and are now life-long friends.

The main body of this book was written with the outstanding support of Peter Vermeersch as my MSC supervisor at the University of Leuven. I also now consider him not only a mentor but a life-long friend. At KU Leuven, I would also like to thank Heleen Touquet, Anwesha Borthakur, Kolja Raube, Kristin Henrard, Ingrid De Wachter, Maaike Vandenhaute and the EU Research Coordination Office. I have received many helpful comments from colleagues and friends on the whole or parts of this book. I would like to thank Peter Vermeersch, Michael Winikoff and Keleigh Coldron for reading the entire developing manuscript. Keleigh has been a fantastic copy-editor for my book who has gone beyond expectations in editing and polishing the final manuscript. I would also like to thank the anonymous external reviewer instructed by Manchester University Press, whose comments have been very insightful and helpful. In addition, my sincere gratitude goes to Fiona Little for her meticulous and patient preparation of the manuscript for the MUP final proofs. I am also grateful to colleagues who have read individual chapters: Aidan McGarry, Stephanie Khoury, Diana Kudaibergenova, Kristin Blainpain, Catherine Baker, Julia McClure, Heleen Touquet, Nuno Ferreira, Rachel Humphris, Ethel Brooks and Gwendolyn Albert. I am extremely happy that I was able to talk about my research also in Kamenci, especially during the workshop co-organised with Julia McClure (who has also offered me enormous support for writing this book in general). I presented an earlier version of Chapter 4 during my short visiting fellowship at the McMullin Centre on Statelessness at the University of Melbourne, where I greatly appreciated comments from Michelle Foster, Christoph Sperfeldt, Timnah Baker and Deirdre Brennan. I presented earlier versions of this book at the 2018 Council of European Studies Convention in Chicago, where I benefited from the comments of Koen Slootmaeckers, Fran Meissner, Jean Beaman and Aitana Guia. I also presented ideas from this book at the 2019 International Studies Association Convention, where I received comments from Karlo Basta and Willem Maas and was introduced to the Yugoslawomen+ Collective (Dženeta Karabegović, Sljadjana Lazić, Vjosa Musliu, Elena Stavrevska and Jelena Obradović-Wochnik), who have been an incredible support while I was finishing the book. I have presented earlier versions of this book at the 2019 Association for the Study of Nationalities Convention (Columbia University), and I am thankful for the comments received there from my co-panellists Ethel Brooks, Anna Mirga-Kruszelnicka and Lucie Fremlová. I also presented at the World Convention on Statelessness and the GlobalCit Annual Conference at the EUI, both in 2019. The book has benefited from discussions with many others such as Can Yildiz, Nicholas De Genova, Eric Fassin, Angéla Kóczé, Huub van Baar, Diana Popescu, Jan Grill, Márton Rövid, Tina Magazzini, Judit Durst, Katya Ivanova, Dominic O'Sullivan, Nick Cheesman and Nyi Nyi Kyaw. Special thanks to Senada Sali, Benjamin Ignac, Samanta Baranja, Sandi Horvat, Tina Friedreich, Aljoša Rudaš, Vinko Cener, Andrej Šarkezi, Bernard Levačić and Nino Nihad Pušija for their support during my fieldwork for the book. I finished the revisions of the book in my current post as Lecturer at Te Herenga Waka – Victoria University of Wellington, and want to acknowledge the support of my mentor Kate McMillan and line manager Xavier Marquez, among others, as well as my colleague and friend Matevž Rašković, who helped me organize the first presentation of the book in Wellington.

As I wrote the final part of this book, one of my closest family members became very sick. I am eternally grateful that they are better now and that all my closest family members are still here with me. I would like to thank my mama and ati (Agata and Dinko Sardelić), who have supported me from my first steps and to whom I dedicate this book with love. I am thankful to my sister Rosemarie and her family Kaja and Branko, and to my second childhood family, the Petkovićes, and Trajche, who is like a brother to me. Thanks also to Judy, Dragon and Dawn. Finally, though no less important for that, besides my parents, my deepest gratitude must go to my husband Michael Sardelić Winikoff, with whom I started sharing life with while this book was in the making. From the first time we met in Liverpool, through our 20,000 km long-distance relationship, to being finally together in Wellington, Michael has been the most supportive, kind and compassionate partner I could have wished for. I owe him more than words can say.

Abbreviations

BIH	Bosnia and Herzegovina
CoE	Council of Europe
CJEU	Court of Justice of the European Union
ECHR	European Convention on Human Rights
ECtHR	European Court of Human Rights
ERRC	European Roma Rights Centre
EU	European Union
EUROPOL	European Union Agency for Law Enforcement Cooperation
FCNM	Framework Convention for the Protection of National Minorities
FRA	EU's Agency for Fundamental Rights
IACHR	Inter-American Commission on Human Rights
NGO	non-governmental organization
NRIS	National Roma Integration Strategy/Strategies
OHCHR	Office of the United Nations High Commissioner for Human Rights
OSCE	Organization for Security and Co-operation in Europe
UN	United Nations
UNHCR	United Nations High Commissioner for Refugees
WeBLAN	Western Balkans Legal Aid Network

Introduction: strangers among citizens

After all, let's be honest, we aren't even capable of integrating our own Romani fellow-citizens, of whom we have hundreds of thousands. How can we integrate people who are somewhere completely else when it comes to lifestyle and religion?

> Robert Fico, Prime Minister of Slovakia, quoted in Romea.cz, 2015

In the autumn of 2015, the European continent witnessed the largest movement of refugees since World War II. Whilst it was first dubbed a 'migrant crisis', by the end of the same year, media outlets across Europe started referring to it as the largest 'refugee crisis' in the European Union (EU).[1] After the Yugoslav wars in the 1990s, EU Member States developed legal mechanisms, such as the Temporary Protection Directive,[2] founded on the idea of sharing responsibility in the case of greater numbers of people seeking asylum in the European Community (Sardelić, 2017a). However, in contrast to these declared EU values, several leaders of EU Member States opposed the accommodation of refugees on the basis that the asylum systems in their countries would become overburdened. These leaders used the populist sentiment of 'putting citizens first' to legitimise their decisions. Robert Fico, the Slovak Prime Minister at the time and the leader of the social democratic party Smer (Direction), expressed this sentiment well in the quotation above that introduces this chapter. Whilst similar to many other statements made at the time,[3] Fico's proclamation was unique in two respects. First, it was not the view of an extreme right-wing populist but of a declared progressive politician.[4] Second, this statement articulated a failure of inclusion as equal citizens for the most marginalised in Europe: the Romani minorities.

Fico's statement points to the central tenet of this book: having equal citizenship status to the majority population has not resulted in equal protection of rights for Roma. Multicultural legislation for minority protection and policies addressing specifically the position of Roma have not significantly contributed to substantive equality. There are three key questions here: (1) why do formally guaranteed rights (in constitutions and other legislation) fail to protect Roma? (2) why does international legislation and policies for inclusion fail to remedy marginalisation? and (3) do these shortcomings only speak to the case of Roma? These questions carry a sense of urgency: the perceived failure of policies targeting the integration of Romani minorities is not only under the scrutiny of (trans)national human rights activists, but is also of interest to extreme right-wing and hate groups who are searching for a justification for why, at best, Roma should remain on the margins of society or, at worst, for how to violently exclude Roma with hate crime (Mirga, 2009; Stewart, 2012; Vidra and Fox, 2014).

Romani minorities, or Roma,[5] have faced societal structures and everyday practices that have marginalised them across Europe throughout history (Pogány, 2012). The contemporary position of Romani minorities in Europe represents an ambiguity in the formation of the EU: whilst Article 2 of the *Treaty of the European Union* highlights the 'rights of persons belonging to minorities' as an EU founding value, the general human rights and special group rights of Romani minorities continue to be violated. Despite their presence in Europe for centuries, Romani minorities have remained on the outskirts of European societies and are marginalised as citizens in their own countries. Roma are mostly citizens but have been constructed as aliens and presented as Europe's own internal outsiders (Powell and Lever, 2015). Romani minorities have not come from 'anywhere else' but have been considered strangers among citizens.

Romani activists around Europe have been addressing ethnic discrimination faced by Roma at least since the establishment of the World Romani Congress (later named the International Romani Union) in 1971 (Nirenberg, 2009; Donert, 2017). However, international organisations started referring to Roma as a marginalised ethnic minority only in the period of postsocialist transitions (Simhandl, 2009). Just prior to the 2004 EU enlargement, the position of Roma as a marginalised ethnic minority was one of the central topics connected to minority protection and human rights (Hughes and Sasse, 2003; Vermeersch, 2003; Guglielmo and Waters, 2005). More recent studies have shown that this was not because the inequality of Roma was completely unaddressed during the socialist period (Sardelić, 2015, Donert, 2017). Rather, previous structures of solidarity and inclusion nurtured under state socialism had been destroyed, and some discursive tropes from socialist systems that equated Roma with 'unadaptable citizens' continued after the collapse of socialism (Sokolová, 2008; Donert, 2018). In the period of the postsocialist EU enlargements, different actors – such as international organisations, European states and civil society organisations – developed a variety of legal documents, policies and initiatives for the 'improvement' of Roma's position. Notable among these are the 2003 *Action Plan on Improving the Situation of Roma within the OSCE Area*, the Decade of Roma Inclusion 2005–15 (henceforth the Roma Decade) and the subsequent *EU Framework for National Roma Integration Strategies NRIS up to 2020*.[6]

Fico made his statement not only in the midst of the 'refugee crisis' in Europe, but also at the end of the Roma Decade in 2015. The evaluation reports on this initiative showed that Slovakia was the least successful state in implementing the Decade's objectives (Kostka, 2018), although other countries too faced significant issues in achieving those objectives (see Brüggemann and Friedman, 2017; McGarry, 2017). Fico's statement came after the 2004, 2007 and 2013 EU enlargements, when eleven postsocialist states, many with significant Romani populations,[7] had already joined the EU. All these states were evaluated as complying sufficiently with the 1993 Copenhagen criteria for accession, which included respect for the rule of law, human rights and minority protection. Nevertheless, Fico's statement did not simply characterise the position of Romani minorities only in his native Slovakia or in just the postsocialist states: EU Member States that joined the European Community before 1993 did not develop adequate minority protection mechanisms for Romani minorities and were also violating their human rights before and after the EU enlargement. France, a founding EU Member State, was accused of violating Article 19 of the EU Charter of Fundamental Rights after it commenced widespread expulsions of Eastern European Roma as part of a crackdown on informal camps in the country in 2010 (Ram, 2014a; Parker and Catalán, 2014; Sardelić, 2017b).

The treatment of Roma as citizens of EU Member States and candidate countries did not significantly improve with the EU NRIS Framework. The integration strategies that these countries developed in response to this framework have not yielded the expected results. In 2016, the EU's Fundamental Rights Agency (FRA) announced that 80 per cent of Roma, who are EU citizens, live in poverty in their own countries (FRA, 2016). Consequently, in 2017, the European Commission called for an audit on how EU anti-discrimination funds had been spent, since they did not eradicate socio-economic disadvantage and discrimination faced by Roma (Stupp, 2017).

Policy reports as well as scholarly studies have shown that across Europe, the position of Roma people continues to deteriorate (Sardelić and McGarry, 2017). Alongside refugees, Roma remain among the main targets for extremist and populist right-wing groups in Europe (CoE, 2016). Whilst latent Romaphobia existed long before that time (McGarry, 2017), it is particularly since 2010 that some of the highest Member States' representatives have found the use of extreme anti-Roma rhetoric unproblematic. For example, in 2018, the Italian Deputy Prime Minister, Matteo Salvini, announced ethnic censuses of Roma in Italy. The goal of these censuses would be the deportation of those who were not Italian citizens. Yet at the same time, he expressed a regret that Roma who were Italian citizens could not be expelled: 'Unfortunately we will have to keep the Italian Roma because we cannot expel them' (Kirchgaessner, 2018). With his populist and openly exclusionary rhetoric, Salvini illustrated a similar point made by Fico earlier: the tension in terms of the politics of belonging did not completely shift to the dichotomy between citizens and migrants, but to the very topologies of citizenship itself (Hepworth, 2014).

As the statements by Fico and Salvini demonstrate, Roma are visible as an exceptional minority in the public space. Romani minorities are also visible as a 'hard case' in policy papers and scholarly literature (Kymlicka, 2002b: 77). In this book, I propose an alternative perspective on the position of Romani minorities as citizens in Europe: I do not intend to conceptualise their position as an exceptional or isolated minority which does not fit in with liberal democratic states and hence is a case of the minority's 'failed belonging'. Instead I aim to scrutinise how, in various European states, legal arrangements and policies on citizenship status and rights produce and maintain the marginality of Roma. Several studies have previously argued that the failure of Romani integration should not be attributed to Roma themselves, nor be ascribed to the presumed incompatibility of Romani culture(s) with liberal democratic societies; instead they have called for a focus on the phenomena of Romaphobia (McGarry, 2017) and antigypsyism (Carrera *et al.*, 2017). Antigypsyism has been defined as follows:

> Antigypsyism is the specific racism towards Roma, Sinti, Travellers and others who are stigmatised as 'gypsies' in the public imagination. Although the term is finding increasing institutional recognition, there is as yet no common understanding of its nature and implications. Antigypsyism is often used in a narrow sense to indicate anti-Roma attitudes or the expression of negative stereotypes in the public sphere or hate speech. However, antigypsyism gives rise to a much wider spectrum of discriminatory expressions and practices, including many implicit or hidden manifestations. Antigypsyism is not only about what is being said, but also about what is being done and what is not being done. To recognize its full impact, a more precise understanding is crucial. (Alliance Against Antigypsyism, 2017)

Carrera *et al.* (2017: 9) argue that the most widely accepted scholarly definition conceptualises antigypsyism as 'a special form of racism directed against Roma that has at its core the assumptions that Roma are an inferior and deviant group'. Taking a parallel approach, McGarry (2017) claims that what he calls Romaphobia has a core of racism similar to that of Islamophobia and antisemitism. However, he contextualises Romaphobia in broader societal processes: 'Romaphobia is a legacy of nation-building and state-building exercises in Europe. The key to understanding why Roma are marginalized across Europe lies in our conception of territory and space as well as processes of identity construction and maintenance' (McGarry, 2017: 7).

For McGarry, marginalisation is then 'a by-product of state making and nation-building, both of which march hand in hand towards a particular vision of progress' (McGarry, 2017: 15). He links marginalisation to the relation between Romaphobia and territory/identity but explicitly signals that his work does not focus on the question of citizenship: 'Romaphobia will unpack the relationship between identity and belonging, but is not principally concerned with the ability of Roma to access citizenship rights; rather, the book intends to shift the focus to antecedent processes of exclusion that have created the context of unequal citizenship' (McGarry, 2017: 35–6).

Whilst acknowledging the importance of studies on Romaphobia and antigypsyism, I argue that instead of looking only at direct and indirect expressions of antigypsyism, we need to also investigate legal arrangements and policies accompanied by discourses and practices in relation to the broader context of citizenship. These may not target Roma directly but are directed at all citizens: they may not be categorised as antigypsyist, yet they end up marginalising Roma. First, whilst I subscribe to the previous conclusions that antigypsyism and Romaphobia do come in covert forms (McGarry, 2017; Carrera *et al.*, 2017: 9), the marginalisation of Roma can also be a product of laws and policies that are neutral and seemingly all-inclusive.[8] Second, I claim that a different light needs to be shed on some policies and laws for the integration of Roma. Member States and international organisations can argue that they have constructed these policies and laws as benevolent for Roma, yet these policies may have adverse effects and contribute to the marginalisation rather than inclusion of Roma. Third, I analyse laws and policies as well as the ways in which state authorities use these laws and policies to justify actions that are clearly racist towards Roma. Here I will investigate official state discourses used to legitimise racism towards Roma.

There has been an emerging consensus that the position of Roma in Europe is a unique one, but can this lead to a conclusion that legal discourses and political practices used for the marginalisation of Roma have also been unique? In this book, I also contest the position of policymakers and public authorities who argue that the status of Roma as marginalised minorities in Europe is unique to such an extent that it is difficult to develop adequate policies for their integration. My claim is that the marginalisation of Roma may appear to be a distinctive European case so long as it is not positioned within a broader context. By scrutinising the policies that were constructed to address the position of Roma, I argue that the processes by which they are marginalised as citizens are in no sense exceptional: similar policies have been used around the globe when addressing the position of marginalised minorities in other contexts within

Western liberal democracies and beyond. The aim of this book is also to situate the treatment of Roma as citizens within a broader, global perspective.

To understand how Roma have become and remain marginalised, this book introduces the concept of invisible edges of citizenship.[9] In my definition, invisible edges of citizenship manifest themselves as unintended consequences of policies and laws that make seemingly unfitting minorities visible. Using a socio-legal approach, I will investigate how the invisible edges of citizenship create what I call the fringes of citizenship: a space where marginalised minorities are manifestly included as a special group but yet latently marginalised as citizens. In the next section, I elaborate how these two concepts are novel in regard to previous discussions within citizenship studies.

Theorising citizenship from the fringe

Aidan McGarry (2017) states that Romaphobia should be discussed from the perspective of broader social science debates and should not remain within the realm of Romani studies. Romaphobia, he argues, highlights the wider processes in which polities and states construct themselves through the concept of territory and identity. This book makes a similar claim about the relationship between the marginalisation of Roma and the construction of citizenship. I analyse the position of Roma and ask broader questions about the marginalisation of minorities from the perspective of citizenship studies. Roma live in different EU and non-EU countries in Europe variously as citizens and non-citizens. The legal statuses of Roma, however, are often exponentially diverse: some Roma are EU citizens who have their freedom of movement hindered (Parker and Catalán, 2014; Sardelić, 2017b); others have multiple forced migrant statuses (such as *Duldung* or the temporary suspension of deportation) in the EU and on its outskirts (van Baar, 2017; Sardelić, 2018); and some are undocumented, legally invisible or even stateless (Sigona, 2015; Sardelić, 2015). All these different legal statuses have something in common: they can be considered precarious citizenship (Lori, 2017) and abject citizenship (Sharkey and Shields, 2008; Hepworth, 2012).

I approach the marginalisation of Roma as citizens from the perspective of global citizenship studies (Isin and Nyers, 2014;

Vermeersch, 2014), understanding citizenship as 'an "institution" mediating between the subjects of politics and the polity to which these subjects belong' (Isin and Nyers, 2014: 1). As Isin and Nyers argue, and Seyla Benhabib (2000) before them, citizenship concerns not only citizens, but also non-citizens who make claims of belonging to the possible future citizenry.

In an age of increased mobility and with diversified legal statuses, citizenship, contrary to expectation, is not losing its grip (Shachar *et al.*, 2017). Instead, the concept of citizenship has undergone significant transformations both in theory and in practice. These transformations have transgressed the previous boundaries of its definition as simply a membership in a sovereign polity. The theory of citizenship, as conceptualised in the classic text by Thomas Humphrey Marshall, *Citizenship and Social Class* (1949), has been criticised by scholars of global citizenship studies for conceptualising citizenship in containment and thus making his theory applicable only to one polity in a specific place and time (Harrington, 2014; Walter, 2014). Citizenship as a concept has been reconstructed within as well as beyond this polity (Gonzales and Sigona, 2017) and beyond the very concept of nationality (Isin, 2012). On the one hand, citizenship has become diversified beyond states because it is also shaped by international and global actors and can be grasped in terms of global studies (Isin and Nyers, 2014); and on the other, citizenship has become differentiated within states primarily with an aim to include those groups previously excluded from enjoying full rights in their own states.

Protection of minority rights, affirmative action and explicit prohibition of discrimination are a few examples of the transformation of citizenship from within. These are interventions that address the subordinate position of marginalised minorities as citizens. Theoretically the debates around these interventions have been conceptualised as multicultural (Kymlicka, 1995) and differentiated citizenship (Young, 1989). In practice, liberal democratic states around the globe have introduced a variety of special rights in their legislation and policies in order to reduce the inequality among different groups of citizens. A number of minorities who have previously been in a subordinated position have benefited from what Kymlicka (1995) calls 'group-differentiated rights' and have been hence more equally included within broader societal cultures. Yet despite the manifest progress in transforming citizenship into a more inclusive endeavour, some minorities remain in a subordinate position even when they have been granted group-differentiated rights in practice. Recent political debates have mainly highlighted inadequate policies for integrating different immigrant groups, in particular refugees and forced migrants, who are not citizens. Migrants have been dubbed multicultural others (Bhambra, 2016: 188). Whilst the official motto of the EU is 'In variate concordia' ('Unity in diversity'), public discourse in Europe has portrayed their others' 'imported multiculturalism' as a threat because they were perceived as incompatible with the liberal democratic order (Bhambra, 2016: 188).

This book argues that it is not just the latest 'newcomers' who face such a predicament. The position of numerous groups identified as national minorities has improved because of the laws and policies attributed to multicultural citizenship. However, there are also traditionally settled minorities in Europe, and around the world, who have been accorded group-differentiated rights and yet are still facing disproportionate scales of inequalities. Romani minorities in Europe, African Americans as well as many Indigenous peoples, experience a very similar quandary and remain at what I call the *fringes of citizenship*.

Earlier theoretical debates have categorised Roma as not fitting the ideal types of multicultural citizenship, such as either 'national minorities' or 'migrants', but claimed that they have certain similarities with the African Americans in the US (Kymlicka, 2002a: 365). The statuses of Roma in different countries were seen as too diverse to be compared to any other possible ideal type category: 'the Roma will probably have to negotiate a new status within each country, and this status may indeed differ dramatically depending on the size, history, internal diversity, and cultural retention of the various Romani communities within each country. There are no Western models for this complicated process' (Kymlicka, 2002b: 76).

Some scholars have subsequently agreed that the position of Romani minorities is so diverse that it cannot be categorised in terms of ideal types of multicultural citizenship: 'It is simply not possible to fit the Roma into the homogeneous and constitutive community model and thus they tend to be excluded from such theoretical remodelling' (O'Nions, 2015: 147). However, in the later attempts to classify Roma in terms of ideal minority type, other authors have labelled them non-territorial (Klímová-Alexander, 2007), transnational (McGarry, 2010) and trans-border (Rövid, 2011a), and have even showed how they were constructed as a stateless minority (Jenne, 2000). Such categorisations have very real effects when it comes to granting certain rights but, as I show in this book, even more so when it comes to restricting them (freedom of movement or rights on the basis of territory, for example). Whilst Western European states did not offer an ideal type model for Romani integration – despite the fact that Romani minorities were citizens in Western European states such as Spain, France and the UK, for example, long before the postsocialist EU enlargement – they did apply similar discriminatory measures to Roma as the postsocialist EU Member States (Parker, 2012; Ram, 2014b; Sardelić, 2017b) despite being 'models' for the rule of law, human rights and minority protection.

Theories of multicultural and differentiated citizenship have highlighted the importance of the diversification of universal citizenship to accord special rights to marginalised groups. For some, other types of diversified citizenship statuses have appeared to further restrict the rights of marginalised minorities: Roma have been categorised as semi-citizens (Cohen, 2009) and abject citizens (Hepworth, 2012) as they do have the citizenship status, but not necessarily the rights associated with that status. Notions of citizenship have been developed within and beyond states in the form of topologies: 'a topological approach emphasised the proliferation of inside-out and outside-in positions that are produced through the act of delimiting the border' (Hepworth, 2014: 112).

Examining the positions of Roma through the lens of citizenship studies has been a fruitful endeavour over the last few decades. There have been two main focuses within this work: (1) on Romani activism (Vermeersch, 2005; McGarry, 2010); and (2) on Romani migrants (Aradau *et al.*, 2013; Çağlar and Mehling, 2013; Faure Atger, 2013). On Romani activism, in 2018 alone there were at least three books published on this subject (Corradi, 2018; Kóczé *et al.*, 2018; Beck and Ivansiuc, 2018). These scholarly debates also included the much-neglected voices of Romani female scholars and activists (Matache, 2018; Kóczé, 2018; Kurtić and Jovanović, 2018;

Mirga-Kruszelnicka, 2018). On Romani migrants, in the last decade alone there have been at least four journal special issues focusing on the position of Romani migrants (see Sigona and Vermeersch, 2012; Yuval-Davis *et al.*, 2017; Yildiz and De Genova, 2018; Durst and Nagy, 2018) as well several edited volumes (Pusca, 2012; Matras and Leggio, 2018; Magazzini and Piemontese, 2019).

Whilst acknowledging the importance of Romani activism and the study of migration, I shift the focus in this book to civic marginalisation for a number of reasons. First, migration of Roma has been an important phenomenon, but the overwhelming amount of literature on Romani migrants gives an impression that most Roma migrate, which is not the case (Sardelić, 2019a). Available data indicate that most Roma do not migrate, but their migration has been of particular interest to policymakers and the media. The 'category of practice' (that is, the focus of the public discourse on Romani migrants) has been converted into a 'category of analysis' (Brubaker, 2012). Second, the scholarly literature has rightly stressed the importance of Romani activism. However, there has been less discussion on how Roma contest the invisible edges of citizenship as non-activists in their everyday lives (Sigona, 2015; Sardelić, 2017b; Humphries, 2019). Third, there is an assumption that within the struggles on citizenship fringes, there are activists contesting the invisible edges of citizenship, whilst the side of law and policies remains static. In the case of Romani minorities, very few studies have shown that this is not the case (van Baar, 2017; Magazzini, 2017; Kostka, 2018). It is also the policymakers and state representatives who interpret and apply the law and policies through 'acts of sovereignty' (Nyers, 2006). It is through enacted laws and policies that they can either enhance marginalisation or contest it.

This book highlights a different angle to performative citizenship (Isin, 2017): that is, how dominant groups maintain their position through the invisible edges of citizenship and contribute to the marginalisation of other citizens. I do not treat Roma as the object of my research nor do I intend to speak on their behalf. Such approaches towards Roma most often reinforce antigypsyist ideologies. However, it is necessary to highlight that concepts like citizenship are the main building blocks of our society with great potential to result in diametrically opposing outcomes: they can lead to more equality or to more marginalisation. Most studies have highlighted how Roma are marginalised along ethnic or socio-economic lines. This book looks specifically at civic marginalisation, which, as David Owen (2013: 328–9) notes, refers 'to the phenomenon of being (or becoming) marginal relative to the abstract norm of equal membership in the democratic state as that norm is concretely instantiated in the figure of the national citizen'. In contrast to Owen, I do not primarily analyse civic marginalisation of migrants, but that of minority citizens, who may in some instances be migrants. However, the 'abstract norm of equal membership in the democratic state' and the question of how citizens of Romani background are critically excluded from this equal membership are at the heart of the analysis. I base the understanding of civic marginalisation on previous intersectional approaches: these do not necessarily refer only to ethnic self-identification or class categorisation. Roma who are not socio-economically deprived or direct targets of ethnic discrimination can still be marginalised as citizens.[10]

The book highlights the cleavages that citizenship regimes create and that contribute to the continued marginalisation of certain minorities. These minorities are perceived as not fitting the liberal citizenship ideal. A number of political theorists have shown that 'colour-blind' liberal conceptions of citizenship are not universal but merely provide a specific outlook from certain cultures that fails to include culturally different minorities (see Taylor, 1994). This book goes a step further. It introduces the concept of the invisible edges of citizenship that seem neutral or even beneficial to margin-alised minorities but, in fact, do not simply exclude the difference, but actively construct it in order to justify the exclusion. In this way, invisible edges of citizenship produce marginalisation not as a by-product of the citizenship concept, but as something that exists at its very core. In other words, the marginalisation and the difference that are in practice incompatible with the ideal notion of citizenship are not simply out there but are created and re-created within it. The aim of this book is to investigate the invisible edges of citizenship and not to create a new ideal type in which Roma would fit.

Instead of attempting to categorise Roma in different ideal types, the book shifts the focus to citizenship itself: it is the way citizenship is constructed in different states that positions the Roma as unfitting, and epistemic violence (Spivak, 1988) redraws the boundaries of citizenship (Mezzazdra and Neilson, 2013; van Baar, 2017) and reinforces civic marginalisation. Following Taylor (1994) on his discussion of the politics of recognition, I challenge the understanding that Roma simply do not fit the liberal notion of citizenship or that their culture is foreign and hence incompatible with it. Multicultural citizenship as it manifests itself in practice creates the invisible edges of citizenship and positions certain marginalised minorities on the fringes. In each chapter of this book, I highlight an example of these edges and the kind of fringes they create. I also show parallels with other marginalised minorities to illustrate that the position of Roma is not exceptional when it comes to practices of exclusion.

The fringes of citizenship are positionalities shaped by *invisible edges of citizenship*. The citizenship fringe is a space where marginalised minorities find themselves. It is a space of an alleged paradox: marginalised minorities in this space have a number of group-specific rights, yet are not equal citizens as their universal citizenship rights are continually violated. The position of these minorities seems to be at the same time visible and invisible. Their position is both over-addressed and under-addressed. Their rights seem manifestly over-protected, but they are at the same time latently under-protected. The fringes of citizenship are not a static and fixed space. They resonate with the performative notion of citizenship as developed by Engin Isin (2017). The fringes of citizenship have multiple manifestations in society: at the fringes of citizenship, marginalised minorities readdress the notion of citizenship as activist citizens through political action that subverts the current system (Isin, 2009). However, I argue that the subversion of citizenship does not happen only through what is usually perceived as the political action (protests and social movement) of manifestly activist citizens, but also includes more everyday mundane acts (Sardelić, 2017b). The inclusion of these practices shows that the repertoire of citizenship subversion is much broader than previously thought and that marginalised minorities cannot be considered apolitical even when they do not fall neatly within the definition of activist citizens (Bhambra, 2015: 104). At the same time, the book shows that it is not only marginalised minorities who subvert citizenship, but that through different interpretations of citizenship laws and policies (and their selective application in practice), the state authorities and the majority population can also either reinforce the invisible edges of citizenship or undermine them.

Socio-legal analysis of civic marginalisation and the approach of connected sociologies

This book offers a socio-legal enquiry into the civic marginalisation of Romani minorities. It seeks to show that similar invisible edges of citizenship have been applied through laws and policies for other marginalised citizens around the globe. Distinct from doctrinal legal research, the socio-legal method is an interdisciplinary approach which focuses on law as a social phenomenon (Cownie and Bradney, 2013). Whilst law can be seen as a set of abstract norms, it is not created in a vacuum but represents a battlefield moulded in a particular context (Wheeler and Thomas, 2000). It is usually understood that 'socio' in the term 'socio-legal' represents a sociological approach. However, it could also mean that it takes a variety of approaches from different social sciences as well as humanities: besides sociology, law can be analysed from the perspective of political sciences, international relations, cultural studies and even anthropology. In relation to the initial commitment of socio-legal studies to deconstructing global power relations (Harrington and Manji, 2017), in this book I take the approach of connected sociologies (Bhambra, 2014) and apply it to the analysis of law and policies that contribute to the marginalisation of Roma as citizens within Europe. The aim of such analysis is to go beyond fitting minorities into ideal types:

> In standard accounts of ideal types, the consequence is a plurality of processes that are disconnected precisely because the function of ideal types is to separate some events and "entities" from others and to represent their internal relationship, thereby making other entities and events mere contingencies from the perspective of those relations. (Bhambra, 2014: 4)

This book takes an approach to the study of citizenship similar to that of Bhambra (2015: 104), who examined 'claims on citizenship where particular connections have been denied by the dominant group, both historically and conceptually, in terms of their very definition of what constitutes citizenship'. Following the approach of connected sociologies and by highlighting the predicament of marginalised citizens in Europe, the book makes a theoretical enquiry into the paradoxes around citizenship that construct exclusion when it should be offering all-encompassing inclusion.

Connected sociologies 'seek to reconstruct theoretical categories – their relations and objects – to create new understandings and transform previous ones' (Bhambra, 2014: 4). In this book, for example, I oppose the understanding of the marginalised position of Romani minorities as a postsocialist problem. Instead, I look at the interconnectedness of international and global interventions in the transforming spaces in Europe after the fall of the Berlin Wall and EU enlargement. Whilst the connected sociologies approach was previously applied to show interconnectedness between different global regions, this book claims that a similar approach should be taken when considering different regions within Europe itself and its diverse citizenry. Instead of looking at Europe as two separate entities, the 'old' democracies in the West and the new postsocialist democracies in the East, it looks at how different ideas about the treatment of Roma are transferred across both. Some authors have previously argued that the position of Roma should be explored through the lens of postcolonial theory (Trehan and Kóczé, 2009). Others argue that after EU enlargement, it is more fruitful to look at the postsocialist citizenship regimes through the lens of postcolonial citizenship (Rigo, 2005). However, a comprehensive study of how Romani minorities are positioned as marginalised citizens in Europe is still lacking.

This book provides a theoretical intervention on the position of Roma in Europe from a global citizenship studies perspective. Nevertheless, I do not intend to compare different positions of marginalised minorities *per se* to show how Roma do not fit either traditional national minorities or Indigenous groups. Instead of examining the position of Roma as a single ambiguity for (supra-) national citizenship in Europe, the book turns to the common invisible edges of citizenship that different marginalised minorities face around the globe as citizens. It maps these invisible edges through a variety of case studies of civic marginalisation, from Roma in Europe to African Americans in the US and Indigenous people in other anglophone settler states. In recent years, scholarly research has highlighted the similarities between Indigenous people and Roma in Europe (see Armillei and Lobo (2017) and Taylor *et al.* (2018) on Indigenous Australians and Roma, and Takacs (2017) on the over-representation of Roma and New Zealand Māori in prisons) as well as Roma and African Americans (Chang and Rucker-Chang, 2020). However, such a comparison from the perspective of citizenship studies is yet to be conducted.

The various case studies presented in this book show the specificities of the positions of different marginalised minorities. Investigating the invisible edges of citizenship offers a parallel insight into how these minorities become marginalised. There are not only parallels between the different positions of marginalised minorities around the globe, including in Europe, but also an interconnectedness in the ways different citizenship regimes construct and address their marginalisation. Similar invisible edges of citizenship that marginalise Roma, Indigenous people, and African Americans exist globally not only for migrant populations, but also for traditionally settled citizens who have been designated as not belonging to the mainstream citizenry. They are positioned on the fringes of citizenship. Yet it is at the fringes of citizenship that the struggles for redefining citizenship occur. I will show that Romani minorities face invisible edges of citizenship similar to those faced by Indigenous people and African Americans when they redefine the core of citizenship status, rights and belonging (Joppke, 2007). Certain developmental approaches primarily established in Europe to deal with the 'developing world' are being imported back to Europe to deal with its own marginalised populations in the process of EU enlargement. The ideas behind marginalisation, as well as the resistance to it, circulate back and forth between Europe and other continents to be (re)used again in this context.

Outline of the book

Chapter 1 discusses the naming and counting of Romani minorities and approaches towards Roma as minority citizens in different EU Member States and candidate countries. Since the 1990s, international organisations have described Roma as 'living scattered all over Europe, not having a country to call their own, they are a true European minority, but one that does not fit into the definitions of national or linguistic minorities' (CoE, 1993). Whilst in the first part of the chapter I look at national legislation on minority protection, in the latter half I examine the reports of the Council of Europe (CoE) and the European Commission to analyse how they describe Roma as a transnational minority. I highlight how the documents of European international organisations use developmental discourse to describe the position of Roma in Europe that is similar to the narrative of the United Nations (UN) on Indigenous people. I argue that the invisible edges of citizenship that have manifested themselves as perceived non-territorialism and alleged underdevelopment of Roma have contributed to a lesser scope of minority rights in some contexts. Finally, the chapter studies the interplay between international and national law in the context of defining the status of Indigenous people. It looks at the invisible edges of citizenship for Indigenous people in Australia, Canada and the US in the wake of the creation of the UN Declaration on the Rights of Indigenous Peoples (2007). It shows that both Roma in Europe and Indigenous people in the four settler colonial states found themselves on the fringes of citizenship where states highlighted their positions as minority groups but at the same time made them invisible as citizens.

Chapter 2 scrutinises the connection between the right to territoriality and the mobility of marginalised minorities. I particularly look at how the perception of Roma as a 'deviant culture' (in particular nomadism) contributes to the forceful restriction of their rights (such as the right to free movement). The chapter first examines the cases of free movement restriction of Roma in the socialist period as a means of inclusion within the socialist citizenry. Second, by analysing the Court of Justice of the European Union (CJEU) case *Dano v. Jobcenter Leipzig* (Case C–333/13, 2014), it pinpoints the invisible edges of citizenship: whilst the court case is seemingly neutral as it does not mention Roma, different states took it to limit the rights of Roma, who are EU citizens. State authorities limit Romani freedom of movement because they construct Roma as a security threat (van Baar, 2017). Third, it looks at the restricted mobility rights of Roma who are citizens of EU candidate countries. This chapter argues that all these cases should be seen not simply in terms of the right to mobility, but in terms of the rights certain groups have on particular territories. It then examines whether there are any similarities in relation to territory and mobility in the case of Indigenous people in Australia. Although both of these groups have rights on the territory where they live, their claims have been suspended when they have been in conflict either with the sovereignty of the states or with the economic interests of the states (as in the case of the Intervention in the Northern Territory in Australia). The chapter concludes that freedom of movement and territorial rights are two sides of the same coin: it is the states that grant or restrict them, and this leads to the positioning of marginalised minorities at the fringes of citizenship.

Chapter 3 focuses on the 'making of citizens' through education. Education in liberal democracies represents a possible corrective mechanism for inequalities among future citizens. Children from disadvantaged backgrounds should get an equal chance of inclusion into society through the education system. However, I argue that in practice education can also be structured in such a way that it actively creates the fringes of citizenship. Using an intersectional reading, this chapter analyses how states justify the school segregation of Romani children as a legitimate measure. It looks at four European Court of Human Rights (ECtHR) cases of school segregation in Europe – *D.H. and Others v. Czech Republic* (2007), *Sampanis and Others v. Greece* (2008), *Oršuš and Others v. Croatia* (2010) and *Sampani and Others v. Greece* (2012) – to argue that state discourses either denied the existence of segregation or portrayed it as a beneficial measure that would allow Romani children to 'catch up' with the majority language. The chapter compares these cases with the reasoning present in US court cases on African American children and school segregation. It shows that in the US case segregation was legal on paper, whilst in the European cases segregation was prohibited. Still, in both cases segregation remains as one of the fringes of citizenship both for Roma and African American children.

Chapter 4 looks at the position of Roma without access to citizenship: those who are stateless. A total of 75 per cent of stateless people belong to minority groups, according to the United Nations High Commissioner for Refugees (UNHCR) (2020). However, not all minorities are equally vulnerable to statelessness. Whilst most stateless minorities have no access to political rights, some do have a broad range of economic and social rights. For example, Russian speakers in the Baltic states are politically marginalised but are not at the fringes of citizenship when it comes to their socio-economic rights. However, other minorities, such as some Roma, cannot prove their citizenship and so have no rights granted whatsoever. They find themselves in a space in between (Sardelić, 2015; Lori, 2017) where they do not fit either the definition of citizen or the definition of a stateless person. I call this position a total infringement of citizenship. The chapter argues that Romani individuals not only are passive observers of this infringement, but they create alternative ways to access rights denied by states (Sigona, 2015; Sardelić 2017b). It explores how states hinder access to citizenship for certain minorities through citizenship laws and other legislation. The chapter argues that statelessness is always a product of state intervention rather than of the lack of it or the lack of interest of stateless minorities in regularising their status. To examine this, the chapter first scrutinises cases where Romani individuals have found their access to citizenship hindered (such as the cases of Yugoslav and Czechoslovak disintegration and in the migratory context where they migrate into other European countries, such as Italy). It then compares the position of stateless Roma with the positions of other stateless minorities around the globe, such as Rohingya from Myanmar, residents of Haitian descent in the Dominican Republic and the children of the 'Windrush generation' in the UK. The question of whether the creation of statelessness in liberal democracies is ultimately different from that in less democratic states (such as Myanmar) is also raised.

The penultimate chapter looks at how states address Roma as (active) citizens and how Roma reconstruct citizenship at its fringes as activist citizens. It exposes how fringes are created by states, by international organisations and through the everyday practices of majority populations. However, the main body of the chapter explores another meaning of the fringe: marginalised minorities on the fringe also subvert and reconstruct the core understanding of citizenship from this fringe. These acts are not necessarily only activism but also include everyday mundane practices that carry the potential of political action. I name this form of enactment citizenship sabotage.

The concluding chapter summarises the main findings of all the previous chapters so as to theoretically grasp the invisible edges of citizenship and the fringes of citizenship. It concludes that in order to understand marginalisation further research on the structural mechanisms leading to marginalisation needs to be conducted. The conclusion rejects the claim that marginalisation is incidental and directly points to the mechanisms that produce it. It also rejects the claim that Roma and other marginalised minorities are themselves to blame for marginalisation, discrimination and their exclusion from society, where they should be included as citizens. It discards the claim that Roma are just passive observers of their position. Rather, they do address it and subvert it: the subversion at the fringes of citizenship, I argue, also carries the potential for the reconstruction of citizenship itself to become truly inclusive and without invisible edges. The conclusion also identifies some critical policy guidelines on how the invisible edges of citizenship could be avoided in the future.

Notes

1 The notion of a refugee crisis is problematic (Anderson, 2016; Sardelić, 2017a; Sigona, 2018). Here I use it to mean a crisis of response to accommodating refugees in Europe and not as a crisis brought by refugees.

2 The full title of the Temporary Protection Directive is *Council Directive 2001/55/EC on Minimum Standards for Giving Temporary Protection in the Event of a Mass Influx of Displaced Persons and on Measures Promoting a Balance of Efforts between Member States in Receiving Such Persons and Bearing the Consequences Thereof.* The directive was developed after the war in Kosovo in 2001 to promote the cooperation and solidarity among the then Member States of the European Community (Sardelić, 2017a).

3 For example, the Hungarian Prime Minister Viktor Orbán stated: 'Hungary's historical given is that we live together with a few hundred thousand Roma. This was decided by someone, somewhere. This is what we inherited. This is our situation, this is our predetermined condition ... We are the ones who have to live with this, but we don't demand from anyone, especially not in the direction of the West, that they should live together with a large Roma minority' (quoted in Kallius *et al.*, 2016: 8).

4 There was a backlash towards Fico's statement from the Group of Progressive Alliance of Socialists and Democrats, which he was part of as a proclaimed Social Democrat: 'Until Robert Fico shows he is a progressive, he does not deserve a place in the Party of European Socialists' (S&D, 2015).

5 In most of the relevant academic literature and policy papers since the 1990s, Romani minorities have been named as Roma. There has been

much academic discussion on what the term Roma means. As Peter Vermeersch notes: '[There is] growing agreement that it makes sense to view Romani identity – as any form of ethnicity – not simply as a matter of isolated group characteristics, but rather as the product of complex classification processes involving both classifiers and those classified as Roma ... In this way, it is also easier to make sense of prevailing exonyms that are used to refer to more or less the same population (such names as Gypsy, Zigeuner, and Tsigane); their equivalents in the Eastern European languages (such as cigán, cikán, cigány, etc), and the self-appellations that serve as subidentities (such as Kalderash, Manush, Caló, Vlach, Romungro, Beash, Sinto, etc). All these categories relate in some way to the overarching term Roma – a term that has historically served as a self-appellation for speakers of the Romani language (sometimes called Romanes) but is now used to encompass a wider group of people, including those who do not speak Romanes but for socio-cultural or political reasons still identify themselves, or are identified by others, as belonging to this group' (Vermeersch, 2017: 227). Following Vermeersch's position, and my previous work (Sardelić, 2015: 174), in this book I use the term 'Romani minorities' when I want to emphasise the heterogeneity and hybridity of this particular minority identity. The notion of Romani minorities also includes individuals who do not identify as Roma (such as Sinti, Ashkali, Egyptians, Manoush, Gitano and Travellers, among others), but are externally categorised either as Roma or derogatively as Gypsies. I use the term 'Roma' when I am referring to the politically engaged term used by either Romani activists or different state institutions and international organisations. The power of naming is discussed in more detail in Chapter 2.

6 The EU NRIS Framework is based on European Commission, 2011b.
7 The EU cites the following estimates of the Romani population in each EU Member State (total number and percentage of the total population for each country): Austria (25,000 or 0.3%); Belgium (30,000 or 0.29%); Bulgaria (750,000 or 10.33%); Croatia (up to 40,000 or 1%); Cyprus (1,250 or 0.16%); Czech Republic (250,000 or 1.93%); Denmark (5,500 or 0.1%); Estonia (1,250 or 0.1%); Finland (11,000 or 0.21%); France (400,000 or 0.21%); Germany (105,000 or 0.13%); Greece (265,000 or 2.47%); Hungary (700,000 or 7.05%); Ireland (37,500 or 0.9%); Italy (140,000 or 0.23%); Latvia (5,600 or 0.3%); Lithuania (3,000 or 0.08%); Luxembourg (300 or 0.06%); Malta (no Romani population according to estimates); Netherlands (37,500 or 0.24%); Poland (12,731 or 0.1%); Portugal (up to 70,000 or 0.52%); Romania (1.85 million or 8.32%); Slovakia (500,000 or 9%); Slovenia (8,500 or 0.42%); Spain (725,000 or 1.57%); and Sweden (42,500 or 0.46%). According to

these estimates, there are approximately 6 million EU citizens identified as belonging to Romani minorities. In the Member States that joined the EU before 2004, there are around 2 million Roma, and in those that joined later, around 4 million (European Union Official Website, 2015). It is not clear how these estimates were calculated.

8 This statement echoes previous positions, such as Young's (1989) notion of 'differentiated citizenship'. However, when I talk about neutral laws and policies I am scrutinising those that have already been observed through the lens of differentiated and multicultural citizenship. Later in this chapter I explain how my understanding of such laws and policies is different.

9 This book acknowledges previous uses of the phrase 'the edges of citizenship' in existing academic literature (especially the extraordinary work of Hepworth (2015), Alderson *et al.* (2005) and Gerald (2019)). Whilst these works do use the term, they do not provide a theoretical conceptualisation of it. It was this lack of a theoretical analysis of 'the edges of citizenship' that formed the basis of my now completed EU Marie Skłodowska-Curie individual fellowship project.

10 There needs to be an awareness that not all Romani minorities can be necessarily labelled as marginalised as not all Roma belong to the most impoverished social class. However, marginalisation works on multiple levels and is not limited only to social class. As some scholars have shown in their work, educated middle-class Roma can face various shades of marginalisation. For example, Durst and Nyírő (2018) have shown that educated Romani women often feel marginalised both from the majority society and from their own communities. Whilst I do not assume that all Romani individuals are marginalised, in this book I am focusing on the majority that are, and the different ways in which this marginalisation can present itself.

1

Visible minorities, invisible citizens

Introduction

Romani minorities belong to Europe's most visible minorities (Szalai and Schiff, 2014). In legal discourses, the concept of 'visible minorities' was associated with non-white migrants in settler states. For example, the Canadian Employment Equity Act (1995) defined members of visible minorities as 'persons, other than Aboriginal peoples, who are non-Caucasian in race or non-white in colour'. Yet Romani minorities have been visible not only as migrants, but also as traditional minorities in their countries of citizenship (Taylor *et al.*, 2018). Recently there has been a growing consensus among scholars that it is predominantly practices and discourses of racialisation that make Roma visible as a minority throughout the European public space (Yuval-Davis *et al.*, 2017; McGarry, 2017; Kóczé and Rövid, 2017; Yildiz and De Genova, 2018): the novel form of racialisation is connected to ascribing fixed cultural characteristics to Roma, which are seemingly incompatible with liberal democratic states. As these scholars have shown, whilst racialisation constructs fixed boundaries around ascribed cultural rather than biological differences (Gilroy, 1987; Balibar and Wallerstein, 1991), it also intertwines concepts like mobility and nomadism (Sigona, 2003; van Baar, 2015) and poverty and benefits abuse (Geddes and Hadj-Abdou, 2016) as interchangeable characteristics of Roma. The merging of such concepts as interchangeable is locally specific and can be different from context to context, yet it serves as a justification for the civic marginalisation of Romani minorities.

This chapter seeks to approach the civic marginalisation of Roma in Europe from a different perspective: it argues that Roma have been a visible minority but invisible as citizens. The EU and its Member States have manifestly constructed (supra)national citizenship on the foundation of fundamental rights and minority protection. Nevertheless, the chapter questions why such a construction still leaves many Roma, who are clearly in need of having their fundamental and minority rights protected (Pogány, 2004), on the fringes of citizenship: can this be attributed to the uniqueness of Roma as a minority?

On the basis of the chapter's analysis, I will show that whilst public discourse might represent a failure to protect Romani minorities as a unique (East) European challenge, the types of civic marginalisation processes that Roma face are not exceptional. Liberal democracies around the globe have employed similar processes with other minority populations and placed them on the fringes of citizenship too. The chapter will focus on three aspects of civil marginalisation. First, it examines the politics around minority naming and counting. Second, it explores the development of targeted 'multicultural' approaches in legislation and policy for minority recognition and how they have contributed to marginalisation rather than protection. Third, it analyses how these multicultural approaches coexist with the breaches of fundamental rights marginalised minorities have experienced as citizens.

A human rights litmus test for East European regimes?

After the fall of the Berlin Wall in 1989, human rights advocates and minority activists dubbed the position of Roma the litmus test for human rights and respect for diversity during the process of democratisation of postsocialist countries (Stewart, 2002).[1] Today, even when human rights – including the rights of minorities, pluralism and tolerance – are enshrined in Article 2 of the Lisbon Treaty as part of the EU's core values and when most of the postsocialist states in Europe have become EU Member States, the position of Roma has become not a litmus test but rather one of the greatest stains on these core values in the EU as a whole. It is not only the 'new' postsocialist EU Member States that have failed to hold up core EU values for all, but also the founding Member States, such as France, which have not achieved these standards in their treatment of Romani minorities (Parker, 2012; Parker and Toke, 2013; Ram, 2014a). In today's Europe, it appears that the original 1993 Copenhagen criteria for accession have not achieved their goal. Although postsocialist states did implement requested legislation, such moves did not necessarily improve human rights in those states (Blitz, 2013). Moreover, evaluations show that subsequent actions, such as those under the European Social Fund 2007–13 (Kostka, 2018) and the EU's soft law approach such as the EU NRIS Framework, have not improved the position of Romani minorities significantly (Carrera *et al.*, 2019) in either the founding or newer EU Member States.

EU policies have contributed to the visibility of Roma as a minority in the Member States and candidate countries (Vermeersch, 2012). However, such visibility has not always been positive: it has also made Roma more visible as a target for hostile politicians and media with antigypsyist stances, who have reinterpreted Roma as the minority privileged by the EU and international organisations (Stewart, 2012; Vermeersch, 2012; McGarry and Agarin, 2014; van Baar and Vermeersch, 2018). A number of politicians have echoed deeply rooted antigypsyist sentiments, present in the majority population, that equate Roma with beggars, thieves, nomads or misfits who are not compatible with the mainstream social order (Okely, 1994; Willems, 1997; Van de Port, 1998, Lucassen *et al.*, 1998).

The increase in the visibility of Roma as a minority was not followed by a discussion as to why certain parts of citizenry do not enjoy equal rights. Debates on citizenship frequently highlighted the position of Romani minorities, but mainly in terms of citizenship exceptionalities far removed from the experience of 'ordinary citizens'. The position of Roma was illuminated as a difficult case of minority integration rather than in terms of equality among fellow citizens.

This chapter examines how even the benevolent policies for integration of Roma can have adverse effects when policymakers do not critically reflect upon their own assumptions about Roma as well as assumptions about all-inclusive citizenship. It analyses commonsense assumptions on citizenship, minority protection and the way Roma are expected to integrate into society as minority citizens. Previous studies and more recent policy analyses claim that antigypsyism positions Roma at the margins of society and citizenship (Alliance Against Antigypsyism, 2017; Cortés Gómez and End, 2019). Here I also look at another angle: the perceived multiple normalities of what a citizen should be and how Roma are excluded from these normalities even when they are ostensibly included. I argue that European states have introduced multiple normalities through their own visions of multicultural (Kymlicka, 1995) or differentiated (Young, 1989) citizenship which include group-differentiated rights and some limited political representation of minorities. Yet all these states, separately, have deemed Roma incompatible with such visions.

I use a similar approach to Morag Goodwin and Roosmarijn Buijs (2013) as well as Tina Magazzini (2017), who have looked at how policies are made for Roma without taking Romani perspectives into account. Romani representatives have usually been included in the consultation processes but have not had a veto power over the position of the community they represent (McGarry and Agarin, 2014). To deconstruct the normalities of citizenship and what the position of Roma conveys about these normalities, I embrace 'critical whiteness' as it has been transposed into critical Romani studies by Violeta Vajda (2015, see also Silverman, 2018; Shmidt and Jaworsky, 2020). Vajda suggests that non-Romani scholars should reflect on their positionality when conducting their research on Roma. I also use Gloria Wekker's ideas on 'white innocence' (Wekker, 2016) and Gurminder Bhambra's line on 'methodological whiteness' (Bhambra, 2017a; 2017b). Wekker shows how the Dutch state and society employed racist discourses and practices even though the state was portrayed as benevolent towards immigrants and its former colonial subjects. Catherine Baker has suggested using this approach when discussing the concept of race in the former Yugoslav region (Baker, 2018). Bhambra (2017b) notes:

> It fails to recognise the dominance of 'whiteness' as anything other than the standard state of affairs and treats a limited perspective – that deriving from white experience – as a universal perspective. At the same time, it treats other perspectives as forms of identity politics explicable within its own universal (but parochial and lesser than its own supposedly universal) understandings.

This chapter shows that the 'dominance of "whiteness"' can be found in discussions of legislation and policies that are either inclusive of all citizens or specifically benevolent towards Roma but, in fact, create invisible edges of citizenship that construct unbridgeable difference and exceptionalism.

The first dilemma that policymakers and scholars face when addressing the position of Romani minorities in any field is the dilemma of naming and of numbers. First, 'Roma' is an umbrella term for diverse populations across Europe: not all of them identify as Roma, and the term itself can unify in a common fight against discrimination, but also can be used to flatten differences among these populations and specific challenges they face in different contexts (Carrera *et al.*, 2019: 29). Second, according to the EU data, Roma are the largest ethnic minority, numbering around 10 to 12 million people in Europe (European Commission, 2018c). Nevertheless, in each individual country in Europe Romani minorities represent a very small proportion of the whole population according to national population censuses. Most of the relevant academic literature and some policy papers acknowledge that many Romani individuals do not identify as Roma in population censuses (Messing, 2014). The underrepresentation of Roma in population censuses shows, on the one hand, that Roma want to avoid being constructed as a visible minority and hence an easy target for extremist groups and, on the other, that these scarcely reliable data are still the basis for certain legislation and policies or the lack thereof (Open Society Foundation, 2010; European Commission, 2018b). The first part of this chapter explores this situation in more detail.

In the second part of the chapter, I examine the laws and policies introduced to protect Roma by analysing primary sources, such as the minority and citizenship acts, country reports and opinions of the CoE's Advisory Committee of the Framework Convention for the Protection of National Minorities (FCNM). I focus particularly on the last cycles of monitoring in each country before 2019 (usually the fourth cycle). In the 1990s, the initial approach that international organisations, such as the CoE as well as the European Commission, recommended that states should take towards Roma was minority protection. The Roma Decade and the NRIS shifted the focus back onto socio-economic integration. At state level, some countries, such as Italy, took a more culturalist approach towards Roma, whilst others, such as Spain, leaned more towards the socio-economic (Magazzini, 2017). Yet both approaches cemented the view of Roma as an exceptional minority. Is the position of Roma unique? I argue that the focus on 'Roma exceptionalism', even when benevolent, has concealed the responsibility of the states and how they have contributed to the placing of Roma on the margins of society and the fringes of citizenship. Such a view is possible only when one ignores minorities around the globe who have faced similar treatments by the states of which they were citizens. Whilst Romani as well as African American civil society activists and scholars (see Jovanović and Daragiu, 2010; Brooks, 2018; Rucker Chang, 2018; Matache and West, 2018; Chang and Rucker-Chang, 2020) have been arguing for decades that there are similarities between different marginalised minorities around the globe, it is only in recent years that some policymakers have become more open to such comparisons. The question, though, remains: what can be set as the common ground for such comparison, given that both the contexts and the histories of marginalised minorities around the globe have their own distinct specificities? The chapter considers the position of Aboriginal people in Australia, New Zealand Māori and Native Americans as citizens to show how states use practices towards Indigenous people similar to those used towards Roma in Europe. The positions of Indigenous people and African Americans are indeed grounded in different contexts.

What is in a number, what is in a name?

The European Commission estimates that 10 to 12 million Roma live on the European continent and around 6 million of them are EU citizens (European Commission, 2018a). However, how are these estimates made? Who counts as Roma, and who counts Roma (Surdu, 2017)? What impacts do external categorisation and self-identification have on Romani minorities in different contexts?

These questions form the foundation of any research examining the position of Roma. As McGarry (2017: 16) comments, '[e]very academic article or book must explain very early on the appropriate nomenclature to refer to Roma. The matter has diverted attention away from the myriad complex puzzles relating to the marginalisation of Roma communities.' Still, the debates on how Roma should be named and counted have real consequences for policymaking

(Messing, 2014) and can either diminish or deepen the stigma around Romani identity.

The designation 'gypsy' was based on the misconception that Roma are a nomadic group coming from Egypt (Tremlett, 2013), whilst the etymology of the word *cigan* (also *cigany*, *cikan* and other similar variations in different contexts) is less clear (Liégeois, 2007: 17). On the basis of a more recent analysis, linguists have shown that the Romani language is strongly connected to Indian languages and have traced the origin of Roma to India (Matras, 2004). In April 1971, Romani activists from around Europe held a congress in London to challenge the name 'gypsy', since it had been given to them by outsiders and had derogatory connotations, choosing instead the name Roma, which in Romanes means a human being (Nirenberg, 2009). There have been disputes around the name Roma also within groups that have previously been known as Gypsies: some wanted to keep the old name, and others claimed that the name Roma privileges certain subgroups and neglects the heterogeneity of subgroups, for example, like the dispute between Roma, Ashkali and Egyptians in post-Yugoslav Kosovo (Lichnofsky, 2013). Yet there has been an agreement by many Romani activists (Costache, 2018) that a certain degree of 'strategic essentialism' (Spivak, 1988) is needed to counter discrimination and the denial of European belonging faced by all these groups despite the fact that they have been present in Europe since the Byzantine Empire at least (Crowe, 2007).

Following my previous work (Sardelić, 2015), I use the term 'Romani minorities' when emphasising the multitude of heterogenous and hybrid identities of minorities around Europe, including those who do not necessarily identify as Roma. For example, here I include minorities who identify themselves as Ashkali and Egyptians from South-East Europe, Manush from France, Gitanos from Spain and Sinti in Germany and elsewhere, among others. Whilst acknowledging the hybridity and heterogeneity of Romani identities (Tremlett, 2014) in different contexts, I also recognise that individuals who might ascribe different identities to themselves have been similarly subjected to antigypsyism. I take the view that antigypsyism is connected to civic marginalisation: this goes beyond the ethnic or socio-economic marginalisation usually highlighted by scholars (Ladányi and Szelényi,

2006) and policymakers. When using the term 'Romani minorities', I underline the varieties, but also ambiguities, of self-identification and external categorisation. By using the term 'Roma', I am highlighting two issues, the first of which is political mobilisation based on a specific identity (Vermeersch, 2006). Anna Mirga-Kruszelnicka (2018), following Stuart Hall's (1996) notion of new ethnicities, has referred to Roma so as to avoid essentialist understandings and also to confirm that what it means to be Roma is continuously being remade by individuals who identify as such. Secondly, this word is used by both international institutions and state authorities that have accepted it as an official umbrella term for Romani minorities in their documents.

The European Commission has identified Roma as the largest ethnic minority on the European continent on the basis of the estimate that there are up to 12 million Roma living in Europe as a whole (European Commission, 2018a). However, in the official state censuses, the number of individuals identifying as Roma rarely exceeds 5 per cent of the population. In Romania, for example, according to the 2011 census, 621,573 residents declared themselves to be Romani, corresponding to 3.3 per cent of the population.[2] Yet according to the CoE estimates, there are 1.85 million Roma living in Romania, just over 8 per cent of the population. Similarly, in Slovakia, the 2011 population census reports that 105,738 individuals self-identified as Roma (European Roma Rights Centre (ERRC), 2012: 7), but EU data stated that there were approximately 500,000 Roma in Slovakia (9 per cent of the total population).[3] Similar high discrepancies occur in Bulgaria, where 335,343 residents (4.4 per cent) identified as Roma but the CoE estimated a total of 750,000 Roma (10 per cent of the total population), and in Hungary, where in 2011 315,000 identified as Roma (Messing, 2014: 814) but estimates go as high as 700,000 (or 7 per cent of the total population).

Both underestimation and overestimation of the number of Roma have very real effects when translated into policy, especially given the drive for policymaking to be based on hard, quantifiable data. Already in 2010, the Open Society Foundation (2010) published a mid-term evaluation report on the Roma Decade which highlighted that ambivalent data on how many Roma live in different countries had caused further difficulties with the gathering of data on the position of Roma in different policy fields (such as the Decade's key areas of housing, education, healthcare access and employment). Similarly, the report on the evaluation of the EU NRIS up to 2020 stated 'that data collection, monitoring and reporting systems should be strengthened. Lack of reliable data disaggregated by ethnicity and lack of transparency and accountability mechanisms are key challenges that make the process of monitoring difficult and unreliable. This makes it difficult to measure progress' (European Commission, 2018b: 11).

Yet the drive for quantifiable data can produce material (Messing, 2019) that can then be used in less than positive ways. An illustrative example is a research project undertaken by the University of Salford in the UK which, on the basis of surveys sent to local authorities, published estimated figures stating that there were 197,705 migrant Roma in the UK (see Brown *et al.*, 2014). Previous estimates had suggested that there were not more than 6,000 Roma from Romania in the UK (Cahn and Guild, 2010). Messing (2019: 24) took issue with the project and its published findings:

> The study is an example of how an academic actor attempted to generate data where it was obviously lacking but missed to carefully consider the implications that such data – collected with several methodological question marks – might be used as 'objective evidence' in a highly hystericized political environment. The question is therefore whether it is worth to produce such vague and methodologically uncertain data about a population that is often in the spotlight in a stigmatising and stereotypical way.

Leggio (2019: 82) noted that 'during the interview that accompanied the report's release, the lead author, Philip Brown, argued that local authorities were struggling to cope with such numbers due to the cuts implemented by Cameron's government. He added that knowing the actual number of Roma migrants was needed for local authorities and third sector agencies to better target EU funds and compensate for the lack of governmental support.' Despite the project leader's call for stronger data, the published figures were used for fearmongering in public debates in 2013 before the UK labour market limitations were lifted for Romanian and Bulgarian citizens and, later, in the Brexit debates on the future of the UK's EU membership.[4] The published figures were used to generate hostile media headlines such as 'UK Roma Population One of Biggest in Europe' (Jenkins, 2013),

'Roma Surge Threatens to Add to Estimated 200,000 Population Already in UK' (Dawar, 2013) and 'Roma Army: 200,000 are Already Here with MORE on the Way' (Perkins, 2013).

Whilst the British right-wing parties, like the United Kingdom Independence Party (UKIP) and the Conservatives, used these figures to create and support a moral panic about the free movement of Romanian and Bulgarian citizens, the left-wing parties issued similar warnings about the difficulties that local authorities would have in dealing with the huge 'inflow' of Romani migrants (Leggio, 2019: 82). Ultimately, the main issue was not whether or not the data were reliable, but the fact that more data did not bring better and more equal inclusion for Romani minorities in the UK. Instead of focusing on integration, political parties from across the spectrum described Roma variously as increasing in numbers in the UK and as 'problematic migrants' for the state (Leggio, 2019: 69–88). Romani migrants themselves and their position were not seen as the significant issue, but rather taken as merely a symptom of a more contentious debate (Sardelić 2019b, 2019c). The very publication of these figures, whether or not they quantifiably overestimated the number of Roma in the UK, raised concerns, and they were used as a proxy for a debate about the nature of EU citizenship and the rights of EU citizens vis-à-vis UK nationals. Arguably, and no doubt regrettably, these then served as precursor debates for the UK referendum on EU membership (Leggio, 2019).

Across the political spectrum, UK politicians portrayed Roma as a 'challenge' exported from an enlarged EU. The assumption was that the new postsocialist EU Member States were not dealing properly with the integration of Roma and, together with the EU Free Movement Directive (see Chapter 2), this had become a problem for the Western EU Member States. UK political representatives, as well as the media, did not reflect upon their own tropes of stereotypes that they held both about Roma as well as Eastern Europeans. In these debates, Roma faced dual stigmatisation: on the one hand, by the UK public as unwanted immigrants generally, and on the other, by other Eastern European immigrants who considered Roma to shed a negative light on them as immigrants. In the UK, they were not positioned as fellow EU citizens, but as a question mark on the very concept of EU citizenship itself. At the same time, other Eastern European migrants distanced themselves and dismissed Romani minorities as their national fellow citizens. Equal EU citizenship was thus shown to be unavailable, and instead there almost existed different taxonomies of EU citizenship, as Rigo (2005) noted in his discussion of postcolonial subjects in the colonial empires. The constructed position of Romani migrants (Magazzini and Piemontese, 2019) in this debate was illustrative of the existence of citizenship taxonomies.

Whilst there is overwhelming agreement among researchers that the most reliable data on the number of Roma should be based on self-identification rather than external categorisation, the fact that self-identification is fluid and contextual (Messing, 2019) can also be used by the state authorities to diminish the rights available to Romani minorities. For example, Croatia amended the 2002 Constitutional Law on the Rights of National Minorities in 2010 and 2011. In 2010, Croatia had amended its Constitution to recognise twenty-two national minorities, and among them Roma were named as a national minority for the very first time. The constitutional recognition of Roma has had to be contextualised within a broader minority politics since Croatian independence. For the Serbian minority, who had been named as a constitutive nation in the Socialist Republic of Croatia before the disintegration of Yugoslavia, recognition as a national minority seemed like a downgraded status and was deemed to be 'constitutional nationalism' (Hayden, 1992). At the same time, Roma had never been recognised as a minority in any of the Yugoslav constitutions (Sardelić, 2013b), but there was a consensus that they belonged to the ethnic groups within the constitutional hierarchisation of constitutive nations–nationalities–ethnic groups. 'Ethnic group' was a designation for territorially dispersed minorities without territorial claims, and this translated into fewer minority rights than those held by nationalities (Sardelić, 2015).

Because of EU conditionality (Sardelić, 2011), Roma were nominally recognised as equal to other minorities in the Croatian Constitution for the first time. In principle, the Constitutional Law on the Rights of National Minorities reflected this recognition and should have given access to a range of minority rights to enhance the presence of minorities in the public space as Croatian citizens. For example, Article 12 gave all the national minorities the right to use their minority language and script in the local administrative units where the number of minority members exceeded at least one third of the total population. According to the Croatian population census, Roma in Croatia did not reach this threshold in any of the local administrative units. Whilst there was a possibility of having this right on paper, in reality it was not reachable. In the FCNM country report (FCNM, 2014b: 66), the Croatian government stated that even in cases where the minorities do not constitute one third of the local population, there are still informal agreements that local administration personnel are sometimes fluent in the minority language. However, the FCNM Advisory Committee's opinion (2016b: 23) in the fourth cycle stated that this did not extend to Roma since the language is not spoken by the majority or spoken as often as other minority languages. Although Roma in Croatia were constitutionally 'upgraded' from an ethnic group to a national minority, this did not necessarily translate into a broader scope of rights.

Yet the question is, why do more individuals not self-identify as Roma? One answer lies in the diversity among Romani minorities. Another answer lies in the widespread fear that identifying as Roma in an official capacity provides very few protections and rights for citizens on the ground despite their having targeted minority protection. There have been numerous cases in Croatia highlighting, for example, ethnic profiling and harassment by the police (ERRC, 2001) as well as the segregation of Romani children in schools (see Chapter 3).

In many European countries, the trade-off between having rights as a minority and having rights as citizens is a very real one for Roma. Self-identification of Roma, as in the case of other minority identities, is not fixed and is context-dependent. In addition, self-identification is not only a part of subjective processes, but is created in dialogue (Messing, 2014). For example, in an interview undertaken for this research, one highly educated woman, who identified as Roma both privately and publicly, noted that when she was looking for employment her employment advisor 'benevolently' recommended she should hide her knowledge of the Romani language (among the listed languages she speaks) in her CV and in any job interviews: 'I think it is still true that no matter if you have education they would rather take someone else, not Roma. The only exception is if the job requires knowledge of the Romani language or is in any way connected to Roma. I still remember when I was at the Employment

Office, the employment advisor there was shocked that I wanted to write in my employment profile that I can speak Romani. She told me between the lines that she was afraid this would be a reason why I would not get a job' (quoted in Sardelić 2019a: 235, for more context, see Chapter 5). As this interview excerpt indicates, being visible as a minority often positions Roma at the fringes of citizenship, in this case with no access to employment.

Minority protection and socio-economic integration: and citizens' equality?

The dilemmas around the numbers and naming of Roma also reflect regional geopolitical developments and policy orientations that international organisations and states have taken towards Romani minorities. Whilst the name Roma emerged from the Romani movement in 1970s, international organisations, especially the European Commission, only gradually started adopting this name rather than 'gypsies' in the 1990s. Before the fall of the Berlin Wall, European Commission documents referred to Roma as a social group which was disadvantaged because of its itinerant lifestyle (Simhandl, 2009). It was only with the prospect of EU enlargement that the discourse changed and EU institutions started using an ethnic denomination, gradually referring to Roma by this name as well as describing them as an ethnic minority especially from Eastern Europe. As argued by Simhandl (2009), the use of Roma as an ethnic denomination served to monitor the progress that former socialist countries were making in following the 1993 Copenhagen criteria, especially with respect to human rights, rule of law and minority protection. Whilst the accession progress reports were initially produced because of fears over minorities with potentially destabilising territorial claims, as in the case of the former Yugoslavia (Vermeersch, 2006: 3), they soon started underlining the position of Roma and their minority rights as the fear of their westward migration grew (Guglielmo and Waters, 2005).

Western EU Member States were not put under the same scrutiny in the 1990s (Donert, 2017). At the end of the 1990s, some of the EU Member States started reintroducing visa restrictions for the postsocialist EU candidate countries because of Romani migrants, which meant compromising the right to seek asylum (Clark and Campbell, 2000). For example, in 1999, the Finnish Ministry of Labour reported that 580 Roma from Slovakia sought asylum in Finland that year. Around 380 of those asylum seekers arrived in the space of a few days, so Finland decided to create a new visa regime for all Slovak citizens. Similarly, the UK briefly reinstated visas for Slovak citizens and threatened to introduce similar restrictions for Czech citizens if they received more asylum applications from those countries. The number of asylum applications in 1999 did not go above a few hundred (ERRC, 1999). Even before the countries with the largest Romani populations joined the EU, there was a strong perception that Roma should remain contained within their own countries and not be 'exported' to Western European states where it was presumed human rights standards were already respected. Indeed, the protection of minorities under the FCNM was part of the EU conditionality for the EU candidate countries (Blitz, 2013), but some founding EU Member States (like France) have neither signed nor ratified this Convention.

There was no shared agreement by the countries that joined the EU before 2004 on whether or not Roma should be legally recognised as a national minority. Spain, Portugal, Denmark, France and Greece did not include a definition of national minority in their legislation at all. Italy recognised linguistic minorities in its Constitution but did not include Roma among these minorities. In the fourth FCNM country report (2014c: 10), the Italian government commented: 'No specific piece of legislation of our legal system recognises and protects the Roma communities living in Italy as linguistic minorities as they lack a stable connection with the territory, as it is well known.' Finland included Roma in its Constitution as a group, next to Sami, who were recognised as an Indigenous group (Section 17 of the Constitution of Finland), whilst Sweden included Roma as a national minority in the National Minorities and Minority Languages Act 2009 with other groups (Article 2). Austria recognised Roma through its 1976 *Volksgruppengesetz* (although not directly mentioned in the Act itself) (FCNM, 2002a); this translates literally as the Ethnic Groups Act, but the FCNM Advisory Committee (2016a: 6) referred to it as the 1976 National Minorities Act. Germany recognised Roma and Sinti as a national minority with a Declaration after signing the FCNM (FCNM, 2002b: 6). In the UK, Roma were recognised as a racial group (to be protected by the Race Relations Act 1976) by the court decision in the case of *Commission for Racial Equality v. Dutton* (1989, see FCNM, 1999: 14) and later by the Equality Act 2010 (FCNM, 2014d: 7).[5] Whilst Irish legislation has previously included special provisions for the Irish Traveller community, it was not until 2017 that the Irish government decided to recognise them as an ethnic group rather than a group with a specific lifestyle (FCNM, 2017: 21). However, Ireland does not recognise Travellers as a national minority.

The FCNM Advisory Committee commented that the legal recognition of minorities as national was not a necessary predisposition for recognising their rights (FCNM, 2014a: 6). For example, the Advisory Committee's Opinion on Spain noted that whilst Spain does not have legal recognition of minorities, it does have comprehensive policies of inclusion for both traditionally settled and migrant Roma (see Magazzini, 2017; Kostka, 2018). Others comment that for migrant Roma the main approach is still forced voluntary return rather than integration (Vrăbiescu and Kalir, 2018). The FCNM Advisory Committee also noted that even though Roma have in many cases been recognised as a minority in national legislation, they were still the most discriminated citizens in their own countries and, faced with school segregation, police harassment and hate crime, experienced hindered access to healthcare and coerced sterilisation, among other issues. All this was caused either directly by the states or by the lack of state protection. According to the opinions of the FCNM Advisory Committee in the period before the 2004 EU enlargement, many postsocialist candidate countries introduced a form of legal recognition of minorities including Roma either in their constitutions or in other legislation or documents. In 1993, Hungary introduced Act LXXVII on the Rights of National and Ethnic Minorities, which was later repealed and replaced by the 2011 Act CLXXIX on the Rights of Nationalities. In the 1993 Act, Roma were named Gypsies, whilst in the 2011 Act they were referred to in the first instance as Roma/Gypsies and thereafter as Roma. Both laws were based on the self-government of minorities and their cultural autonomy. However, although legislation has in theory introduced Roma national self-government (McGarry, 2010), it has been criticised by the Romani non-governmental organisations (NGOs), which have claimed that this structure, rather than representing the interests of Romani minorities, complies with the practices of the leading party in Hungary:

> In 2017 as many as 29 representatives out of the 47 belonged to the *Lungo Drom Roma* minority party which is associated with the current government of *Fidesz*. Through the years the ÖRO [Romani Minority National Self-Government] has faced many accusations and fraud cases over not being able to be accountable for billions of forints. Viktor Orbán himself notified the Ministry of Human Capacity of allocating over HUF 1.3 billion to the ÖRO, so the self-governance can finance their debt accumulated by fraud, deceit and embezzlement. (Carrera *et al.*, 2019: 69)

Whilst in Hungary Romani minorities were recognised as nationalities from 2011 (in the previous Act they were included in the list of ethnic and national minorities), Slovakia and the Czech Republic included Roma as national minorities in their legislation. In the Czech Republic, Roma were recognised as one of the national minorities in the 2001 Act on Rights of Members of National Minorities. In Slovakia, the term 'national minorities' was mentioned in Articles 33 and 34 of the Constitution. The article requires a specific constitutional Act to further elaborate the rights of minorities. Yet such an Act was, according to some scholars, never introduced (Constantin, 2010). There was a similar situation in Slovenia. Article 65 of the Constitution of Slovenia mentions the 'Romani community', yet the specific rights given to this group were not defined in the Constitution but required a new legal act. In the subsequent legislation adopted in Slovenia, Roma were recognised as an ethnic community, whilst other minorities, such as Hungarians and Italians in Slovenia, were recognised as national communities. Whilst Italian and Hungarian minorities had their rights recognised by the Slovenian Constitution (Article 64), that was not the case for Roma minorities. In contrast, Poland made a similar distinction between ethnic and national minorities, but constitutionally recognised their rights as equal (Article 35). In the 2005 Act on National and Ethnic Minorities and on Regional Languages, Roma were recognised as an ethnic group, as in Slovenia, but without the hierarchy of rights that Slovenia established for national and ethnic minorities.

In 2007, Slovenia became the only country in Europe to introduce a special Roma Community Act after a 2006 pogrom of a Romani village committed by the local majority population (Vidmar Horvat *et al.*, 2008). However, the Act only confirmed the hierarchy of rights between constitutive nation, national communities and Roma as an ethnic community, with far less scope for minority rights (Sardelić, 2013a). For example, whilst bilingual education was possible for national communities, Roma do not enjoy a similar right in Slovenia. National communities in Slovenia have a representative in the parliament, whilst Roma only have councillors at the municipal level. Furthermore, the Roma Community Act only recognised some Romani minorities living in Slovenia: it did not give rights to Romani minorities who were not arbitrarily considered to be autochthon in Slovenia. The reason for this was to deprive internal migrants and migrants from other parts of the former Yugoslavia to Slovenia of rights (Janko Spreizer, 2004; Sardelić, 2012a).

Whilst Slovenia clearly introduced a hierarchy of rights for different types of minorities, it allowed so-called dual voting for recognised minorities. Members of Italian and Hungarian national minorities can vote for their representatives in parliament, but they can also vote for general representatives. For Roma, this form of dual voting is possible at the municipal level: they can vote for a minority representative and for a general representative. The Venice Commission (2008) published a report on dual voting by national minorities which found that only Slovenia allows dual voting for minorities whereas other EU Member States do not, as they see it as a deviation from the 'one person – one vote' rule. For example, in Croatia, Roma have a representative in parliament (the same MP also represents other national minorities), but they cannot vote for a general representative. In 2010 the Croatian Constitutional Court decided, 'in these cases it does not seem plausible that recognition of the dual voting rights would advance the relationship between the "*privileged minority*" and other citizens. Actually, such a privilege in a legal sense could lead to conflict' (Constitutional Court of Croatia, 2011, my emphasis and translation[6]). Whilst the decision of the Croatian Constitutional Court was mainly focused on dual voting by the Serbian minority, Romani minorities were affected as well. In this case, minorities could vote either as a minority members or as general citizens but not as both.

After the most substantial EU enlargement in 2004, the policy towards Romani inclusion shifted the discourse once again: whilst

Roma remained named as an ethnic minority, the social and economic disadvantages they faced were again among the prominent themes before minority protection was enforced in legislation. Some scholars argued that Roma needed more social and economic inclusion than group-targeted rights (Pogány, 2006). Bulgaria and Romania did not introduce specific minority legislation that would include Roma prior to their accession to the EU. However, they were party to initiatives for the 2005–15 Decade of Roma Inclusion. The Roma Decade introduced new international actors, such as the Open Society Foundation, the World Bank, the United Nations Development Programme, the CoE, and the Organization for Security and Co-operation in Europe (OSCE) in collaboration of some EU and non-EU states as the main drivers of Romani inclusion (Brüggemann and Friedman, 2017). The Roma Decade specifically targeted Roma but had a similar logic to the ten-year Millennium Developmental Goals (MDG) plan: 'As a result, in Europe, concerns about Roma exclusion have been, at the heart of the concerns about inequality in MDG implementation' (UN, 2013: 1). Besides the aforementioned international organisations, the Roma Decade was a partnership with countries such as Albania, BIH, Bulgaria, Croatia, the Czech Republic, Hungary, North Macedonia, Montenegro, Romania, Serbia, Slovakia and Spain. Whilst these countries were full members which needed to introduce and implement action plans that would improve access to education, housing, healthcare and employment for their Romani minorities, Slovenia and the US took part as observers. One of the agreed successes of the Roma Decade was that there was a clear continuation of the EU NRIS Framework (Brüggemann and Friedman, 2017). However, it did not achieve the main goal that was set: to close the inequality gap between the Romani and non-Romani population. Željko Jovanović, director of the Roma Initiative Office at the Open Society Institute, stated that the reason was institutional antigypsyism: 'Anti-Gypsyism, as a form of exclusion, is not haphazard. It is embedded in our domestic institutions and structures. It runs through public offices, schools, hospitals, the labour market, the welfare system, police, and elections. A Roma child denied schooling with everyone else is not the result of one rogue, racist teacher – a whole system, built and entrenched over time, has led to this' (Jovanović, 2015).

The EU institutions, particularly the European Commission and the European Parliament, started developing parallel mechanisms for Romani integration, such as the Roma Inclusion Platform and the EU NRIS Framework (Brüggemann and Friedman, 2017). Like the Roma Decade, the EU institutions focused on four areas where there was a perceived gap between the majority population and Romani minorities: (1) education; (2) employment; (3) access to healthcare; and (4) housing. The EU NRIS Framework functioned as a form of 'soft law' for the EU Member States and also candidate countries. The countries were required to design their own national strategies and then report to the European Commission, which would conduct an evaluation of the progress they made.

The EU NRIS Framework was adopted in 2011 as a policy response to the evictions and expulsions of migrant Roma from postsocialist countries (Romania and Bulgaria in particular; see Carrera *et al.*, 2019). Just before the adoption of the Framework, the EU action plan in the field of justice and home affairs – the so-called Stockholm Programme 2010–2014 – categorised Roma as a vulnerable group (Article 2.3.3): 'The EU and the Member States must make a concerted effort to fully integrate vulnerable groups, in particular the Roma community, into society by promoting their inclusion in the education system and labour market and by taking action to prevent violence against them' (European Council, 2009). However, soon after its establishment, the vision of integration proposed by the NRIS Framework came under criticism from a number of scholars and policymakers. For example, Goodwin and Buijs (2013) analysed the Framework, concluding that it took a set of majority values and expected assimilation rather than integration of Roma. Iusmen (2018) argued that instead of taking minority protection, anti-discrimination and the human rights of Roma as valuable in themselves, the Framework repeated the previous assumptions of organisations such as the World Bank that Romani integration is framed in terms of the economic prosperity of the EU: here, Roma were not seen as EU (and Member States) citizens, but primarily an impediment to the EU's economic goals.

Another criticism of the Framework was that, as with its predecessor, the participating states did not address antigypsyism, instead putting the burden of the integration of Romani minorities onto the rather power-limited responsible authorities (especially those at state level) and majority population (Carrera *et al.*, 2019). Different civil society actors, such as the European Romani Grassroot Organisations Network, emphasised that any further policies on 'Romani integration' should not only include measurable results, but also redress the antigypsyism of state actors when such policies are implemented (ERGO, 2020). The two major achievements in relations to the EU NRIS Framework did not come from the states, but from the Romani and the pro-Roma civil society: An Alliance Against Antigypsyism was formed out of a plethora of such organisations, and this supported a new definition of antigypsyism (Alliance Against Antigypsyism, 2017).

The other underlying issue with the EU NRIS Framework is its perpetuating narrative of underdevelopment. In the EU accession processes, the question of underdevelopment was addressed as the democratisation of postsocialist candidate countries. When the countries joined the EU, the narratives shifted to representing Roma as a vulnerable community that needed development so that it could catch up:

> Much like the post-colonial developmentalism … the postsocialist developmentalism which has logic of gradual progress and on that of a developmental continuum, according to which the Roma are on the same trajectory as 'we', the 'developed' Europeans, are. 'They' are 'only lagging behind', but this can and will be solved because 'they' will undergo a passage through several stages of socio-economic and human development that will ultimately connect them to 'our' modern, competitive, multicultural, and unified Europe. Whilst they were once the externalised outsiders of Europe, against whom Europe defined itself, they have now become the 'internalised outsiders' who will slowly but surely become included as true Europeans. (van Baar, 2019: 172–3)

Both the approaches of minority protection and socio-economic integration were addressed in a project-oriented manner (spanning in decade cycles), as if the inequalities of Roma as citizens could be eradicated by working on their position rather than addressing and deconstructing the structures that led to such inequalities. In addition, as international organisations have become the main financial supporters of advocacy for Romani rights, they have expected Romani NGOs to follow their developmental vision as to what Romani integration should look like (Plaut, 2016, see also Chapter 5). The developmental discourse in EU approaches towards Roma in Eastern Europe was dubbed 'Europeanised hypocrisy' (Ram, 2014b) and portrayed as neocolonialism (Trehan and Kóczé, 2009) because it had double standards on Romani inclusion in Western European countries that also failed to protect Roma. The developmental approaches towards Roma in Eastern Europe also produced a backlash from Eastern Europe itself: the local political elites started portraying Roma as a minority privileged by the EU who, consequently, were then seen as neglecting the predicament of the majority population in this region (Vermeersch, 2012). As Vermeersch (2012) showed, Roma were described as an EU minority, but at the same time alienated from their national fellow citizens. Whilst the (trans)national legislation and policy made them visible as a minority, Roma remained invisible as citizens at the fringes of their own national citizenship.

Roma as an exceptional minority? Names and numbers

Building on Alana Lentin's (2004) theory (see also Lentin, 2020), van Baar (2019) shows that one of the main challenges of the Roma inclusion programs – both of the Roma Decade and of the NRIS – was the assumed superficiality of antigypsyism (anti-Roma racism): in their policy documents, states as well as international organisations highlighted the exceptionality of antigypsyism, which goes against principles on which these states are founded. They did not recognise antigypsyism as something deeply embedded within society. Exceptionality of antigypsyism can be understood also in another way. Antigypsyism has been ascribed to encountering Roma as an exceptional minority, and has not been primarily understood as a violation of rights that all citizens are supposed to have regardless of their background. In the early 1990s, Václav Havel claimed that antigypsyism is a 'gypsy problem' that remains salient even when functioning democracies have been established (Kamm, 1993) and therefore is a litmus test for a civil society in postsocialist countries. Yet the Romani civil society and the Romani movement (Vermeersch, 2006; McGarry, 2010) had been strongly present in the postsocialist EU Member States even before the fall of the Berlin Wall (Donert,

2017). Nevertheless, the structural inequalities that Roma face across the EU remain intact.

Structural inequalities are, I claim, a product of the current liberal democratic states and their citizenship regimes rather than the alleged underdevelopment of Roma or the lack of critical civil society. This can be shown by comparing the position of Roma with that of other non-immigrant minorities in liberal democratic states around the globe. Whilst Romani minorities are arguably in a different position from Indigenous people and African Americans in postcolonial contexts, the treatment of these minorities that states and international organisations have applied has been strikingly similar. The first similarity can be seen in the controversies around naming and numbers of marginalised citizens. For example, in the cases of both Native Americans and African Americans, states have used derogatory naming in legal documents that have made both groups visible as minorities but marginalised as citizens. Albeit based on misconceptions of the first colonisers, the term 'Indian' remains present in Canadian legislation, such as the Indian Act, despite the fact that the activists' and representatives' preferred term is First Nations (Ramos, 2006). One of the Smithsonian Museums in the US is officially named the National Museum of the American Indian. Like Roma in Europe, Native Americans (including those categorised as Indian Americans) in the US do not represent more than 5 per cent of the total US population according to the 2010 US population census (Leavitt *et al.*, 2015).

As Leavitt and her colleagues (2015) point out, Native Americans remain invisible as citizens in the US context. They are, however, represented in a stereotypical manner in the mainstream public domain. This is best illustrated by controversies of naming mascots and sports teams, such as the Washington Redskins. Native American civil society activists have been advocating a change to this name since 1940 (Phillips, 2017) as it reinforces a derogatory term in the public domain. The owner of the Washington Redskins asserted that he would not change the name because of the majority's support of this name: 'In justifying his continued support for the team's name, Snyder asserted that the overwhelming public support for the continued use of the term "Redskins" was reason enough to retain the name' (Nteta *et al.*, 2018: 474). Whilst Native American civil society, with the support of professional organisations such as the American Psychological Association, has been successful in limiting the use of mascots and derogatory names in the educational sector through legislative battles, it has had less success when it comes to registered trademarks: according to the First Amendment on free speech, the Washington Redskins could retain their name; in mid-2020 Snyder decided to change the name to Washington Football Team (Washington Football Team, 2020).

Whilst civil society activists have been advocating against using the term Indians for Native Americans, according to the 2010 US census there is a larger group in the US that identifies as American Indian rather than Native American (Leavitt *et al.*, 2015). Similarly, in some countries in Europe, such as Spain, the traditional minority refers to itself as *Gitano* (Gypsy) rather than Roma. However, whilst there is a proven link between derogatory names and the marginalised position of certain minorities (Stegman and Phillips, 2014), the politically correct name does not necessarily diminish exclusionary stereotypes and practices towards these minorities. For example, both Native Americans and Roma have been portrayed as savages on the one hand and as being noble and free through positive stereotypes on the other. Certain cultural practices have reinforced the former image in the media. For example, scalping has been described as one of the cultural practices of Native Americans, despite originating from the settlers (Ganje, 2011), just as nomadism was seen as a cultural practice of Roma (Sardelić, 2019b). As Leavitt and her colleagues point out (2015), Native Americans do remain invisible as citizens, but they are also depicted as 'frozen in time' and as a community not on the same developmental level as mainstream society.

Human rights breaches and the biopolitics of citizenship

Besides the problems with names and numbers, the human rights breaches that different marginalised minorities face as citizens are similar in content. Whilst monitoring the minority rights situation and socio-economic integration of Roma, the FCNM Advisory Committee also continuously marked systematic breaches of rights that Roma experience as citizens. As the Advisory Committee has noted, Romani children have been systematically placed in either segregated classes or segregated schools in both Western and Eastern Europe. The US formerly treated its African American populations in a similar manner (this is discussed in Chapter 3). The next chapter shows how liberal democratic states have systematically limited the rights of minorities on their territories when they clashed with other state's interest. Chapter 4 discusses how Romani minorities and other similarly marginalised minorities around the globe experience impeded access to citizenship.

Women identified as belonging to marginalised minorities have often been faced with violence that needs to be studied with an intersectional approach (Yuval-Davis, 2011). One of the practices that Romani women have faced in order to prevent the 'wrong' biological nation being reproduced (Yuval-Davis, 1997; Kóczé, 2009) is coerced sterilisation. Throughout the twentieth century, several countries (such as Sweden, the Czech Republic, Hungary and Slovakia) employed coercive sterilisation for Romani women who were described as having too many children. Whilst this new century has banned coerced sterilisation as a state-sponsored practice, it still occurs because of deeply ingrained prejudice against Romani minorities. The ERRC has taken the Czech Republic, Slovakia and Hungary to court over this issue. Coerced sterilisations have happened without Romani women's informed consent, as they have usually been requested just before they undergo caesarean sections and are already under the influence of painkillers and sedatives. In Hungary, a woman who underwent sterilisation without informed consent was given compensation by the state. However, in *I.G. and Others v. Slovakia* (2012), the ECtHR did not recognise the practice of coerced sterilisation as a direct discrimination of Romani women: 'The Court decided that in view of the documents available, it could not be established that the doctors involved acted in bad faith, that the applicants' sterilization were a part of an organized policy, or that the hospital staff's conduct was intentionally racially motivated. At the same time, the Court insisted that shortcomings in legislation and practice relating to sterilisations were liable to particularly affect members of the Roma community, so their discrimination in these cases would be only indirect and unintentional' (ERRC, 2016: 20).

The practice of coerced sterilisation existed in different Canadian provinces throughout the twentieth century (Dyck, 2013). In 2018, two Indigenous women from the Canadian province of Saskatchewan filed a class action lawsuit after they were sterilised without prior free and informed consent. However, in this latest class action lawsuit the similarities between the experience of the two Indigenous women is strikingly similar to those Roma women: they were both sterilised whilst undergoing caesarean sections. Similarly, like some European countries, some Canadian provinces formerly had eugenics laws that included coerced sterilisation. Whilst such laws were abolished, the practices of coerced sterilisation continued: 'The practice has continued into the 21st century. Approximately 100 Indigenous women have alleged that they were pressured to consent to sterilisation between the 1970s and 2018, often whilst in the vulnerable state of pregnancy or childbirth' (Stout, 2019). The authorities in both Czechoslovakia and Canada eugenically justified forced sterilisation as a means of control over the under-developed population and as a method of preventing poverty prevention among large families. As activists against the coerced sterilisation of Romani women have stated, this act was 'racism's cruellest cut' (Rorke and Szilvasi, 2017). In Foucauldian terms, coerced sterilisation can be seen as the biopolitical act (van Baar, 2016) of cleansing citizenry. In both cases, the responsible authorities legitimised such procedures as practices 'for their own good' (Stout, 2019).

The developmental logic of decades

The 'Decade' approach was not an original invention for international intervention for 'improving' the position of Roma. Other marginalised minorities around the globe were scrutinised by the 'Decade' approach as well. In December 1993 the UN General Assembly adopted Resolution 48/163, which established the first International Decade of World's Indigenous Peoples (1995–2004). A year later, the Office of the UN High Commissioner for Human Rights (OHCHR) was appointed as the coordinator of the Decade and an action plan for how to improve the position of the world's Indigenous peoples was introduced. The aim of the Decade was to enhance international cooperation to address the pressing issues faced by Indigenous people in the realm of human rights, territorial rights, development education and access to healthcare. In 2004, at the end of the first Decade, the coordinator submitted a report to the Economic and Social Council which emphasised that the Decade had brought about institutions, programmes and projects that highlighted the position of the world's Indigenous peoples, but the general conclusion was distressing:

> However, despite the important institutional developments that have taken place in the framework of the Decade, the report acknowledges that Indigenous peoples in many countries continue to be among the poorest and most marginalised. It also notes that the adoption of a declaration on the rights of Indigenous peoples, one of the main objectives of the Decade, has not been achieved. The report considers that further efforts are needed by the Member States concerned and the international community to ensure that all Indigenous peoples everywhere enjoy full human rights and enjoy real and measurable improvements in their living conditions. (OHCHR 2004: 1)

Whilst also addressing specific challenges that Indigenous communities around the globe face, the conclusion drawn after the first Indigenous Decade has been strikingly similar to that after the Roma Decade. The General Assembly adopted another resolution in 2004 to start a second Decade of the World's Indigenous peoples (2005–14). Over this period, the most important international document relating to the position of Indigenous peoples came into existence: the UN Declaration on the Rights of Indigenous Peoples of 2007. The Declaration identified specific rights that should be guaranteed to Indigenous peoples around the globe by their states. Besides the general anti-discrimination provisions, it included Article 3 on self-determination of Indigenous people, Article 8 on mechanisms for prevention and redress, Article 19 on the necessity that the states acquire informed consent from Indigenous people and Article 26 on the right of Indigenous people to their traditional lands. This corpus of rights was specifically designed to address the position of Indigenous people around the world. However, Australia, the US, New Zealand and Canada voted against the adoption of the declaration and did so in a clear action to protect the current structures of their liberal states (Moreton-Robinson, 2011; Lightfoot, 2012; O'Sullivan, 2020). The four countries where the largest number of the world's Indigenous populations live presented multiple arguments: against self-determination because it could destabilise the territories of their countries; against returning traditional lands to Indigenous people because it would ignore current ownership; and finally, against prior informed consent in matters concerning Indigenous people, which was interpreted as causing inequality among citizens by giving Indigenous people a 'veto right' which other majority citizens do not have. In subsequent years, the four countries in question supported the declaration, albeit without changing their position on it: they claimed they would abide by the Declaration, which is legally non-binding, as long as it is not in contradiction with their pre-existing national laws (Lightfoot, 2012).

The Second International Decade of the World's Indigenous Peoples (2004–14) ran alongside the first Roma Decade of 2005–15. There was no second Roma decade, but the EU instead formulated the EU NRIS Framework, which concluded in 2020. In the penultimate year of the EU NRIS Framework, under the leadership of the Romani MEP Soraya Post, the European Parliament introduced a Resolution (2019/2508) that would acknowledge not only that the EU NRIS Framework did not fully succeed in its goal but also that it failed to address the underlying cause of Romani marginalisation: antigypsyism. The Resolution showed some awareness that Member States – like those states in the case of the UN Declaration on the Rights of Indigenous Peoples – are willing to go along with multicultural protection as long as it does not question the very fundamentals upon which the states are based, even if those fundamentals instil the marginalisation of some of its citizens.

Conclusion

The analysis of law and policy documents as well as public discourses and practices shows that there are parallels in how states position marginalised minorities on the fringes of citizenship both in settler colonial contexts and in the context of the expanding EU. States are willing to support benevolent policies towards marginalised minorities but only if they do not address the original structures (which may well be racist) upon which these states themselves are built. It is these invisible edges of citizenship, which position some groups as a visible problematic minority rather than shining the light on the problematic policies that create inequality among citizens. Despite existing liberal democracies and fundamental rights, it is precisely within such systems that civil marginalisation occurs. The FRA (2018) itself compared the position of Roma in Europe to that of individuals living in Third World countries. However, this masks the fact that their position is not a product of underdevelopment but arises in the most developed states in Europe. Similar observations have been made about alleged underdevelopment of Indigenous people in Australia, New Zealand, the US and Canada (Cooke *et al.*, 2007). In this chapter, I have analysed (inter)national legislation and policies introduced for the protection of minority rights of Roma. I have shown how plans to improve the position of Roma in Europe as well as other marginalised minorities around the globe were anchored by the invisible edges of citizenship and put these minorities on the fringes of citizenship: while legislation and policies gave the appearance of their minority rights being over-protected, at the same time the rights of these minorities as citizens remained under-protected despite the legislation on minority protection that was introduced. In the next chapter, I look at a different angle: I show how states willingly violate their own laws and international legislation in respect of marginalised minorities in order to serve their preferred greater interests.

Notes

1 The idea of Roma representing a litmus test of human rights in postsocialist countries has been voiced by several scholars, policymakers and civil society activists on numerous occasions. The original statement was made by Václav Havel, then the Czech President, in 1993 in the *New York Times* (Kamm, 1993). Havel was referring to the racist hate crime attacks targeted at Romani individuals after the collapse of the Berlin Wall: 'The Gypsy problem is a litmus test not of democracy, but of civil society.' Whilst defending the rights of Roma, he still referred to them as a 'Gypsy problem' and shifted the burden for protection of human rights of Roma from states to civil society (see Donert, 2017: 247–70).

2 All the numbers from the official censuses as well as the estimates are available at the European Commission's website: https://ec.europa.eu/ info/policies/justice-and-fundamental-rights/combatting-discrimination/ roma-and-eu_en.

3 See n. 2 above.

4 Following a referendum in 2016, the UK voted to leave the EU. The UK's membership of the EU was officially terminated on 31 January 2020.

5 For the purposes of the Equality Act 2010, Roma, Gypsies and Travellers are recognised as an ethnic group, which is a racial subcategory according to this Act.

6 Croatian original: 'U takvim slučajevima, ne čini se vjerojatnim da će priznavanje prava na dvojno glasovanje "privilegiranoj manjini" unaprijediti njihov odnos s ostalim građanima. Zapravo bi takva privilegija, u pravnom značenju pojma, mogla voditi sukobu.'

2

Irregularised citizenship, free movement and territorialities

If all the Gypsies were to steal, Tour Eiffel would disappear

from 'Sarkozy versus Gypsy' sung by VAMA, featuring Ralflo,
as a protest against the 2010 expulsions of Roma from France,
quoted in Romea.cz, 2010

Introduction

In her 2007 journal article, Linda Bosniak argued normatively that all residents in liberal democratic states should have equal rights on the same territory irrespective of their formal legal status: she called this the principle of 'ethical territoriality' (Bosniak, 2007). In practice, policies and laws of different states have oscillated between granting a broader scope of rights for migrants at one extreme, and restricting the rights of some citizens at the other. This chapter offers a descriptive enquiry into restrictions on ethical territoriality and its clash with the other meaning of territoriality: the ability of the state to exercise its sovereign power over its territory (Bosniak, 2007: 404). To investigate the clash between these two meanings of territoriality, the chapter highlights the case of trans-border minorities and minorities that have been present on a territory before current borders were formed. It specifically examines how states move away from the ideal of ethical territoriality and deem not only migrants but some of their citizens as having 'less-than-complete-membership' (Bosniak, 2007: 392) with a position closer to that of foreign residents. Echoing Nyers' (2019) theory on irregular citizenship, the chapter examines acts of sovereignty (Nyers, 2006) and how states, through such acts, irregularise the citizenship of marginalised minorities and restrict some of the rights they should have as citizens (van Baar, 2016; Sardelić, 2017b; Nyers, 2019).

This chapter first looks at how states restrict the free movement of Roma in the enlarged and enlarging EU and justify this restriction by abiding with broader universalist principles and protecting the rights of all citizens. I show that this was the case in the debates on EU citizenship as well as the visa liberalisation for the Western Balkans. As a first case study, the chapter analyses the expulsions of Romani Bulgarian and Romanian citizens from France in the summer of 2010. It continues with an examination of the CJEU case *Dano v. Jobcenter Leipzig* (C–333/13, henceforth the *Dano* case) of 2014. In this case, the court was seemingly neutral towards all citizens, including Roma. However, the chapter shows how the court's decision led to public discourses that claimed it was Roma in particular who needed to have their rights limited in regard to free movement. The chapter then presents two interrelated cases where marginalised minorities were either prevented from leaving the country where they were citizens or not allowed to stay in the country where they had lived for most of their lives.

The main argument of this chapter is that the restriction of freedom of movement needs to be looked at within a broader context of restricting the rights of marginalised citizens, rather than in terms of problematic migration practices. I claim that restricting the rights of Romani individuals who are mobile falls in the same category as restricting the rights of Indigenous people in Australia under the 2007 Northern Territory Emergency National Response Act or the so-called Intervention (Altman and Hinkson, 2007; Calma, 2009; Watson, 2011; Armillei and Lobo, 2017). Both were based on a misconception of the cultural characteristics of marginalised minorities allegedly in conflict with the norms of human rights guaranteed by liberal democratic states.

Imagining nomadism: migration or the right to free movement?

Whilst no country in the world at this point fully subscribes to the principle of ethical territoriality, there have been trends in different regions that approximate rights of certain foreigners to those of citizens (Kostakopoulou, 2008). Examples of such approximations include the 2004 Citizens' Rights Directive (Maas, 2013) and the 2003 Long-Term Residence Directive (Acosta Arcazaro, 2015) which arguably speak to notions of postnational citizenship (Soysal, 1997) in the EU. Nevertheless, this chapter aims to show that such approximations retain tensions as to the level of national citizenship possible and how they can even support inequalities among national citizens. At the same time, when the states are moving towards ethical territoriality with a specific category of foreigners, they are producing new practices that restrict the rights of some other foreigners and even their own citizens.

The restriction of rights for certain citizens echoes the debate between Will Kymlicka and Susan Moller Okin (Okin, 1999) on multiculturalism versus feminism, especially the question of whether multiculturalism and specific practices of minorities limit the freedom of minorities within minorities, for example minority women and children. However, in the case of Romani minorities and the right to free movement, the multiculturalism debate was twisted into another direction: it was no longer about a practice of limiting special group rights, but about restricting rights that all citizens should possess.

Historically, as well as in the contemporary context, states have legitimised the restricting of universal rights of Roma as a means to address their alleged cultural characteristics: that is, their non-sedentary lifestyle or nomadism (Lucassen *et al.*, 1998; van Baar, 2015; Donert, 2017). Indeed, there have been cases of Romani minorities, especially Irish and British Travellers, who have defended a (semi-)nomadic lifestyle as their cultural right (O'Nions, 2011). However, in today's Europe most Roma are not nomadic (O'Nions, 2011: 378), yet still the representation of Roma as nomads persists and has consequences for legal policies and practices.

Even the most paradigmatic ECtHR case, *Chapman v. the United Kingdom* (2001), on the right to a nomadic lifestyle, in fact primarily dealt with the right to equal access to housing. The representative of the ERRC commented that this is where the importance of the case lies: 'At first sight, these cases appear to be only of relevance to those European countries where Roma continue to live a pre-dominately nomadic way of life. However, in fact the cases raise issues of significance for all Roma' (Clements, 2001). In *Chapman v. the United Kingdom*, the applicant Sally Chapman sought a permit to place her family caravan on the land she owned. The local authorities refused the permit. The statistics presented in the case showed that whilst 80 per cent of non-Roma applicants got permits to build their houses on their land, only 20 per cent of Romani applicants were allowed to place caravans on their land. As Clements (2001) argued, the case was not primarily about the special rights of a specific Romani group, but about the right not to be discriminated against under supposedly neutral laws that do not take the special position of Romani minorities into account.

State control measures towards Roma on account of their alleged nomadism have a long-standing history (van Baar, 2011). For example, during the period of the Enlightenment under the rule of Maria Theresa (between 1740 and 1780), the Habsburg monarchy adopted a number of decrees with the intention to assimilate Roma and include them as new but equal sedentary citizens of the monarchy. The decrees included the prohibition of nomadism, the prohibition of marriage between Romani individuals, and the removal of Romani children from their families and their placement in peasant families so that they would learn the ways of sedentary families (Barany, 2002: 93). In the socialist period, a number of states also took the approach of controlling the movement of their Romani citizens. As Donert uncovered (2017: 133), in socialist Czechoslovakia 46,000 Roma were identified as nomads and conscripted into the 1959 Nomad Register, although most of them did not live a nomadic lifestyle. Although the state officially opposed nomadism, it relocated Romani individuals from one part of the federation to another. Most Roma from the Czech territories were killed during World War II, which meant that in post-war Czechoslovakia a much larger number of Roma lived in the Slovak part. As the Czech part became industrialised, the government introduced a policy of relocating Slovak Roma to the Czech Republic in the Czechoslovak Federation, so that they could be evenly distributed and not concentrated in only one part (Kochenov, 2007). This governmental decision had significant consequences for the citizenship status of relocated Roma (see Chapter 4).

In the former Yugoslavia, a similar collective relocation of Romani minorities occurred after the devastating 1963 earthquake in Skopje, which resulted in much of the city being rebuilt. The reconstruction of Skopje also dismantled a part of the centuries-old Romani settlement Topaana in the centre of Skopje, and the local authorities gave its inhabitants two options, as the historian David Crowe (2007: 224) commented:

> Shuto Orizari began as a temporary American-built Quonset hut community in the aftermath of an earthquake on July 26, 1963 that destroyed three-quarters of the Macedonian capital and left 200,000 homeless. Reconstruction of the old Rom quarter Topana, entailed 'the addition of two intersecting freeways' and officials gave Gypsy leaders two choices: they could move into new integrated neighbourhoods, or they could move into their own suburb on the outskirts of Skopje.

Shuto Orizari, colloquially known as Shutka, later became a model of multicultural coexistence in multi-ethnic Skopje, usually without showing any historical reflection of its establishment as a temporary campsite built with American donations. The inhabitants of Topaana were not nomads but had lived there for centuries, yet the prevailing image of Roma as nomads made it possible to design a policy according to which they were able to be removed from the centre of the city. This predominantly affected the long-standing Romani community in Skopje (Sardelić, 2018). A similar relocation, indirectly sponsored by the EU, took place in the Serbian capital, Belgrade. Roma who lived under the Gazela bridge were relocated to other informal settlements around Belgrade while the bridge was being reconstructed with the support of the European Bank for Reconstruction and Development and the European Investment Bank. As van Baar (2016: 215) notes, in order to enhance the mobility of all EU citizens and connect them with citizens of EU candidate countries, Roma who lived under the 'connecting bridge' had to be forcedly relocated.

Despite available data showing that most Roma are sedentary and are no more mobile than majority populations (Cahn and Guild, 2010), the mass media as well as much research focus on the small population of Romani migrants (Balch *et al.*, 2013). Although most of the academic literature is critical of discourses and practices faced by Roma as migrants (Magazzini and Piemontese, 2019; Messing, 2019; Leggio, 2019; Humphris, 2019), the unrelenting focus on Romani migration also contributes to the reproduction of the image of the Romani migrant. In my previous work I have argued that whilst very few Roma are migrants, and it is questionable whether there is such a thing as Romani migration, the politics around Romani migration certainly exists (Sardelić, 2019b). This has become especially clear in debates on the free movement of EU citizens.

Among the most celebrated achievements of the EU were the 2000 Charter of Fundamental Rights (EU, 2012) and the 2001 Citizens' Rights Directive or EU Free Movement Directive as it is sometimes named (EU, 2004, henceforth the Citizens' Rights Directive). Both documents were EU legal manifestations to bring the EU closer to the ideal of ethical territoriality recognising rights of residents and citizens alike living in all Member States. The major breakthrough that both documents brought was the extension of social and economic rights to all citizens living in another EU Member State than their own. The free movement of EU citizens was initially conceptualised as a free movement of workers in the 1957 Treaty of Rome, which through Article 48 prohibited the discrimination of workers in question: 'Such freedom of movement shall entail the abolition of any discrimination based on nationality between workers of the Member States as regards employment, remuneration and other conditions of work and employment' (Treaty of Rome 1957, a. 48). However, it was only with the 2004 Citizens' Rights Directive that the rights of EU citizens were statutorily decoupled from the economic logic and labour market demands of an individual EU Member State (Carrera, 2005). With the EU Charter of Fundamental Rights and the 2004 Citizens' Rights Directive, the freedom of movement was transformed into the fundamental right of all EU citizens and their family members (even if the family members were third-country nationals). In Article 27(1) of the Citizens' Rights Directive, there is an explicit prohibition of the restriction of the free movement rights based on economic demand: 'Subject to the provisions of this Chapter, Member States may restrict the freedom of movement and residence of Union citizens and their family members, irrespective of nationality, on grounds of public policy, public security or public health. These grounds shall not be invoked to serve economic ends' (EU, 2004, a. 27). The expulsion of EU citizens and their families can occur only when there are serious threats to public health, public policy and public security, and the Directive included several procedural safeguards in Article 15 against such expulsions.

The perceived mobility practices place Roma with notional EU citizenship status close to the position of foreigners as they are stripped of their citizenship rights. More concretely, even in cases where Roma were EU citizens, the host states have used their 'acts of sovereignty' (Nyers, 2006) to irregularise them as EU citizens (Sardelić, 2017b) and appropriate their rights to those of third-country nationals (van Baar, 2016). It is important to note that the question of mobility and nomadism is never a stand-alone question but is always connected to the bigger puzzle of what rights citizens who are mobile have in a certain territory. States have securitised and criminalised the alleged problematic mobility practices of Roma in order to justify restricting their free movement rights (van Baar, 2015, 2019; Carrera and Faure Atger, 2010; Sardelić, 2017b). The criminalisation of Romani migration is not only perpetuated by states themselves, but has also often been uncritically reinforced in the reports of international organisations, as for example in the following 2016 report from the EU's Agency for Law Enforcement Cooperation (EUROPOL) on human trafficking:

> Criminal networks of Roma ethnicity are extremely mobile. Young women and minors of this group are especially vulnerable to exploitation and trafficking, which is sometimes arranged by their own families. This happens quite frequently in cases of child trafficking, where parents and close relatives are part of the recruitment circle. Destination countries for trafficked minors from Roma communities are mainly the United Kingdom and France, where they are subjected to sexual exploitation, labour exploitation, forced begging, petty crimes, and to a lesser extent the systematic defrauding of the social security and welfare benefit systems. The perpetration of property crimes is the main activity and source of income. Women and minors are mainly engaged in street crimes such as pick pocketing, bag-snatching and shoplifting in crowded and tourist areas, while men are in charge of the logistical and organisational management of the criminal activities (e.g. document forging, recruitment of new members, trade of high value vehicles and management of belongings). (EUROPOL, 2016: 18)

Two clear examples of such entanglement between mobility rights and alleged problematic nomadism took place during the so-called *l'affaire des Roms* (Carrera and Faure Atger, 2010; Balch *et al.*, 2013) and in the subsequent 2014 CJEU decision in *the Dano case*.

In the summer of 2010, French authorities initiated a plan instated by the then president, Nicolas Sarkozy, in a speech in Grenoble (La Croix, 2010). The speech was connected to a general crackdown on crime and irregular migration, but it shifted its attention to Romani EU citizens. In August 2010 French authorities expelled a thousand Romani individuals who were Romanian and Bulgarian citizens (BBC, 2010) after dismantling their informal settlements, and between 2009 and 2011 up to twelve thousand Roma were expelled each year (Ram, 2014a: 207). The justifications for dismantling these settlements were not only poor living conditions, but also the perception that these were the 'breeding grounds' for criminal activity of mobile groups, such as human trafficking and the exploitation of women and children (Gunther, 2013; Aradau *et al.*, 2013; Faure Atger, 2013; van Baar, 2015). In August 2010 the French Ministry of the Interior published a circular that included guidelines allowing the police to specifically target Roma from other EU Member States when demolishing informal settlements. When the circular was leaked to the press, later documents omitted a reference to Roma but did not prevent the demolition of their settlements (Carrera and Faure Atger, 2010: 4).

In 2010 a provisional measure was still in place that restricted the right to work of Bulgarian and Romanian citizens in other EU Member States. This measure was enacted so that the citizens of the new EU Member States who joined in 2007 would not migrate *en masse* to other EU countries in order to seek employment. However, the 2004 Citizens' Rights Directive was already in place, and this provided a safeguard against the expulsion of those Romanian and Bulgarian citizens who were already in other EU Member States. Any restriction on free movement had to be framed in connection to a threat to public policy, public security and public health, and not simply in terms of formal economic activity. With the dismantling of informal settlements, French authorities actively irregularised the status of Roma EU citizens of other Member States in order to create grounds for expulsion (Sardelić, 2017b). However, it became clear very soon that these expulsions were not made on a case-by-case basis, but were collective and therefore in breach of Article 19 of the EU Charter of Fundamental Rights and the Citizens' Rights Directive itself (van Baar, 2016).

Vivian Reding, who at the time was the Vice President of the European Commission and the Commissioner in charge of the Directorate for Justice, criticised France heavily over the collective expulsion of EU citizens of Romani background (Reding, 2010a; Balch *et al.*, 2013; and Ferreira, 2019) which also constituted a breach of the EU's 2000 Race Equality Directive (O'Nions, 2011). This Directive prohibits indirect discrimination on the basis of race or ethnicity. Following Article 258 of the Treaty on the Functioning of the European Union, the European Commission announced an infringement procedure against France on 15 October 2010 because it was not abiding by the fundamental legal principles of the EU. However, by 19 October the European Commission had revoked its decision, and it did not start the infringement procedure against France since it claimed that the French authorities had made official commitments to halt the collective expulsions of Roma from France (Reding, 2010b).

Whilst collective expulsions stopped in the eyes of the media, the French Office for Immigration and Integration continued its 'voluntary repatriation' project funded by the European Commission with a budget of €34,760,077 (Sardelić, 2017b: 339). Each Bulgarian and Romanian citizen who decided to 'voluntarily' leave France to return to their country of citizenship was awarded a one-way ticket and €300 in cash bursaries as a social inclusion measure for integration back into their country of origin. At the end of the project in 2012, France and Romania signed a repatriation agreement: 'France and Romania have signed a deal on the voluntary repatriation of Roma to Romania, with both sides saying that 'time' and 'patience' were needed to solve *Roma migration problems* (Euractiv, 2012; my emphasis). The European Commission report evaluated the project on voluntary repatriation as positive: '[t]he Project has had a positive impact: it facilitated return on a voluntary basis, ensuring the rights of migrants and initiating both sustainable return and reintegration in the individuals' country of origin. With the financial allowance, migrants were able to establish a new economic activity in their home country' (European Commission, 2011d).

Whilst it is not clear from the project description whether France's assisted voluntary return programme for Romanian and Bulgarian citizens was funded by the European Commission, the logic of returning them to their countries of origin was very similar to that of the return of third-country nationals funded by the European Return Fund. It received heavy criticism from civil society and Romani individuals themselves (Faure Atger, 2013). For example, in its punk rock song 'Sarkozy versus Gypsy', quoted in the introduction to this chapter, the Romanian band VAMA featuring Ralflo, with Romani members, mocked such politics with the following lyrics:

> We're looking for the better way
> But you decide we cannot stay ...
> You take the right to dream, to work ...
> Three hundred euros won't buy hope ...
> The fingerprint is not our soul
> We're human beings first of all ...
> If all the gypsies were to steal ...
> Tour Eiffel would disappear ...
> The world belongs to all the people
> Gypsy people is not people?
> (VAMA featuring Ralflo, 2010, quoted in Romea.cz, 2010)

Further responses by the European Commission to the European Parliament, the EU Council, the European Economic and Social Committee and the Committee of Regions led to the establishment of the EU NRIS Framework (European Commission, 2011b: 173). Whilst this was a response to the approach France took towards Romani migrants (Carrera *et al.*, 2019), it did not address the position of Romani migrants *per se* but rather reinstated the logic that each EU Member State should primarily be responsible for the integration of its own Romani citizens (Magazzini and Piemontese, 2019). As Dragos Ciulinaru (2018: 1059) explains, there was a 'shift from protection against discrimination to the issue of integration'. In 2013 the EUs NRIS Framework became operational (for more details see Chapter 1). In parallel with the operationalisation of this strategy, however, the CJEU dealt with the *Elisabetta and Florin Dano v. Jobcenter Leipzig* case and reached a decision in November 2014. The *Dano* case concerned a Romanian citizen and her son who had moved to Germany under the Citizens' Rights Directive. According to the data the CJEU possessed, Elisabeta Dano had had only three years of primary schooling, did not have a profession, had limited knowledge of the German language and was not formally working or seeking formal work in Germany, but was economically supported by her sister. In its discussion of the prohibition of discrimination on the basis of nationality, the court omitted any reference to her ethnicity or possible discrimination she might have faced in her country of citizenship as a basis for being mobile. However, the CJEU did reach the decision that since she was not seeking formal work, in accordance with Articles 14 and 24 of the Citizens' Rights Directive, Germany was not obliged to provide any social assistance to her or her son: 'It is apparent from the documents before the Court that Ms Dano has been residing in Germany for more than three months, that she is not seeking employment and that she did not enter Germany in order to work. She therefore does not fall within the scope *ratione personae* of Article 24(2) of Directive 2004/38' (*Dano v. Jobcenter Leipzig* 2014, para. 66).

The court's decision in the *Dano* case became prominent in the debates about the UK's membership in the EU, popularly known as Brexit. As Euractiv reported: 'EU Member States can block jobless immigrants from receiving specific welfare benefits, Europe's top Court said on Tuesday (11 November), in a ruling likely to aid British Prime Minister David Cameron's efforts to tackle so-called "welfare tourism"' (Euractiv, 2014). Like the CJEU decision in *Dano*, Euroactiv made no reference to Dano's Romani ethnicity. However, the article did include a photo of a beggar on the street with the caption: 'Roma panhandler in Sweden, 2013' (Euractiv, 2014). There was no discussion on how the photo of a Romani beggar allegedly from Sweden related to the *Dano* case, if it was not for the previous reports that mobile Romani migrants commit social assistance fraud as 'welfare tourists' (Geddes and Hadj Abdou, 2016). Most of the newspaper articles on welfare tourism ignored practices such as 'dental tourism' (Österle *et al.*, 2009), whereby British citizens travel to Eastern European countries for cheaper dental healthcare. Yet the British tabloids did identify Elisabeta Dano as a Roma and even labelled her a 'gypsy': 'Wrapped up warm for a day out in town, this is the Roma gipsy whose refusal to work has spurred a crackdown on benefits tourism. Elisabeta Dano, 25, has found herself at the centre of a landmark European case, which has apparently given Britain the green light to block welfare claims from migrants who refuse to work' (Bentley, 2014). Whilst the CJEU wanted to avoid any reference to ethnicity, the media, especially the British tabloids, were explicitly stereotypical in this manner. The tabloids also quoted from her statement that she was a babysitter for her sister, yet this was not considered to be work as it was informal.

Besides being portrayed as benefit tourists, Romani migrants, particularly those from non-EU countries, have been increasingly depicted as 'bogus asylum seekers'. Roma had already been represented as asylum seekers before the 2004 EU enlargement (Clark and Campbell, 2000; see also Chapters 1 and 5), but the main discussion on restricting the rights of Romani asylum seekers emerged during the process of the Schengen visa liberalisation for the Western Balkan countries. The Schengen visa requirements for the three post-Yugoslav countries (Serbia, Montenegro and North Macedonia) were lifted in late 2009, and, in late 2010 they were lifted for Albania and BIH also (Kacarska, 2015: 363). As stated by one of the reports from the European Migration Network, an EU-funded group, on the visa liberalisation's impact on destination countries: 'Several Member States of the EU (Germany, Sweden, Belgium) have notified that within a year from launching visa liberalisation had to deal with significantly increased, doubled and tripled asylum applications. Majority of asylum applications belonged to minority groups of Roma and ethnic Albanians, who appeared less integrated within local societies, having fewer chances for improving living conditions' (European Migration Network, 2018: 5).

After the change in the visa regime for the countries in the Western Balkans, the number of asylum seekers from these countries did indeed significantly increase: in 2009, before the visa restrictions were lifted, EU Member States received 5,460 asylum applications from Serbia, and, by 2014 they had received 30,810 applications from the same country. More than three quarters of these asylum applications were received in Germany (Kummrow, 2015: 21). As many as 90 per cent of the individuals who applied for asylum from the Western Balkan countries self-identified as Roma, though it was not clear whether these individuals were in fact all Romani or whether they included non-Romani asylum seekers wishing to secure asylum-seeking status (Sardelić, 2018: 499).

However, the increased number of asylum seekers caused a heated debate in the European Parliament, which in September 2013 voted on a visa-free suspension mechanism that would reintroduce the visa regime for the Western Balkan countries should the number of asylum seekers continue increasing. The mechanism was legally introduced through EU Regulation 1289/2013: 'This Regulation should establish a mechanism for the temporary suspension of the exemption from the visa requirement for a third country listed in Annex II to Regulation (EC) No. 539/2001 ("the suspension mechanism") in an emergency situation, where an urgent response is needed in order to resolve the difficulties faced by at least one Member State, and taking account of the overall impact of the emergency situation on the Union as a whole.' As Article 2 of the Regulation specified, the suspension mechanism could be enacted in the following scenarios:

> A substantial and sudden increase in the number of: (a) nationals of that third country found to be staying in the Member State's territory without a right thereto; (b) asylum applications from the nationals of that third country for which the recognition rate is low, where such an increase is leading to specific pressures on the Member State's asylum system; (c) rejected readmission applications submitted by the Member State to that third country for its own nationals. (EU, 2013, a. 2)

As Euractiv reported, '[a] mechanism allowing the suspension of visa-free travel for third countries was adopted by the European Parliament last week, but controversial legal issues remain over the increasing problem of "fake" asylum-seekers, often Roma from the Western Balkan countries'. The article continued: 'Several EU countries were affected negatively by the visa liberalisation policy. In particular, a wave of asylum-seekers from Macedonia and Serbia, mainly of Roma or Albanian ethnicity, hit Sweden, Belgium and Germany' (Milevska, 2013). The debate in the European Parliament highlighted that the Western Balkan countries had to strengthen their minority and human rights protections should they want to keep a visa-free regime for the Schengen zone. However, such an approach had an adverse effect. Serbia, for example, started putting up billboards with the message 'I do not want to seek asylum in the European Union' at the border controls in Serbian, Albanian and Romani languages (Sardelić, 2018: 499).

North Macedonia went one step further and started blocking its own Romani citizens from leaving their country, which was against Article 13 of the Universal Declaration of Human Rights (1948).

As reported by several international NGOs (such as the ERRC), a number of Romani individuals were not allowed to leave North Macedonia if they were identified as potential asylum seekers. Their passports were marked with an 'AZ' stamp which indicated that the holders should not be allowed to leave the country. Instead of introducing a comprehensive and adequate minority protection framework, the countries in question responded to the EU institutions by violating the human rights of ethnic minority citizens in order to preserve the rights of free movement for all other citizens: 'The [North Macedonian] Government argued that the passport revocation measure was necessary to prevent or minimise the risk of individuals violating the immigration laws of other countries, thus damaging the country's reputation' (ERRC, 2014). In 2014 the Constitutional Court of Macedonia deemed the racial profiling taking place on the border unconstitutional, as well as the law on travel documents that permitted certain citizens to exit their own country (ERRC, 2014).

All the cases on the free movement restriction of Romani minorities reveal the discrepancy between ethical territoriality and the other meaning of territoriality, referring to a space where states can practise their sovereign power. The ways in which the states deal with alleged problematic types of mobility and migration are myopic: these cases show how expanding rights for all can effectively limit such rights for certain minorities despite the fact that they are actual citizens themselves. The invisible edges of citizenship reinforce the perception of Romani individuals as migrants rather than citizens and position them at the fringes of citizenship. However, it is a debate about citizenship rights that should transcend the debate about a particular migration or mobility pattern.

Irregularising citizenship globally: the Intervention in Australia

In his book *Irregular Citizenship, Immigration, and Deportation*, Nyers (2019) showed that processes of legal status irreguralisation do not apply only to migrants in particular countries, but also to citizens with a migrant background even if they have never been migrants themselves. The Romani individuals whose freedom of movement was limited fall into the category of irregularised citizens rather than migrants. It was the rights they possessed as citizens that were infringed in all the cases analysed, although the discussion mainly focused on the portrayal of Romani individuals in question primarily as migrants. In this case, states ascribed nomadism as a specific and essential characteristic of Romani culture that needed to be controlled.

In contrast to Nyers, this chapter claims that citizenship status can become irregularised even in cases where minorities predate the current borders and cannot be conceived as having migrant status at all. In 2013 around 20,000 former Yugoslav citizens of Romani background became at risk of statelessness (see Chapter 4) even though they had never crossed a border that was internationally recognised at the time, as the post-Yugoslav states' borders were established later (Sardelić, 2017b). In general, Roma are rarely regarded as a minority that predates the borders of the Westphalian state order, and are not classified as Indigenous (Olivera, 2012), although there are records of the presence of Roma in Europe before current states emerged (Crowe, 2007). However, citizenship irregularisation does appear also in cases of Indigenous citizens, who can be deprived of rights in a similar manner to Romani citizens in Europe. I examine this claim through an analysis of the 2007 Northern Territory Intervention enacted by the Australian federal Government. The Intervention targeted specifically Indigenous communities in the remote areas of the Northern Territory in Australia.

The Northern Territory Government held an inquiry that resulted in a report entitled *Little Children are Sacred* (Wild and Anderson, 2007). The report was published in mid-July 2007 and dealt with the disadvantages Aboriginal people face in remote areas of the Northern Territory. Its main focus, however, was on the alleged sexual abuses that children suffered because of these disadvantages, and also on the lack of governmental control over Indigenous communities. The inquiry research team consulted forty-five Aboriginal communities, who suggested possible means of addressing child abuse in these communities, such as: 'dialogue, empowerment, ownership, awareness, healing, reconciliation, strong family, culture, law' (Wild and Anderson, 2007: 15). The team then designed a number of long-term sustainable principles for protecting women and children in the remote Indigenous communities. Among these principles, the most important were the improvement of governmental services to remote Aboriginal communities, the recognition of diversity and possible barriers to dialogue, and authentic consultations between the Aboriginal communities and the Northern Territory Government as well as the Australian federal Government. The report stressed the urgency of these measures, recommending that: 'Aboriginal child sexual abuse in the Northern Territory be designated as an issue of urgent national significance by both the Australian and Northern Territory Governments, and both governments immediately establish a collaborative partnership with a Memorandum of Understanding to specifically address the protection of Aboriginal children from sexual abuse. It is critical that both governments commit to genuine consultation with Aboriginal people in designing initiatives for Aboriginal communities' (Wild and Anderson, 2007: 22).

With no immediate response by the Northern Territory Government to the *Little Children are Sacred* report, the Australian Government took the initiative and introduced the 2007 Northern Territory National Emergency Response Act (henceforth the Intervention Act). The Intervention Act was introduced by the Liberal government of John Howard in a pre-election period, but the measures continued after Kevin Rudd's Labour government came into power. The Intervention started in the year the UN passed the Declaration on the Rights of Indigenous Peoples with the opposition of Australia, New Zealand, US and Canada (O'Sullivan, 2020) and continued in 2008, at the same time as Rudd issued a governmental apology for the 'Stolen Generations', the children from the Aboriginal communities who were forcedly removed from their families by the Australian governments and church missions until the late 1960s (Barta, 2008; Moses, 2011).

As noted by a number of scholars and activists (Altman and Hinkson, 2007; Watson, 2011; Macoun, 2011; Armillei and Lobo, 2017), the Intervention Act took up the sense of emergency in the *Little Children are Sacred* report but ignored its recommendations about informing, consulting and obtaining proper consent from the Aboriginal communities on the matter. Section 132 of the Intervention Act proclaimed its content as 'special measures' and stated, '[t]he provisions of this Act, and any acts done under or for the purposes of those provisions, are excluded from the operation of Part 2 of the Racial Discrimination Act 1975' (Northern Territory National

Emergency Response Act 2007, para. 132). Part 2 of the Racial Discrimination Act 1975 includes the 'prohibition of racial discrimination' (Racial Discrimination Act 1975, Part 2). This part refers to paragraph 4 of Article 1 of the 1969 International Convention on the Elimination of All Forms of Racial Discrimination:

> Special measures taken for the sole purpose of securing adequate advancement of certain racial or ethnic groups or individuals requiring such protection as may be necessary in order to ensure such groups or individuals equal enjoyment or exercise of human rights and fundamental freedoms shall not be deemed racial discrimination, provided, however, that such measures do not, as a consequence, lead to the maintenance of separate rights for different racial groups and that they shall not be continued after the objectives for which they were taken have been achieved. (UN, 1969, a. 1.4)

The special measures and the exception clause of the Racial Discrimination Act 1975 were revoked so that the Intervention Act could specifically target Aboriginal communities in the Northern Territory. Among other measures, the Intervention Act introduced additional control over alcohol consumption (Part 2) and special filters on publicly funded computers (Part 3) in order to limit pornography access, five-year township leases for the land previously owned by the Aboriginal communities (Part 4) and finally an income management system (Article 126) to control how individuals spent their welfare benefits. As some scholars argued, the abolition of some of the previous successful programmes – such as the Community Development Employment Projects – made more Indigenous individuals dependent on social benefits (Perche, 2017). Overall police presence was increased in the Aboriginal communities, but at the same time, infrastructure (like medical facilities) was not significantly improved as the report recommended. The special measures over the remote Northern Territory continued after the Intervention Act was no longer in force, as a result of the Stronger Futures in the Northern Territory Act 2012 introduced by the Labour government in 2012 (Baehr and Schmidt-Haberkamp, 2017; Perche, 2017). The key change, though, was that this Act no longer targeted Indigenous communities directly (by suspending the Racial Discrimination Act 1975) but focused on disadvantaged communities (Stronger Futures in the Northern Territory Act 2012). Yet all the key elements of the

Intervention Act remained intact despite the claim in the Act that it was supposed to be temporary (Baehr and Schmidt-Haberkamp, 2017), and there was no clear evidence that these measures were in fact protecting children and women, as they had been initially intended to do (Watson, 2011) A similar 'concern' was raised in EUROPOL's report that 'Romani criminal itinerant gangs' were abusing their children and women; yet there is no evidence that limiting the rights of Roma as EU citizens brought an improvement in the position of Romani women and children. The emergency response became a long-term policy towards remote Indigenous communities in the Northern Territory (Armillei and Lobo, 2017). To protect the human rights of the most vulnerable and to prevent criminal activities by some individuals in the community, entire communities were deprived of rights that non-Indigenous Australians take for granted.

The Intervention Act irregularised Indigenous people as Australian citizens, in a similar manner to how Roma have been irregularised as citizens in various European states. A few scholars have recognised the similarities between the Northern Territory Intervention and the so-called 'nomad emergencies' in Italy which occurred around the same time (Armillei and Lobo 2017; Hepworth 2012: 431). The emergency was called a 'nomad emergency' because it targeted Roma who were Bulgarian and Romanian citizens. Two additional parallels have remained under-analysed until now: first, although directly discriminatory emergency laws had been repealed, other manifestly more neutral laws took on the same function; and second, the political discourse around the Northern Territory Intervention constructed child abuse as a problematic part of aboriginality, that is, a key feature of Indigenous culture that needs to be controlled (Macoun, 2011). As in the case of Roma, it was the alleged problematic cultural practices of Indigenous people that were the basis for the violation of their citizenship rights and more general human rights (overriding the Racial Discrimination Act 1975 too).

Conclusion

This chapter has scrutinised concepts of ethical territoriality and irregularised citizenship. It has argued that whilst a number of countries are moving in the direction of ethical territoriality to extend certain citizenship rights to (some) aliens, they are also moving away from them by irregularising the status of some citizens. I have shown this through the example of Roma whose migration has been reinterpreted as a problematic cultural practice. I have argued that rather than looking at this through the lens of migration, we need to examine it through the prism of restricting citizenship rights. I have compared the restriction of free movement of Roma in Europe to the Northern Territory Intervention in Australia, which restricted certain rights for Indigenous communities by using the 'excuse' of protecting children and women from 'problematic' aboriginal culture. Previously, scholars have argued that there are different categories of citizenship and conceptualised them as semi-citizenship (Cohen, 2009). However, this chapter argues that the cases described do not simply correspond to citizens having different levels of rights. These are cases where citizens were supposed to have equal status but governments, through acts of sovereignty, irregularised their position. When critical voices have pointed out that the legal acts in question were racially discriminatory, states have usually transformed them so that they appear neutral but have kept the invisible edges of citizenship that position marginalised minorities at the fringes of their own citizenship.

3

Citizens in the making and inequality of opportunity: school segregation of Romani children

Inequality of opportunity is unfair and inefficient. Although there is much debate on whether and to which extent public policy should aim to level outcomes (for example, being poor), there is consensus that all individuals – irrespective of the socioeconomic circumstances into which they are born – should be allowed the same chances to be successful in life. Equality of opportunity is not only the right thing to do for societies that want to call themselves fair, but also a smart economic choice.

2016 report *Being Fair, Faring Better: Promoting Equality of Opportunity for Marginalized Roma* published by the World Bank (Gatti *et al.*, 2016: xix)

Introduction

Between 31 May and 2 June 2019, Pope Francis paid a visit to Romania and made a historical apology to all Roma in Europe. He apologised for the harm inflicted on Roma by the majority populations and institutions affiliated with the Roman Catholic Church. Prominent international media in Europe and around the globe reported on the Pope's apology, among them the *New York Times*: 'Pope Francis, on the last day of his trip to Romania, on Sunday asked for forgiveness on behalf of his church for the suffering endured by the Roma people, saying his heart was "weighed down by the many experiences of discrimination, segregation and mistreatment" they have experienced' (Gillet and Horowitz, 2019). This was not the first time Pope Francis expressed remorse for the mistreatment of Romani minorities. Earlier in May the same year, he spoke against the violence inflicted on the Omerović family, who fled from BIH to Italy during the post-Yugoslav wars. When the Italian state authorities relocated the refugee Romani family from the segregated camp on the fringes of Rome to a more centrally located apartment in the city, neofascist and extreme-right groups protested against the decision. There were numerous media reports about the protests: 'The mayor of Rome, Virginia Raggi, also visited the family to show her support after some of the protesters said they wanted to see the family "hanged and burned"' (Lakić, 2019). The Pope welcomed around 500 Roma and Sinti to a service at the Vatican, including the family in question, in his own protest against the xenophobic attacks, much to the disdain of the Italian Deputy Prime Minister at the time, Matteo Salvini. During the service, as reported by Vatican News, the Pope said the following words: 'Yes, second-class citizens exist here, but those who are really second-rate are those who reject people because they are unable to accept them' (Vatican News, 2019). With this gesture, along with his previous gestures of support for refugees, Pope Francis clashed with the global extreme far-right movement and became 'a hate figure for the far right' (Baldwin *et al.*, 2019).

The news of the Pope's visit to Romania and his apology to Roma also made the national headlines in Europe. The media reported it in, among others, the newest EU Member State, Croatia, whose population predominantly identifies as Catholic (Perica, 2006). However, on exactly the same day, a local event in connection to Roma was in the media spotlight in Croatia. Whilst the Pope was visiting Romania on 1 June, a protest under the banner 'I want a normal life' (Telegram, 2019; my translation)[1] was taking place in the Croatian county of Međimurje, where the highest number of Roma live (Šlezak, 2009: 67). The protest, which attracted around a thousand people, was organised by two men: an eighteen-year-old supporter of the radical right-wing parties' coalition, and a Croatian war veteran who stated, 'I have put my life in danger, sacrificed in war, but I do not want, speaking in the name of all peaceful and hard-working citizens of Međimurje, to suffer the *Roma terror*, which has lasted over twenty years' (*Međimurjepress*, 2019; my emphasis and translation).[2] The organisers claimed that their protest was to highlight the problem of petty crimes alleged to be mostly committed by the local Roma in Međimurje. They claimed that Romani petty criminals were violating the human rights of the local majority population, especially the right to a normal life (Vlasić, 2019). Whilst some local Romani representatives supported and even joined the protest, international NGOs, such as the ERRC, and the member of the Croatian parliament representing the Romani minority, Veljko Kajtazi, called it 'pure racism' (Duhaček, 2019). The Pope's apology in Romania and the local protest in the Međimurje county were reported side by side on the same day, and yet the connection between the two was never made, either by the media or by any of the local Croatian politicians.

The Croatian Interior Minister at the time, Davor Božinović, came to Međimurje county and promised extra police support to patrol Romani settlements, but emphasised that much more needed to be done to improve the situation in the county, especially in the education sector. Government websites too echoed Božinović's comments: 'The key to solving the *Roma problematics* in Međimurje is education' (Government of Croatia, 2019; my translation and emphasis).[3] Božinović declared that in this situation where only four out of 318 Romani high school pupils finished their schooling, 'there must be something terribly wrong. These young people have disqualified themselves from the race of life so they are not equal any more, they do not fulfil the basic conditions for jobseekers, and this problem needs to be solved' (Government of Croatia, 2019; my translation).[4] Some newspaper commentators agreed with the minister: 'Božinović is right, Roma have disqualified themselves!' (Vlasić, 2019; my translation).[5] Yet what was absent from these debates was the fact that Croatia had been charged with discrimination against Romani children in education in 2010 by the ECtHR, less than a decade previously. Similarly, as in other European countries, the minister and the public in Croatia engaged in the 'politics of forgetting' (Gándara, 2005) and returned to the view that Roma themselves were responsible for their own marginalisation. Whilst the Pope publicly apologised for the segregation of Roma, none of the political representatives of the states where Romani children were segregated in schools made a similar gesture, and they instead sought to legitimise it as a benevolent approach (O'Nions, 2010).

This chapter looks at the 'citizens in the making' in education and analyses the invisible edges of citizenship on which state authorities rely to argue that they offer equal opportunities for all of their citizens. By examining the segregation of Romani children, it highlights how through such invisible edges of citizenship the educational system not only maintains but also actively constructs the civic marginalisation of minorities such as Roma. The chapter shows how governments have legitimised the segregation of Romani children in public educational systems. It argues that policies based simply on either socio-economic disadvantage or ethnic discrimination are often myopic and cannot fully explain the dynamics and reasons behind such marginalisation. The chapter explores the justifications that state lawyers have used in ECtHR court cases on educational segregation of Romani children. Previous scholarly accounts have examined the successful arguments that advocates of Romani applicants have used to prove discrimination (Goldston, 2010). This chapter focuses specifically on the following ECtHR cases: 2007 *D.H. and Others v. Czech Republic* (henceforth the *D.H.* case); 2008 *Sampanis and Others v. Greece* (henceforth the 2008 *Sampanis* case); 2010 *Oršuš and Others v. Croatia* (henceforth the *Oršuš* case); and 2012 *Sampani and Others v. Greece* (henceforth the 2012 *Sampani* case).[6] In all these cases the states justified segregation as a legitimate non-discriminatory measure: they denied that spatial separation equals discriminatory segregation and that it had been organised specifically for Roma so that they could 'catch up' and secure the same chances of inclusion through education as the majority population. I claim that the practice of segregation has been structured through the invisible edges of citizenship in such a way that it actively creates the fringes of citizenship. Placing Romani children in separate educational facilities contributes to the positioning of Roma on the fringes of citizenship. Besides analysing governmental discourses that legitimised segregation, I also look at the dissenting opinions of ECtHR judges who disagreed that Romani children had been discriminated against in school systems, focusing in particular on the dissenting opinions in the *D.H.* and *Oršuš* cases. In the two cases from Greece, the ECtHR Chamber judges reached unanimous decisions.

Contemplating the societal implications of educational discrimination

The link between educational opportunities and the social inclusion of Roma has been well documented and widely discussed in academic literature (Rostas and Kostka, 2014; O'Nions, 2015; Van Den Bogaert, 2018). More broadly, different liberal theories from Rawls (1971) to Nozick (1974) have underlined the importance of equal opportunities, as have international organisations (Gatti *et al.*, 2016) and NGO activists (Albert, 2019), However, not everyone sees the greater value in embracing equal opportunities and striving for social inclusion, as Albert (2019: 44) notes: 'It is regrettable that whilst many changes to education policy have been undertaken in response to the need to make educational opportunity more equal, the [Czech] Government has done a poor job of explaining to the public why these changes will actually improve education for all children, not just for those who have been excluded and educated in segregated, separate settings.'

International policymakers have taken equality of opportunity as a theoretical assumption, such as the World Bank, which published the report *Being Fair, Faring Better: Promoting Equality of Opportunity for Marginalized Roma* (Gatti *et al.*, 2016). This report followed the logic that education in liberal democracies should serve as a corrective mechanism to mitigate the inequalities faced by children from disadvantaged backgrounds, who are still 'citizens in the making'. In addition, it argued that equality of opportunity was not simply a moral responsibility for the state but also a rationale for economic growth, especially in Central and Eastern European (CEE) states with significant Romani minorities:

> Equality of opportunity is not only the right thing to do for societies that want to call themselves fair, but also a smart economic choice. A growing body of evidence shows that equity is associated with improved growth prospects. This is especially the case in the context of countries such as those in CEE, where aging, emigration, and low fertility are leading to a decline in working-age populations and where the young and growing Roma populations represent an increasing share of new labour market entrants. (Gatti *et al.*, 2016: xix)

The report used economistic logic to justify the inclusion of Roma and portrayed it as a possible benefit for the entire wellbeing of wider society, including majority populations. This logic was also prevalent in EU policies on Romani integration, including the EU NRIS Framework (Goodwin and Buijs, 2013; Iusmen, 2018). The argument that desegregation has potential benefits for state economies was not an original one: in the US, different actors had made similar arguments around half a century earlier in the context of racially segregated education. In 1947 President Truman's committee issued a report in which it stated 'three reasons, why civil rights abuses should be redressed: a moral reason – discrimination was morally wrong; economic reason – discrimination harmed the economy; and an international reason – discrimination damaged US foreign relations' (Dudziak, 2011: 79).

According to the economistic perspective contained within the World Bank report, the main problem Roma face with regard to educational discrimination is the fact that it leads to their exclusion from the labour market later in life. The logic here is inherently neoliberal: the exclusion of Roma from the labour market is damaging for the local economy as it leads to more dependency on social benefits and welfare. At the same time, the description of the educational system as reproducing the labour force echoes a classic neo-Marxist text by Louis Althusser (1971) entitled *The Ideological State Apparatus*, where school serves as a mechanism for ideology production which is necessary for the continued functioning of the capitalist system. However, some anthropologists, such as Judith Okely (1994: 71), have argued that whilst Romani minorities have been outcasts from the capitalist system, this can be perceived as liberating rather than as a disadvantage: 'Their outsider status is imposed, but also chosen.' Okely refers specifically to Althusser and to schooling as a state's ideological apparatus, but claims that Romani minorities have actively avoided being included in educational and labour market structures; rather, they have formed alternative and sometimes competing niches in the official systems, and that is why state officials have particularly scrutinised their position (Okely, 1994: 66–7).

However, when considering these claims, I argue that the segregation of Roma children in schools needs to be analysed in terms of civic marginalisation in a European as well as a more global perspective, which goes beyond the question of socio-economic calculus and ethnic discrimination. It is also problematic to analyse it simply as an individual or even group choice without understanding the context in which these choices have been made. I claim that the case of school segregation shows that Romani minorities are not only discriminated against because of their socio-economic status and ethnic belonging but also discriminated against as citizens.

Global parallels

Legal activists and advocates focusing on the educational segregation of Romani children have drawn their inspirations from the earlier US Supreme Court cases on the school segregation of African American children, especially the 1954 case *Brown v. Board of Education of Topeka* (henceforth the *Brown* case) (Bader Ginsburg, 2005; Greenberg, 2010; Minow, 2012; Goldston, 2017). Indeed, the *D.H.* case has been referred to several times as the 'European *Brown* case' (ERRC, 2019; Chang and Rucker-Chang, 2020: 122). This chapter compares the reasoning of the states in question, which claimed that segregation does not mean discrimination and, in both cases, argued along the lines of 'separate, but equal'. However, whilst there have been a number of works published that show the similarities between the two cases, I also highlight important differences that have not been raised until now. The most obvious difference lay in the question of addressing direct and indirect discrimination (see Hepple, 2006; Farkas, 2014; O'Nions, 2015; Arabadjieva, 2016, Chang and Rucker-Chang, 2020: 129): in the US, segregation was entrenched in law with the 1896 *Plessy v. Ferguson* decision of the Supreme Court, whilst the segregation of Roma did not have a legal basis but was present in practice. Nevertheless, some legal scholars have argued that the Roma segregation cases did amount to direct discrimination according to EU law (Farkas, 2014). Finally, from the perspective of connected sociologies (Bhambra, 2014), this chapter looks at the segregation cases in the frame of global politics at the time. Whilst some scholars point out that the US desegregation process has to be understood within the broader Cold War context (Dudziak, 2004; Bader Ginsburg, 2005; Goldston, 2017), Romani school segregation cases played an important role in shaping the global politics of postsocialist transitions and EU integration (Chang and Rucker-Chang, 2020: 38–51). Nonetheless, global politics has not had such a decisive role for these European cases as it has in the American context, even to the present day.

This chapter looks at how the invisible edges of citizenship are produced and reproduced through the education system and how they put marginalised minorities on the fringes of citizenship. It argues that discrimination created by the segregation of Romani children in state education systems can be considered one of the most prominent examples of the invisible edges of citizenship. In a similar vein to the pronouncements made by the Croatian minister Božinović discussed earlier, in the broader public discourse education is often described as a corrective mechanism for the inequalities that children inherit from their parents. However, in this chapter I show how the educational system can also create new inequalities and contribute to civic marginalisation despite claiming to use benevolent approaches towards marginalised children from minority backgrounds. Civic marginalisation does not simply happen to migrants or citizens with a migrant background as a result of their inherent cultural differences and their belonging to a different society incompatible with liberalism, as Taylor (1994: 62) claimed. The cases of both African Americans and Romani children show that liberal democratic states produce this difference by imposing invisible edges of citizenship against the minorities who have been part of these wider societies for centuries.

US school segregation

In 2018 two Harvard academics, Margareta Matache, a Romani scholar and activist, and Cornel West, an African American civil rights scholar and activist, wrote an article which argued that 'Roma and African Americans share a common struggle' (Matache and West, 2018). The piece mostly focused on the parallels with regard to the slavery that Roma endured on the territory of present-day Romania until the mid-nineteenth century:

> Since 1853, Mihail Kogălniceanu, one of the most progressive Romanian intellectuals of all time, has pointed out the comparable struggles of African Americans in bondage and enslaved Roma people. His preface about Roma slavery and the translation of Uncle Tom's Cabin – the first American novel to be published in Romanian – increased a consciousness of shame about the brutality of slavery across a few strands of Romanian society. Kogălniceanu was one white intellectual

among many in both Europe and the Americas who, along with fellow abolitionists, denounced slavery and advocated for its eradication. (Matache and West, 2018)

Besides slavery, scholars have also highlighted other parallels between the position of Roma and other marginalised minorities, such as the spatial segregation of Aboriginal people in Australia (Armillei and Lobo, 2017; Taylor *et al.*, 2018), the high incarceration rates of Māori in New Zealand (Takacs, 2017) and the coercive sterilisation of women belonging to First Nations of Canada (Stote, 2015). Yet the parallels that have received the greatest attention among scholars and activists is that with educational segregation. These parallels have been noted by Jack Greenberg (2010), a lawyer in the original *Brown* case, Ruth Bader Ginsburg (2005), an associate justice of the US Supreme Court until 2020, and the lawyer in both the *D.H.* and *Oršuš* cases, James Goldston (2017).

Whilst there have been several cases dealing with educational segregation in the US, the one receiving the most attention as relevant for the Romani movement and legal activism is the *Brown* case of 1954 (Goldston, 2017; Chang and Rucker-Chang, 2020). The *Brown* case overturned the decision of 1896 *Plessy v. Fergusson* (henceforth the *Plessy* case), which upheld the policy of 'separate but equal' (the understanding that the separate facilities for African American do not mean unequal treatment) as the legal doctrine on the federal level. Whilst the 'separate but equal' policy of the *Plessy* case did not deal with education, it did influence segregated schooling, and it soon not only became a practice but was institutionalised legally. The *Brown* case overturned *Plessy* with the decision that the 'separate but equal' position was in breach of the Fourteenth Amendment (the provision on equal treatment). The court in the *Brown* case reached the following conclusion:

> Segregation of white and colored children in public schools has a detrimental effect upon the colored children. The impact is greater when it has the sanction of the law, for the policy of separating the races is usually interpreted as denoting the inferiority of the Negro group … Any language in contrary to this finding is rejected. We conclude that in the field of public education the doctrine of 'separate but equal' has no place. Separate educational facilities are inherently unequal. (Warren in *Brown v. Board of Education of Topeka*, 1954)[7]

Whilst it was a landmark legal case, *Brown* did not ignite a huge desegregation process. There was major opposition to the desegregation process, as witnessed, for example, in the case of the so-called Little Rock Nine, a group of nine African American students who were blocked from entering the previously all-white Little Rock High School in Arkansas in 1957 by the state governor, Orval Faubus (Epperson, 2014). The US President at the time, Dwight Eisenhower, had to federalise Arkansas's national guard so that it could protect those nine students from protestors at the entrance in order to execute the Supreme Court decision. As Epperson (2014) argues, Governor Faubus initially stated that he would not give up his state power to federal authority. Subsequent education laws in Arkansas were amended to prohibit segregation in theory, yet in practice the desegregation process never took place. One of the reasons for this was that some African American parents feared that their children would not be safe in mixed schools. In the subsequent 1958 case *Cooper v. Aaron*, Governor Faubus changed his tactics and attempted to suspend desegregation on the basis of the very protests themselves, claiming that the safety of the African American children in question could not be guaranteed. The court did not endorse these arguments:

> Today, *Cooper* is taught in almost every constitutional law class around the country to highlight the role of judicial supremacy in our constitutional structure. In declaring that the US Constitution is 'the supreme law of the Land', and the federal judiciary is 'supreme in the exposition of the law of the Constitution', Cooper also emphasized the 'fundamental and pervasive' right of children to a desegregated education. It provided a clear disavowal of state-inspired violence as a mechanism to thwart educational opportunity. (Epperson, 2014: 696–7)

The *en masse* desegregation process started only gradually, but it did yield positive results despite the initial disbelief, as Pettigrew (2004: 525) notes: '[f]rom 1970s to 1990s, Black high school completion rates rose sharply. Although less than half of Black students finished high school in 1950, the percentage now approaches that of White students. During these same years, the mean difference between Black and White achievement test scores steadily narrowed.' However, a number of authors, including Danielle Holley-Walker (2004) and Wendy Parker (2000), have argued that several cases from the 1970s onwards almost prompted a re-segregation, starting with the 1974 *Milliken v. Bradley* case (hereafter the *Milliken* case) – a Supreme Court case on the planned desegregation of state school students across school districts by means of busing in Detroit, the city with the greatest African American majority in the US – that departed from *Brown* by arguing that *de facto* district segregation did not represent *de jure* segregation (Pettigrew, 2004: 523). As Orfield and his colleagues (1994) note, the separate *de facto* segregated facilities were a reality not only for African American students, but also for Hispanic pupils.

From American to European segregation cases

A number of prominent US lawyers have claimed that European court cases concerning the segregation of Romani children in education have been influenced by desegregation developments in the US. For example, Bader Ginsburg (2005: 501) declared: '*Brown*'s example or inspiration on the tight tie between education and democracy, and on the role courts can play in advancing change in long-standing societal structures, is evident in a current controversy concerning the schooling of Romany children in Central and Eastern Europe.' Parallels were also pointed out by Jack Greenberg, the original lawyer in *Brown*, who himself took an interest in the segregation of Romani children in his later life: 'After *D.H.* was decided, many European lawyers and Roma rights advocates referred immediately to *Brown*' (Greenberg, 2010: 940). However, Greenberg also underlined an important difference between the two cases: 'whilst the *Brown* case was arguing against the existing legal doctrine of "separate but equal", the European cases against Roma segregation were claiming that the states in question are not abiding by their anti-discrimination legislation' (Greenberg, 2010: 940–1). Another American legal scholar, Bob Hepple, claimed that whilst *Brown* was about direct discrimination within the law itself, Roma segregation cases were about 'disparate impact' or, in the European context, 'indirect discrimination' (Hepple, 2006: 612; see also Chang and Rucker-Chang, 2020: 129). In this regard, Hepple argued that *D.H.* bore more resemblance to the Supreme Court case *Washington v. Davis* of 1976, which ruled that laws that were not established with racially discriminatory motives are valid (Hepple, 2006: 612). However, the EU's Race Equality Directive carries a slightly different view on indirect discrimination vis-à-vis US case law. According to Article 2 of the Directive, indirect discrimination occurs 'where an apparently neutral provision, criterion or practice would put persons of a racial or ethnic origin at a particular disadvantage compared with other persons, unless that provision, criterion or practice is objectively justified by a legitimate aim and the means of achieving that aim are appropriate' (European Commission, 2000, a. 2). Whilst many have celebrated the *D.H.* case as an achievement, other legal scholars have been particularly critical of how its decision was formulated and concluded that this case was in fact a missed 'European Court of Human Rights at *Brown v. Board of Education* moment' (Goodwin, 2009: 93). The ECtHR cases on the segregation of Romani children in schools did not raise the same question as *Brown* in the US context did: rather than examining whether segregation is an acceptable practice, all the ECtHR cases asked when segregation represents an unequal treatment and discrimination of the marginalised minority (Goodwin, 2009; Arabadjieva, 2016). In the next section, I will examine how the European governments did not deny the existence of segregation but, instead, argued that it was a justifiable practice because it was not based on ethnic or racial grounds. In some cases, like 2008 *Sampanis* and *Oršuš*, government representatives went further and argued that segregation is actually beneficial for children who belong to marginalised minorities.

Narratives on justifiable segregation in Europe

The *D.H.* case received an ECtHR Grand Chamber ruling in 2007, after the Czech Republic had joined the EU. The case was initially examined by the Constitutional Court in the Czech Republic in 1999, but this court did not find discrimination on ethnic grounds. The representatives of the applicants from the town of Ostrava claimed they had been discriminated against on ethnic grounds as they had been placed in special schools for children with learning disabilities solely because they were Romani. The applicants' lawyers argued that the Czech Republic violated Article 14 (Prohibition of Discrimination) and Article 2 of Protocol 1 (Right to Education) of the European Convention on Human Rights (ECHR). Whilst officially there was no law stating that Romani children should be placed in such schools, the applicants presented the court with the following statistics:

> the total number of pupils placed in special schools in Ostrava came to 1,360 of whom 762 (56%) were Roma. Conversely, Roma represented only 2.26% of the total of 33,372 primary school pupils in Ostrava. Further, although only 1.8% of non-Roma pupils were placed in special schools, in Ostrava the proportion of Roma pupils assigned to such schools was 50.3%. Accordingly, a Roma child in Ostrava was 27 times more likely to be placed in a special school than a non-Roma child. (*D.H. and Others v. the Czech Republic*, 2007, para. 18)

The Czech government argued that the placing of Romani children in separate schools was not a violation of the European Convention. Initially, it argued that school placement was based solely on the 'intellectual capacity' of the child applicant rather than their belonging to a particular ethnic or social group. Furthermore, it maintained that it had the consent of the parents of the children who were placed in special schools for this action. The government argued that according to the Czech legislation, oral parental consent was adequate in these cases (*D.H. and Others v. the Czech Republic*, 2007, para. 46). The court heard opinions from a number of organisations working in human rights protection, including the CoE's Commissioner for Human Rights, who underlined that such practices of discrimination diminish equality of opportunity for Romani children because they hinder their success in the labour market later in life (*D.H. and Others v. the Czech Republic*, 2007, para. 50). It also cited a UK asylum law case heard in the House of Lords that effectively confirmed that discrimination against Roma had occurred when the UK's immigration officer did not allow Roma to travel to the UK more often than other Czech citizens, because of an assumption that they would seek asylum in the UK (para. 105).[8] The ECtHR referred to a US Supreme Court decision in the case of *Griggs v. Duke Power Co.*, which stated that there was a disparate impact on African American applicants with lower education (*D.H. and Others v. the Czech Republic*, 2007, para. 43).

The Czech government argued that the applicants did not use all the domestic legal instruments in this case. For example, it claimed that none of the parents appealed against the placement of their children in special schools. However, its main argument was that although there were many Romani children in special schools, these schools had been established for all children with specific learning disabilities. The government argued that this did not discriminate against Romani children but that, rather, it did the opposite: it gave more equal access to education for *all* children in a similar position (*D.H. and Others v. the Czech Republic*, 2007, paras. 110–23). However, the applicants replied that although the intention to discriminate could not be directly proven, Romani children were disproportionately affected and the government had to prove that it did consider protection against discrimination (para. 130) rather than the applicants having to prove they had been subjected to unequal treatment. The court agreed with this and shifted the burden of proof onto the Czech government.

The government's lawyer argued that the state representatives were aware that it was not necessarily the case that having anti-discrimination legislation was always effective and was always implemented in practice. However, he also repeated that in the case of special schools, ethnic background did not play any role in the placement of children. He reiterated that the main criteria for placement were intellectual capacity and parental consent and, on that basis, he also claimed that Romani parents were not particularly interested in the education of their children (*D.H. and Others v. the Czech Republic*, 2007, para. 197). He rejected the statistics presented by the applicant's lawyers, arguing these did not constitute adequate or conclusive evidence of discrimination since they were taken from interviews with head teachers as opposed to official state data (para. 148).

According to the numerous reports cited in the court, all the applicants belonged to a vulnerable minority, and so the ECtHR decided against examining the individual appeals of applicants but concluded that all the children's parents lacked capacity to give informed consent about their children's schooling. The Grand Chamber decided that the Czech government had violated Article 14 of the ECHR in conjunction with Article 2 of Protocol 1:

> Furthermore, as a result of the arrangements the applicants were placed in schools for children with mental disabilities [sic] where a

more basic curriculum was followed than in ordinary schools and where they were isolated from pupils from the wider population. As a result, they received an education which compounded their difficulties and compromised their subsequent personal development instead of tackling their real problems or helping them to integrate into the ordinary schools and develop the skills that would facilitate life among majority population. Indeed, the government have implicitly admitted that job opportunities are more limited for pupils from special schools. (*D.H. and Others v. the Czech Republic*, 2007, para. 207)

Thirteen ECtHR judges agreed with this decision, with four expressing their dissenting opinions. Boštjan Zupančič, the judge appointed by the Slovenian government at the time, expressed a dissenting opinion in defence of the Czech policies. He suggested that it was inappropriate to blame the Czech Republic for discrimination against Romani children when it was the only country willing to work to improve their position. He claimed that the ECtHR was being abused for political games rather than serving justice (Zupančič in *D.H. and Others v. the Czech Republic*, 2007). Karel Jungwiert, a judge appointed by the Czech Republic, presented a more elaborate dissenting opinion defending his own country. He claimed that the Czech Republic had guaranteed the right to education for Romani children where older EU Member States before 1989 had failed to do so. Citing CoE statistics, he argued that a large proportion of children belonging to Romani minorities in Western Europe were never included in any education system at all, but that his country had managed to overcome this exclusion: 'In a way, the Czech Republic has thereby established an educational system that is inegalitarian. However, this inegalitarianism has a positive aim: to get children to attend school to have a chance to succeed through positive discrimination in favour of a disadvantaged population' (Jungwiert in *D.H. and Others v. the Czech Republic*, 2007). He then asked the following question: 'which country in Europe has done more, or indeed as much, in this sphere?' (Jungwiert in *D.H. and Others v. the Czech Republic*, 2007).

In his dissenting opinion, Judge Borrego Borrego highlighted the discrepancies between the case and the court's decision. He criticised the court's decision not to examine individual cases and its conclusion that none of the parents in this case had the capacity to decide about their children's schooling. He claimed that the latter echoed earlier practices of rulers in Europe who had taken Romani children away from their parents, who they proclaimed to be unfit to decide about their children's education. To fight discrimination, Borrego Borrego underlined, the court itself was essentialising the position of Romani parents as all being unfit to make decisions about their children's education. Furthermore, he questioned whether the lawyers themselves really represented the interests of the applicants in question, asking whether they were too far removed from them and had ulterior motives that had very little to do with the applicants themselves: 'An example of the sad human tradition of fighting racism through racism ... How cynical: the parents of the applicant minors are not qualified to bring up their children, even though they are qualified to sign an authority in favour of British and North American representatives whom they do not even know!' (Borrego Borrego in *D.H. and Others v. the Czech Republic*, 2007).

The next case dealing with the segregation of Romani children that reached the ECtHR was the 2008 *Sampanis* case. It was heard by the ECtHR Chamber, which decided that Greece, an older EU Member State, had discriminated against Romani children when it put them in a separate annex of the school they attended. The government's argument in this case resembled that in the US Supreme Court case *Cooper v. Aaron* of 1958. In 2004, with the support of the ERRC amongst other NGOs, Romani parents from the Psari camp wanted to enrol their children into primary schools in the nearby town of Aspropyrgos. According to the applicants, the schools refused to enrol the children: the schools' justification was that the relevant ministry did not require them to enrol any Romani children, but if the order was issued, they would send the invitations to the parents in question. After a visit by the ombudsperson, who responded that there was no justification for the Romani children from the Psari camp not to be enrolled in those schools, their enrolment did begin in 2005 (*Sampanis and Others v. Greece*, 2008, para. 8). However, at the start of the academic year, when Romani children arrived to attend the Aspropyrgos school that they were assigned to, they were met with protests from non-Romani parents who prevented them from entering. On one occasion the non-Romani parents put up a sign on the school that stated, 'The school will remain closed because of the *Gypsy problem*' (para. 19, my emphasis). On other occasion, the Romani children could enter the school only when escorted by the police (para. 20). The school authorities decided to move the children to a separate building to protect them from the protests of the majority population (para. 23). In this separate building they attended 'preparatory classes' that would help them to attain the level required for mainstream schooling in the future (para. 29).

The argument for such a placement was that it was implausible from a 'psycho-pedagogical' perspective that these children would mix with other children: most of the Romani children were older than the other children in the same grades. As well as not having attended school previously, they were, according to the school authorities, not able to mix with other children. The official reason that the school gave to the ministry was that there was not enough space and that the parents had agreed that the children could be in a separate building in order to be closer to their camp. The government lawyer repeated these arguments and claimed that the classes in question were not put there to segregate Romani children, but to offer additional help so that they could catch up with other children before being placed into ordinary classes (*Sampanis and Others v. Greece*, 2008, para. 61). However, the court noted that the Greek government had not proven that any of the children would be transferred into the mixed classes after successfully attending the preparatory classes (para. 90). The Chamber unanimously decided that the Greek government was not providing an acceptable justification for the differential treatment of Romani children, as the preparatory classes were based mainly on the criteria of children being of Romani origin. In this case, there were no dissenting opinions from any judges (para. 98).

Both the *D.H.* case and the 2008 *Sampanis* case were referred to in the *Oršuš* case. At the time both of the hearings and of the decisions (in 2009 and 2010 respectively), Croatia was a not an EU Member State but a candidate country. Following the 1993 Copenhagen criteria, the protection of minorities such as Roma was one of the topics highlighted during Croatia's accession period (Bračič, 2016; Sardelić, 2019c). In the 1990s, during the post-Yugoslav wars, which significantly affected Croatia, Roma were not the main minority of concern for international organisations. Instead the organisations focused more on the Serbian minority, because of the potential territorial instability and because this group had been recognised as the ultimate Other in Croatia (Sardelić, 2015: 168; Vermeersch, 2006: 3). The position of Roma was also not a primary concern for minority protection in the post-conflict and postsocialist transition, despite the fact that a number of international organisations and NGOs (such as the ERRC, Open Society Foundation and CoE, for example) had urged Croatia to stop the educational segregation of Romani children. This, perhaps unsurprisingly, changed during Croatia's negotiations for EU membership (Sardelić, 2011; 2019).

The *Oršuš* case was initially addressed by the local courts in Croatia and finally by the Constitutional Court. The representative of fifteen applicants of Romani origin from Međimurje county claimed that their right not to be discriminated against (Article 14 of the ECHR) and their right to education (Article 2 of ECHR Protocol 1) had been violated (*Oršuš and Others v. Croatia*, 2010, para. 4). In contrast to the *D.H.* case and the 2008 *Sampanis* case, here Romani children were not placed in separate educational facilities (different schools or separate annexes), but in Roma-only classes in the same schools as majority children (para. 10). The main argument from the government was that they were not placed in these classes because of their ethnicity but because they did not speak the majority language (that is, Croatian) competently. According to the government's lawyer, these were so-called 'catch up' classes to give Romani children extra support with their Croatian language skills (para. 123).

Like the Croatian courts, the ECtHR Chamber concluded in 2008 that there had been a violation of ECHR Article 6 (Right to Fair Trial) owing to prolonged judicial procedures (*Oršuš and Others v. Croatia*, 2010, para. 99). However, the ECtHR Chamber did not find discrimination or the violation of the right to education. In 2009 the Grand Chamber revisited the case. The applicants represented at the ECtHR Grand Chamber attended two primary schools in Međimurje county: Podturen and Macinec. In the school year of 2001, 47 Romani children were enrolled in the Podturen. The school had the 463 students in total, of whom 47, or around 10 per cent, were Roma. Of these 47 Romani students, 17 were placed in a Roma-only class and 30 in mixed classes. The school authorities reported that there were no more Roma-only classes two years later. The school included a statement from a Romani assistant who was working in a Roma-only class to prove that members of the Romani community themselves were aware of the language issues among pupils. The assistant stated that in addition to their inadequate command of the Croatian language, she had observed many behavioural issues and poor school attendance which were due to the disinterest of parents (paras. 11–17). Macinec primary school also called upon Romani assistants, but the statistics for Roma-only classes here were different: there were 194 Romani pupils out of a total intake of 445 (43.5 per cent) in the school year of 2001. Of these, 142 Romani pupils were in six Roma-only classes whilst the remaining 52 were in mixed classes. One of the justifications the school offered was that in the lower four grades, Romani children represented 50 to 75 per cent of the total number of all students in those classes (paras. 11–17).

This case ended up at the ECtHR after the expedited case at the Constitutional Court of Croatia in 2007. The initial case was lodged in the lower courts in 2002. The Constitutional Court acknowledged that the placement of Romani children in separate classes was an exception rather than a rule, since 93 per cent of Romani children in Medmurje county attended school with their non-Romani peers. It argued that the qualified experts had placed the children in the classes that they believed would benefit the children's development the most: '[s]eparate classes were not established for the purpose of racial segregation in enrolment in the first year of primary school but as a means of providing children with supplementary tuition in the Croatian language and eliminating the consequences of prior social deprivation' (*Oršuš and Others v. Croatia*, 2010, para. 60). In the case at the ECtHR Grand Chamber, the court implicitly agreed with the assumption that spatial separation itself does not necessarily equate to a breach of the right to education and discrimination. The parties involved had to prove or disprove discrimination, which according to the ECtHR meant 'treating differently, without an objective and reasonable justification, persons in relevantly similar situations' (para. 149).

The Croatian government representatives at the ECtHR argued that there was no discrimination and sought to show that there was in fact an 'objective and reasonable justification' for putting the children in question in separate classes from their non-Romani peers. First, she claimed that the school was not enrolling Romani children and Croatian children as such, but was testing their knowledge of the majority language, which was the necessary prerequisite for attending the school in Croatia. She built on the argument of the Constitutional Court that these classes were an exception that applied only to the schools in question. The claim was that in the case of these two schools, the board of experts, after careful deliberation and after assessment of each individual child, had decided that the applicants' knowledge of Croatian was insufficient to allow them to be placed in the same classes as the majority of children. The government representative tried to prove that the best remedy for addressing the language inequality of the children in question was to apply differential treatment in the form of separate classes (*Oršuš and Others v. Croatia*, 2010, para.123). She stated that the quality of education in Romani classes did not vary beyond that permissible by legislation, which permits the omission of up to 30 per cent of the curriculum (para. 163). Furthermore, the government representative argued that such classes were needed to develop the basic social skills of Romani children, as, in comparison with Croatian children, they were lacking in such skills (para. 123), and stated that the teachers in these particular schools had to deal with poor attendance, low interest among parents in their children's education and disruptive behaviour from the children who were put in the Roma-only classes (para. 13). The representative also claimed that the parents of the children in question did not object to the placement of their children in the Roma-only classes. She also asserted that Romani children in Roma-only classes had numerous opportunities to mix with other children, especially during extra-curricular activities (para. 122), and that the schools in question had showed respect for Romani culture by celebrating International Romani Day (para. 135).

However, the applicants' representatives argued that putting children in Roma-only classes translates into other forms of spatial segregation in later life as it normalises parallel societies of Romani and the majority population. They presented statistics showing that only 16 per cent of Romani individuals finished primary schooling in comparison to 91 per cent of the total population in the school year 2006/07 (*Oršuš and Others v. Croatia*, 2010, para. 18) and also that in the present environment the vast majority of Romani children did not have friends who were non-Roma (para. 53). They argued that for the Romani children to efficiently learn a language they needed to have maximum opportunities to mix with all other children, which in this case they did not have. The applicants' representatives also stated that their knowledge of the Croatian language was never properly tested and that their right to education was violated since the curriculum in Roma-only classes was significantly reduced. The representatives doubted that the separate classes helped the Romani children to progress in the Croatian language when they only sporadically included additional Croatian lessons. Further, the lawyers questioned whether these classes were transitional given that no Romani children transferred to mixed classes throughout their schooling period. The government representative responded to that point by claiming that classes were not broken up, because evidence suggested it was important for the children's development to ensure the homogeneity and stability of the class throughout their (lower-grade) schooling (para. 119).

The ECtHR Grand Chamber agreed with the government representative and the previous conclusion of the Constitutional Court that spatial separation does not necessarily mean discrimination or a breach of the right to education. However, it questioned whether proper safeguards had been put in place to ensure that these measures would not disproportionally affect Romani children. It reiterated that the special position of Romani minorities needed to be considered (*Oršuš and Others v. Croatia*, 2010, paras. 147–8). It brought forward statements from various international expert bodies, including the CoE's Human Rights Commissioner at the time, who had visited Croatia in 2002. His statement was presented to the court:

> The year 2002 saw the worsening of problems around the town of Čakovec [capital of Međimurje county] which applied a practice of separating Roma and non-Roma pupils in schools. An atmosphere of intolerance took hold; non-Roma parents went so far as to stage a demonstration in front of a school at the start of the 2002/2003 school year, denying entry to the Roma children. Under strong national and international pressure, the authorities recognised that these practices existed and undertook to review this question. ... Difficulties over Roma pupils' Croatian language proficiency were also reported to me. I would stress the importance of putting all pupils through the same syllabus and the same teaching process in one class. Nonetheless, the knowledge gap problem is not to be evaded. As a remedy to it, it could be useful to set up at national level pre-school classes for children whose mother tongue is not Croatian. (*Oršuš and Others v. Croatia*, 2010, para. 72)

The ECtHR Grand Chamber asked whether it was only Romani children who were placed in separate classes or whether there was any evidence that other children who lacked Croatian language skills were also placed in such classes. The Grand Chamber could find no evidence that there were any other children in separate classes at the time besides Roma (para. 158). It also concluded there were no tests for specifically assessing the children's knowledge of the Croatian language, but that the assessment was based on a broader psychological test on school entry (para. 159). Another contradiction was that some of the applicants were initially in the mixed class but were only later put into the Roma-only class, which seemed to indicate that the teachers did not notice initial difficulties with the Croatian language, but this seemed unlikely to the court (para. 161). Furthermore, when the government representative claimed that the curriculum was the same in both cases, the court asked why, if that was the case, the children needed to attend separate classes. The court indicated that there was no evidence of progress reports for children who lacked Croatian language skills, as well as no evidence that they could be transferred into the mixed class if their progress was sufficient:

> a number of European States encounter serious difficulties in providing adequate schooling for Roma children. The Croatian authorities have sought to tackle the problem. However, in their attempts to achieve the social and educational integration of the disadvantaged group which the Roma form, they have had to contend with numerous difficulties as a result of, *inter alia*, the *cultural specificities* of that minority and an alleged degree of hostility on the part of the parents of non-Roma children. (*Oršuš and Others v. Croatia*, 2010, para. 180; emphasis added)

However, eventually the Grand Chamber made the following decision:

> In sum, in the circumstances of the present case and while recognising the efforts made by the Croatian authorities to ensure that Roma children receive schooling, the Court considers that there were at the relevant time no adequate safeguards in place capable of ensuring that a reasonable relationship of proportionality between the means used and the legitimate aim said to be pursued was achieved and maintained. It follows that the placement of the applicants in Roma-only classes at times during their primary education had no objective and reasonable justification. (*Oršuš and Others v. Croatia*, 2010, para. 184)

In a marginal vote of 9 to 8, it decided there had been a breach of ECHR Article 14 in conjunction with Article 2 of Protocol 1. Eight judges – from the Czech Republic, Croatia, the Russian Federation, Armenia, Germany, the Netherlands, Monaco and Montenegro – wrote a joint partial dissenting opinion that stating that they did not agree that there was no justifiable reason for the separation of the Romani children in question and their placement into Roma-only classes, as the applicants did not state that their command of the Croatian language was adequate. They also reiterated that these classes were established to address the 'special needs' of children and were benevolent, and could be understood as a type of affirmative action. They argued that these actions applied only to the children who had difficulties with the language, not to all Romani children. The dissenting judges emphasised that the efforts of the schools in question could not be denied: the schools organised parent–teacher meetings to deal with low school attendance, employed Romani assistants and redirected the blame for the disinterest in schooling to the parents. They argued that the authorities had done their best to address a culturally specific minority and that the judgement did not mention the rights of majority 'Croatian-speaking children' and how their education would have been disrupted if they had been in a classroom with a large number of children with 'special language needs' (dissenting opinion in *Oršuš and Others v. Croatia*, 2010). The dissenting judges stated that, rather than the Romani minority being looked at as a whole, there should be more focus on specific cases. They claimed that the ECtHR Grand Chamber had overstepped its role in these matters and that it went against a well-reasoned judgement of the Constitutional Court of Croatia (dissenting opinion in *Oršuš and Others v. Croatia*, 2010).

After *Oršuš* had been concluded, the ECtHR Chamber had to decide on another Greek case, which implied that the Greek government was not abiding by the initial 2008 *Sampanis* judgement. The segregation of Romani children continued, and in 2009 a new *Sampani* case was presented to the ECtHR. The 140 applicants were represented by the Greek Helsinki Monitor, and some of them were the same applicants as in the initial *Sampanis* case (lodged in 2005). After the initial 2008 *Sampanis* case had been concluded, the non-Romani parents and the Mayor of Aspropyrgos (the town where the original case took place) addressed a letter to the Greek Ministry of Education. The letter was presented to the ECtHR Grand Chamber in the *Sampani* case:

> The creation of the 12th primary school did not aim to ... segregate Romani students from other students in the district schools. It has, however, become an inevitable necessity because Gypsies living in tents have chosen to live a nomadic life, in dumps they have created themselves, without worrying about basic standards of hygiene, and indulging in illegal activities which have a negative impact on vulnerable social groups and, more generally, on the inhabitants of Aspropyrgos ... in spite of all this, [the Romani children] dare to demand to share the same classrooms as the other students of Aspropyrgos, a considerable percentage of whom are sensitive social groups or children of economic immigrants. (*Sampani and Others v. Greece*, 2012, para. 18)

The ECtHR Chamber unanimously decided that Greece had violated ECHR Article 14 in conjunction with Article 2 of Protocol 1.

Shifting global contexts of racial segregation: from Cold War to postsocialist and EU integration narratives

Comparing the two examples of strategic litigation, James Goldston, who was one of the lawyers in both the *D.H.* and *Oršuš* cases, commented that in the European context segregation was met with less political disapproval than in the US: 'While the European Court's condemnation of segregation was important, it is less revolutionary than *Brown* – and may have less immediate impact on the public consciousness – at least in part, because the law had not been entwined with segregation in Europe as it has been in the United States'(Goldston, 2017: 182). Yet the other reason, as Goldston mentions too, was the Cold War as the geopolitical framing in the period of the *Brown* case (Goldston, 2017: 182). Dudziak (2004) has similarly confirmed in their legal historical research that the Cold War played a significant role in cases such as *Brown* and the American civil rights movement more generally (Dudziak, 2011): segregation of African Americans did not put an impressive international light on the US as a global moral leader, especially on the African continent, where it was rivalling the then Soviet Union for influence. The Soviet Union used the case of US segregation for its political gains in the Cold War as well. Whilst *Brown* itself did not directly cause the desegregation process, it served as a signal to the world that the US had deemed segregation to be 'unAmerican' (Dudziak, 2004: 34–5). The American media described the *Brown* case as 'the blow to Communism' (Dudziak, 2004, 35). At the same time, there was initially massive public resistance to desegregation at the local level, some even describing desegregation as a communist plot (Dudziak, 2011).

The question is whether the two contexts of desegregation can be directly compared, as they occurred in different time periods. However, it is clear that countries on the other side of the Berlin Wall were similarly concerned with their public image with regard to discrimination. That is why, according to Donert (2017: 54), socialist Czechoslovakia gave special attention to how Roma were treated and to the public image of their position within Czechoslovak society. Other socialist countries, such as the non-aligned Yugoslavia, had divergent policies towards Romani children's schooling and integration: whilst the wealthier republics of Slovenia and Croatia clearly practised segregation of Romani children, North Macedonia and Kosovo embraced ethnic integration policies (Sardelić, 2016). Media at the time, however, portrayed the position of Roma as improving as part of the development of socialism (Sardelić, 2016). However, since school segregation was not enshrined in law, even during the socialist period, it remained invisible. After the fall of the Berlin Wall, the US State Department scrutinised the position of Roma in countries such as the Czech Republic, describing it as the remains of human-rights-violating communist regimes (Schlager, 2017). However, as Donert (2017: 247) showed, the 1990s human rights violations were also a product of the human rights vacuum created during the transition period.

As segregation was not enshrined in law and did not happen systematically to all Romani children, the European cases resembled the 1974 *Milliken* case in the US, which is now studied as a case that deems *de facto* segregation permissible. The European cases confirmed that the court deemed 'spatial separation' *per se* unproblematic it had a justifiable cause. Another important difference is the distinction between the power of the US and the federalism of the EU. First, in the US it was not the state itself that was on trial but either individuals or educational institutions, whilst in the European cases the countries themselves were on trial. The US could turn the story of desegregation into a victorious story of progress to enhance its international image as the protector of human rights (Dudziak, 2011), whereas the European countries charged with discrimination did not have the same opportunity and were shamed as human rights violators in the international arena. There was no consensus that the ECtHR represented the ultimate legislator in Europe as the Supreme Court did in the US. Furthermore, there was no consensus in the countries in question that discrimination was taking place; but even if it did take place, there was no agreement that it is morally wrong or that it is bad for the economy, foreign relations or the international standing of the countries in question.

The desegregation process involving Romani in a number of postsocialist Central and Eastern European countries began in the anticipation of EU accession at the turn of the millennium, and not during the postsocialist transition in the 1990s:

> [O]ne of the most important factors in putting Roma school desegrega-tion on the agenda of the governments in Bulgaria, the Czech Republic, Hungary, Romania and Slovakia was the move toward EU membership. In fact, with the publishing of the Agenda 2000 of the European Commission in July 1997 and the opening of negotiations with the accession countries, issues faced by Roma got on the agenda of these governments due to the 'Copenhagen criteria'. (Rostas, 2012: 353)

Yet the efforts for school segregation remained mainly in the hands of Romani activists (Rostas, 2012: 353) rather than the actual burden being extensively taken by the state authorities, which treated it more as a tick-box in the EU accession negotiation processes (Rostas, 2019).

In terms of strategic litigation, all but one of the cases at the ECtHR were decided on when the countries in question had already joined the EU; the *Oršuš* judgement was delivered a year and a half before all the negotiation chapters were closed for Croatia at the end of June 2011 (Croatia joined the EU two years later). Just after the decision had been made, the two principals commented on it in some of the Croatian newspapers: 'I categorically deny there was ever anyone discriminated in this school, but if there was ever anyone discriminated, it was the children of non-Roma nationality' (Jutarnji, 2010; my translation).[9] Another newspaper opinion piece from the region stated that the problem in Međimurje was 'not segregation but *Roma terror*' (Međimurje, 2010; my translation and emphasis),[10] showing that these phrases had been used before the protests in 2019.

The EU had warned Croatia previously that if it did not fully cooperate with the International Criminal Tribunal for Former Yugoslavia it might jeopardise its accession to the EU. There was a similar opportunity for the EU to force Croatia to develop an effective strategy to end the segregation of Romani children (Sardelić, 2019c). However, three months before the negotiations were concluded, the interim report on the progress of Croatia on judiciary and fundamental rights barely mentioned Roma (European Commission, 2011c). The final Croatia report commented: 'There has been progress as regards the protection of minorities and cultural rights. The commitment to the rights of minorities, reaffirming their place in Croatian society, continues to be expressed at the highest level' (European Commission, 2011a: 12). The report continued:

> As for the Roma minority, there have been some further improvements in education, particularly in pre-school education. Improvements to the infrastructure of some Roma settlements have continued. However, the Roma still face discrimination, particularly regarding access to education, social protection, health, employment and adequate housing. Segregation persists in some schools. Progress towards ensuring that Roma children complete primary and secondary education has been modest. (European Commission, 2011a: 12)

In November 2015 the FCNM Advisory Committee published an opinion that despite progress in the field of education, the segregation of Romani children in schools was increasing, even after Croatia had joined the EU: 'the number of classes where only Roma are educated has increased, despite the 2010 *Oršuš* judgment of the European Court of Human Rights that bans segregation of Roma in schools' (FCNM, 2016b: 25). Taking into account all the chapters in the EU negotiations, the European Commission did highlight the position of Romani children who were segregated, but presenting a viable plan for desegregation was not a condition for Croatia to join the EU.

Most of the scholarly literature and policy reports at least implicitly connect school segregation to the legacies of communism. However, this does not explain the persistence of segregation that has been reported in older EU Member States such as Greece and others. Whilst there was some reluctance among the ECtHR judges to decide on discrimination in the *D.H.* and *Oršuš* cases, in the Greek cases the decision was already unanimous at Chamber level. Yet in its NRIS Framework for Roma, the Greek government did not mention segregation even once, merely stating that drop-out rates and low attendance were among the most serious issues in the education of Romani minorities. In 2014 the European Commission's evaluation of Greece's NRIS highlighted that desegregation remained an issue in Greece. In 2014, ten years after the decision in the *D.H.* case, the European Commission started infringement procedures against the Czech Republic for not abiding by the Race Equality Directive. Similar procedures have been started against Hungary and Slovakia (Chang and Rucker-Chang, 2020: 119). Yet in 2018 the evaluation report on the NRIS noted that whilst there had been some improvement in the field of education, at the same time segregation of Romani children was increasing at the European level, not only in Central and Eastern Europe but also in the older EU Member States. Another European Commission report on the implementation of anti-discrimination law (Chopin *et al.*, 2017) showed that patterns of segregation exist in seven post-2004 EU Member States as well as in the seven pre-2004 EU Member States.

Taken together, this all shows that the segregation of Romani children cannot be understood simply as a postcommunist legacy but is a broader reality of the wider EU today. The segregation of African American children (as well as other minorities in the US) was not simply in the past and did not end with the Cold War, but continues in the present day in a different form. Similarly, the segregation of Romani children has continued, even after the postsocialist countries allegedly complied with the Copenhagen criteria test for EU membership. Additionally, the older EU Member States were never subjected to the same test as the postsocialist countries seeking to join the EU.

Conclusion

This chapter has explored the cases of educational segregation of Romani children in Europe both in some newer EU Member States (Croatia and the Czech Republic) and in an older one (in Greece). It has particularly scrutinised the ECtHR cases on educational discrimination, focusing specifically on the states' justification of why segregation does not equal discrimination. It has also contextualised the educational discrimination of Romani children within international and global narratives on the segregation of other marginalised children, that is, our future citizens.

The socio-legal analysis of the ECtHR cases and especially the states' justifications have revealed both an embeddedness in and a detachment from global narratives when it comes to the segregation of Romani children. I started the chapter with the discrepancy between the local and the global: whilst the Pope was apologising on behalf of the Catholic Church and the majority population for the segregation of Roma in Europe, a local political elite in Croatia blamed Roma for their own lack of education. The fact that Croatia was charged with educational segregation and discrimination of children in Roma-only classes seemed absent from the public's memory after a decade. According to the Croatian public discourse in 2019, it is Roma who allegedly choose their own lack of education and therefore it is Roma who actively resist any involvement in the formal labour market.

In all four cases, the states followed a similar line of reasoning on why spatial segregation was not only permissible for the Romani children in question, but also beneficial as it addressed their 'special needs': either their intellectual capacity (as in the Czech Republic), their incomprehension of the majority language (as in Croatia) or the security risks and need for preparation before integration (as in Greece). In all the cases, the state authorities argued that this was not racial segregation since it did not apply explicitly to Romani children and, moreover, it was not only Romani children who were subjected to such treatment. According to the states' arguments, the main difference from the earlier Supreme Court cases on segregation in the US was that the latter was entrenched in laws and applied to all African American children. In the case of Roma, the states' representatives argued that it was qualified pedagogical experts who decided on the placement of children and that their decisions were not based on ethnicity but on objective educational criteria. However, the states' representatives could not explain the invisible edges of citizenship, that is, why Roma were disproportionally represented in schools for children with special needs (as in the Czech Republic) and why only Romani children had to be in separate classes (Croatia) or in a separate annex (Greece). No other children were treated in such a manner. In the NRIS, the Czech Republic and Croatia did recognise Romani educational segregation as a challenge that needed to be addressed. The Czech Republic even linked African American desegregation with the plight of Romani children. Yet the Greek NRIS did not mention segregation as a challenge in the educational system, despite the three ECtHR cases proving that segregation did exist. This also shows that the global context in the case of Roma segregation cannot be simply understood through dichotomies of new versus old EU or socialist versus capitalist Europe. Segregation and discrimination had, on one hand, local specificities, while, on the other hand, they transcended previous Cold War divisions. Neither did the EU accession represent a clear-cut 'carrot' for the postsocialist countries to stop segregation.

The case of Romani segregation in educational systems provides a window through which to explore a broader question of how state authorities and international organisations create citizenship fringes in which they situate marginalised citizens: how Croatian politicians in 2019 'forgot' that ten years previously the ECtHR had confirmed the existence of segregation and discrimination against Romani children, so that Roma could be again blamed for their own exclusion from the labour market. There is a broader neoliberal idea, too, promoted by the World Bank, that marginalised citizens should be included as they can enhance the economy, without questioning the basic premise: should their potential economic contribution be the measurement of whether rights are granted to marginalised minorities? Such questions point to the ways in which citizenship is constructed through its fringes. In this process, as Bhambra (2015: 110) explains, it is not enough simply to grant equal rights to marginalised minorities previously deprived of such rights:

> The exclusions and modes of subjugation that provided the context for the emergence of particular ideas of equal citizenship need to be recognised as integral to those forms today. ... The injustices of displacement, dispossession, enslavement, and domination are not, and have not been, overcome by simply extending 'equal citizenship' to those who were previously excluded from it and subjugated by it. Citizenship itself needs to be rethought in the context of its wider history, its connected histories and sociologies, and new conceptual forms developed from those reconstructed accounts.

This chapter shows that even introducing the practices of multicultural citizenship and the politics of recognition – such as celebrating International Romani Day – does not necessarily address the underlying discrimination that Roma face as citizens. It is at its fringes that citizenship establishes its boundaries, and it is there that it has to be reconstructed.

Notes

1 Original Croatian text: 'Želim normalan život.'

2 Original Croatian text: 'Izložio sam svoj život, žrtvovao kao i u ratu, ali ne žalim u ime svih mirnih i radišnih građana Međimurja trpjeti romski teror koji traje preko 20 godina.'

3 Original Croatian text: 'Ključ rješenja romske problematike u Međimurju je obrazovanje'.

4 Original Croatian text: 'Smatra kako je ključ u obrazovanju jer ako četvero od 318 srednjoškolaca završi školu onda nešto "deblo ne štima". "Ti mladi ljudi su sebe diskvalificirali iz utakmice u životu jer oni više nisu ravnopravni, ne ispunjavaju temeljni uvjet za traženje posla i taj problem treba riješiti", naglasio je ministar.'

5 Original Croatian text: 'Božinović je u pravu, Romi su se sami diskvalificirali iz života.'

6 The chapter omits analysis of two other ECtHR cases that dealt with discrimination of Romani children in education: 2013 *Horváth and Kiss v. Hungary* and 2013 *Lavida and Others v. Greece*. Whilst both cases are relevant, they are sufficiently similar to the analysed cases. I distinguish between the two cases from Greece by prefixing the case name with the relevant year.

7 Verbatim quotation.

8 See *Regina v. Immigration Officer at Prague Airport and Another, ex parte European Roma Rights Centre and Others* (2004).

9 Original Croatian text: 'Ako je netko u ovoj školi diskriminiran, a odlučno demantiram da je diskriminacije ikad bilo, onda su to učenici koji nisu romske nacionalnosti.'

10 Original Croatian text: 'Nije segregacija nego romski teror.'

4

Minority statelessness and racialised citizenship: total infringement of citizenship

I have made more than 20 formal applications for documents since 1991. I even visited the Ombudsman's Office. They [the authorities] didn't explain things to me, they just asked for documents that I don't have.

Haidar Osmani, stateless Roma in North Macedonia, quoted in UNHCR statelessness report (UNHCR, 2017c: 27)

This is a problem many believe has been resolved, but living without nationality and rights is a harsh reality for thousands of Roma in the EU. Roma children born in Italy to parents who've fled there during the Balkan wars are still facing the scourge of statelessness, even though their families have been living there for decades. We, as members of the European Parliament need to make sure that this remains a priority on the EU agenda until all Roma can enjoy their rights as European citizens.

Soraya Post, Swedish Member of the European Parliament of Romani background, 2014–19, quoted in Jovanović, 2017

Introduction

In 2014, on the sixtieth anniversary of the UN Convention Relating to the Status of Stateless Persons (UNHCR, 1954; henceforth the 1954 Statelessness Convention), the UNHCR set a goal of readdressing the position of world's stateless people. These are the people who are literally 'citizens of nowhere' (Lynch and Cook, 2006: 1): according to the 1954 Statelessness Convention (Article 1.1), they are 'not considered as a national by any State under the operation of its law'. The final aim of the renewed interest in the position of stateless people was to eradicate statelessness by 2024, that is, by the seventieth anniversary of the Convention. In order to reach this goal, the UNHCR introduced a *Global Action Plan to End Statelessness 2014–2024* (UNHCR, 2014a). The plan lists ethnic discrimination as one of the causes of the lack of nationality (UNHCR, 2014a: 14) but does not single out any particular stateless group. However, the cover of the *Global Action Plan to End Statelessness* itself included a photo of what seemed to be a frightened child looking through the glass window. The caption read: 'Roma girl in Croatia already knows the difficulties of being stateless. She lives with her family in a makeshift room with no running water, electricity or sanitation. They survive by collecting scrap metal' (UNHCR, 2014a: cover photo). The caption tried to capture the value of citizenship that Hannah Arendt (1968: 298) described as the 'right to have rights'.

Three years after the *Global Action Plan to End Statelessness* was published, the UNHCR issued a report that estimated that 75 per cent of stateless people belonged to minority groups (UNHCR, 2017c). Among the minority groups vulnerable to statelessness that the report specifically highlighted was Roma in North Macedonia, currently an EU candidate country which was established after the disintegration of Socialist Yugoslavia. Whilst portraying statelessness as a global problem, the report ended with examples of statelessness from countries on the outer edge of the EU, which could suggest that minorities in the EU do not face a similar predicament.[1] However, the issue of minority statelessness in the EU has been raised in the European Parliament by the then Swedish MEP Soraya Post, as quoted at the start of this chapter. Similarly, the predicament of minority statelessness in Europe has been raised by a number of NGOs (such as the European Network on Statelessness, the Institute for Statelessness and Inclusion and the ERRC, among others) at the 2018 UN Minority Forum in Geneva, which that year addressed statelessness as its main topic.

Romani minorities throughout Europe face challenges when accessing the rights they have been granted as citizens, as I have explored in previous chapters. Even when Roma have possessed minority rights, these have not guaranteed a more equal position as citizens either in the national or in the broader European context. Two main conclusions emerged from the analysis in the EU NRIS Framework and the states' actions based on it: (1) despite some local stories of success, the Framework had not achieved its main goal of eradicating the inequalities Romani minorities face as citizens of the EU Member States (European Commission, 2018b); and (2) the main reason for this failure was that it had no comprehensive strategy for how to recognise and address systematic antigypsyism, a special form of racism targeting Romani minorities (see Chapter 1). The link between anti-Romani racism and limited access to rights granted to Roma has been very well researched (McGarry, 2017). Yet it has only been in recent years that policy itself has started catching up and recognised the severity of this form of racism. At the end of the EU NRIS Framework, the European Parliament published a Resolution stating that future initiatives dealing with the position of Roma need to first address antigypsyism. Nevertheless, whilst having an extensive focus on the rights dimension of citizenship (Joppke, 2007), the EU NRIS Framework completely ignored the status dimension and its relationship to citizenship. It assumed that all Roma in the EU have some national citizenship even when they are not EU citizens (European Commission, 2011b: 2).

Against this backdrop, the chapter examines two issues: first, whilst much scholarly and activist literature has focused on antigypsyism and its consequences, very few studies have made direct reference to the formation of racialised citizenship (Kóczé and Rövid, 2017: 688). Does the example of stateless Romani minorities show that citizenship itself can be a covert racialised formation? Second, it explores the formation of racialised citizenship on the status dimension axis (that is the access to citizenship itself), underscoring in particular how it contributes to the phenomenon of minority statelessness.

Hannah Arendt (1968) highlighted the connection between the position of minorities and statelessness in *The Origins of Totalitarianism*. Here she also conceived the theoretical foundations for statelessness research. Yet the question of why certain minorities are specifically vulnerable to statelessness has remained under-researched. After analysing the contexts in which Roma have become at risk of statelessness (in particular countries such as the Czech Republic, the former Yugoslav space and Italy), this chapter asks what the similarities and differences in the production of minority statelessness are in other contexts. It compares the position of stateless Roma with that of Russian-speaking minorities in the Baltic states, which constitute Europe's most well-documented case of minority statelessness. Second, it compares the position of stateless Romani minorities with two other well-researched cases of minority statelessness beyond Europe: the Dominicans of Haitian descent in the Dominican Republic and the Rohingya minority in Myanmar. It finishes with a comparison with another less-examined case of minority statelessness in Europe, the children of the Windrush generation in the UK.

The contexts in which these minorities have become stateless are very diverse – both geographically and politically – yet I claim that the mechanisms that states used to render them stateless were very similar: state authorities applied their 'acts of sovereignty' (Nyers, 2006) to construct these minorities as stateless by introducing legislation, discourses and practices that retroactively transformed them from citizens to irregular or illegitimate migrants. However, I also argue that these transformations did not necessarily translated the lack of citizenship into the lack of 'the right to have rights' (Blitz, 2017; Swider, 2017): that is, what I call the *total infringement of citizenship*. I argue that the total infringement of citizenship follows from minority statelessness when racialised citizenship formation is already in place. This chapter initially illustrates some of the main ambiguities around statelessness in general. It then highlights how selected scholars have theorised racialised citizenship; following a the comparative analysis of minority statelessness examples, it explores the question of when the total infringement of citizenship occurs.

The ambiguities around statelessness

Statelessness, both as a legal status and as sociological reality (Sigona, 2015), generates many ambiguities. The first concerns the number of statelessness people in the world and how can they ever be counted. The 2016 UNHCR Global Trends report estimated that at least 10 million people were stateless but, at the same time, noted that different countries around the world documented only 3.2 million (UNHCR, 2017a). There are at least two reasons for the discrepancy in numbers and for why so many stateless people do not have a recognised statelessness status. First, states are sometimes not aware of their existence or, more often, they do not recognise that these people are stateless and see them as potentially citizens of another state (Minority Rights Group International, 2017). In later publications, the UNHCR acknowledges that 'millions of people around the world are denied nationality' (UNHCR, 2020). As a part of the *Global Action Plan to End Statelessness*, the UNHCR started highlighting the issue of statelessness with an '#IBelong Campaign', in which UNHCR teams conducted interviews with stateless people around the world in order to make these minorities visible.

The second ambiguity important for this chapter concerns minority statelessness: not all minorities are equally at risk of statelessness, and not even all the people who are recognised as members of the same minority are at risk. It is the minorities who are caught in the circle of marginalisation (Kingston, 2017) and who are reconfigured from traditional minorities to foreigners (Hayes de Kalaf, 2019). Can we then talk about racialised citizenship regimes if not all who are categorised as members of a minority are subjected to the same treatment? Until recently, statelessness has been an under-theorised non-citizenship status (Belton, 2011; Staples, 2012; Tonkiss and Bloom, 2015). Although Arendt (1968) set the theoretical foundations for the scholarly enquiry into statelessness, less research has been conducted on the position of stateless persons than on the status of refugees and other migrants (Belton, 2011; Foster and Lambert, 2019). Stateless people have also not been at the forefront of debates in the international community. Whilst 145 states are parties to the 1951 UN Convention Relating to the Status of Refugees, and 146 to the 1967 Protocol, only 91 are parties to the 1954 Convention Relating to the Status of Stateless Persons, and just 74 to the 1961 Convention on the Reduction of Statelessness. However, more recently there have been more theoretical debates and research on statelessness (Weissbrodt, 2008; Sawyer and Blitz, 2011, Blitz and Lynch, 2011; Staples, 2012; Lawrance and Stevens, 2017; Bloom *et al.*, 2017; Owen, 2018; Gibney, 2019). These debates have shown that the status of a refugee and the status of a stateless person do not necessarily overlap. Moreover, a great number of stateless persons have never left the territory where they were born and so, rather than being stateless in a migratory context, they are stateless *in situ* (Belton, 2015; Vlieks, 2017).

The concept of statelessness has multiple definitions, and this can lead to confusion. The 1954 Statelessness Convention offered the following legal definition of *de jure* statelessness in Article 1.1: 'the term "stateless person" means a person who is not considered as a national by any State under the operation of its law' (UNHCR, 1954). Yet in practice, some groups have been considered to be stateless in a political but not necessarily in a legal sense. For example, some political science scholars have argued that the Scottish in the UK and Catalans in Spain are stateless nations (Keating, 2001). However, they are not legally stateless as they possess citizenship of the UK and Spain respectively. Roma, Kurds and Palestinians are similarly categorised as stateless nations in political terms, and often they are also stateless legally or are at least lack effective citizenship that would secure their rights (Jenne, 2000; Molavi, 2013; Fiddian-Qasmiyeh, 2015).[2]

The second puzzle around the definition of statelessness arises from the distinction between *de jure* and *de facto* statelessness. David Weissbrodt (2008: 84) has stated that '[p]ersons who are de facto stateless often have nationality according to the law, but either this nationality is not effective or they cannot prove their nationality'. Human rights activists have been critical of the concept of *de facto* statelessness, as some states have used it in order to refrain from recognising individuals who were *de jure* stateless (Van Waas and De Chickera, 2017; Manby, 2015). The 2010 UNHCR *Prato Conclusions* offered another definition of *de facto* statelessness: 'de facto stateless persons are persons outside the country of their nationality who are unable or, for valid reasons, are unwilling to avail themselves of the protection of that country' (UNHCR, 2010). As for *de jure* statelessness, the UNHCR *Prato Conclusions* of 2010 and 2014 UNHCR *Handbook on Protection of Stateless Persons* urged the authorities responsible for determination of statelessness not to leave the definition to endless legal acrobatics but to carefully consider the states with which an individual could have genuine links (UNHCR, 2014b).

Recent research has shown that the reality of statelessness and the lack of citizenship can be much murkier in practice and needs to be analysed beyond the scope of the legal definition

(Sigona, 2015; Sardelić, 2015; Bloom *et al.*, 2017). As a result, David Owen (2018) has introduced a new concept of *de jure* statelessness as either structural or administrative: structural *de jure* statelessness arises from the right of a state to determine its own citizenry, whilst administrative *de jure* statelessness derives from the lack of relevant documents, especially birth certificates. Unlike Weissbrodt's definition, Owen's conceptualisation recognises individuals who are not able to prove their nationality as *de jure* stateless.

The *Global Action Plan to End Statelessness* did not specifically talk about minority statelessness, but it hinted that there were people who belonged to minorities that were stateless. It identified 'prevailing social views regarding ethnic, racial, religious or other minorities' (UNHCR, 2014a: 15) as one of the main obstacles to implementing its plan for reducing and ultimately ending statelessness. Both the 2014 *Global Action Plan to End Statelessness* and the 2017 UNHCR statelessness report (UNHCR, 2017c) highlighted that minorities were at increased risk of becoming stateless. These documents also captured the position of those people who have not been legally recognised as stateless in the states where they reside, but are nevertheless without access to citizenship (Sardelić, 2015). Both publications also follow Arendt's assumption that stateless minorities lack the protection of human rights and that it is only with citizenship that these rights can be guaranteed. However, this chapter analyses the reasons why not all minorities are equally vulnerable to statelessness. Whilst some lack political rights (Swider, 2017), others also have no official access to social and economic rights, for example the right to education, work and healthcare. The chapter argues that it is individuals in the latter group who usually also fall into the regime of deportability (De Genova, 2002) and irregularisation (De Blois *et al.*, 2015), even in cases where the stateless minorities in question have never crossed any borders themselves. These stateless minorities have been reinterpreted as aliens and stripped of rights on the basis of practices of racialised citizenship regimes.

I apply the theoretical conceptualisation of racialised citizenship regimes to the socio-legal analysis of minority statelessness. The cases of stateless Romani minorities and Russian-speaking minorities are generally connected to the postsocialist state disintegration, and those of the Haitian Dominicans and Burmese Rohingya to post-colonial contexts. To analyse the acts of sovereignty, I examine how the citizenship acts and other relevant pieces of legislation have been constructed, as well as exploring the policy reports of international organisations (such as the UNHCR, the CoE, and the Inter-American Commission on Human Rights (IACHR) that deal either with statelessness or with the position of minorities. Research on stateless Romani minorities in this area has already been done before (Cahn, 2012; Sardelić, 2015; Sigona, 2015; Bhabha, 2017), so this chapter aims to shed a new theoretical light on it by applying the concept of racialised citizenship. The chapter then compares the position of stateless Roma with the position of Russian-speaking minorities who are Latvian and Estonian non-citizens: can their statelessness also be considered a product of a racialised citizenship regime? In a different postcolonial context, around 200,000 Dominican citizens of Haitian descent were stripped of their citizenship retroactively and pronounced illegal immigrants. Similarly, the Rohingya in Myanmar were previously thought of as a traditional minority, but were not recognised as such in the 1982 Myanmar Citizenship Law. The chapter concludes with the case of the Windrush generation as a window onto the link between racialised citizenship regimes and minority statelessness.

Enquiry into racialised citizenship regimes

How can racialised aspects of citizenship regimes contribute to minority statelessness in a legal sense? I follow the socio-legal definition of citizenship regimes introduced by Shaw and Štiks (2010: 6): 'the concept encompasses a range of different legal statuses, viewed in their wider political context, which are central to exercise of civil rights, political membership and – in many cases – full socio-economic membership in a particular territory'. In its 2017 report *Denial and Denigration: How Racism Feeds Statelessness*, the Minority Rights Group International highlighted minority statelessness as 'often an outcome of discrimination and racism' (Minority Rights Group International, 2017). The question, though, remains: what is the connection between minority statelessness and racism, or racialised citizenship to be more exact?

David FitzGerald indirectly connected racialised citizenship to statelessness by arguing that the racialisation of citizenship emerges 'through rules of birthright acquisition, naturalization and denationalization'. Racialised citizenship can also manifest itself as a preferential treatment of a more dominant group and not only as discrimination of the group subjected to racism (FitzGerald, 2017: 130). He defines racism and race in the following way:

> Racism refers to the sorting of social groups by their supposedly inherited and unchangeable physical attributes and/or phenotype, attributing differential moral and mental capacities to those physical characteristics, and then using those putative differences to legitimate the unequal distribution of resources and treatment. Race is a subset of ethnicity ... What makes race distinctive from other forms of ethnicity is the perceived inalterability of belonging to the category and/or emphasis on phenotype. (FitzGerald, 2017: 130)

The 'inalterability of belonging' is the most important feature of racialised citizenship, according to FitzGerald, and this feature defines it as a particular subset of ethnic discrimination. Whilst forced assimilation might be discriminatory, he claims, it is not a feature of racialised citizenship as it implies that the boundaries between groups can be altered (FitzGerald, 2017: 132). FitzGerald identifies the trend of deracialisation of citizenship over history, but points out that racialised citizenship still appears in contemporary contexts, as in the case of the mass denationalisation of Dominicans of Haitian descent (FitzGerald (2017: 132).

In another attempt to classify racialised citizenship, Paul Silverstein (2008) connects it to Balibar and Wallerstein's understanding of 'racism without race' or cultural racism. Cultural racism is founded on perceived cultural differences that classify groups but not necessarily biological features. In other words, Balibar and Wallerstein connect racism to alleged 'insurmountable cultural differences' (Balibar and Wallerstein, 1991: 28–9). Whilst analysing the manifestly neutral content of French citizenship, Silverstein identified racialised practices towards citizens from former colonies and especially citizens with Muslim backgrounds. In a more recent attempt to classify racialised citizenship, Nelson Torres-Ríos (2018) uses doctrinal legal research to claim that Puerto Ricans are second-class US citizens. Although according to the 1917 Jones Act they are US citizens, Puerto Ricans have no right to vote at the US national level if they reside in Puerto Rico (Torres-Ríos, 2018: 7). Studying US Supreme Court decisions, Torres-Ríos argues that Puerto Ricans have been described as racially inferior as a justification for second-class citizenship (Torress-Ríos, 2018: 22).

Another account of racialised citizenship maintains that racialised citizens are not mere observers of their predicament but contest it both in public and in private spheres (Erel and Reynolds, 2018; Bauer 2018). None of the previous theoretical comprehensions of racialised citizenship has explicitly dealt with whether and how it is connected to the creation of stateless minorities. There is research that discusses statelessness and racialisation (Molavi, 2013; Kingston, 2017; Hayes de Kalaf, 2019), but it does not go into sufficient depth to offer a definition of the concept of racialised citizenship itself. This chapter also acknowledges previous research which showed that stateless minorities are not simply passive observers of their own predicament, but also search for alternative ways to access rights that are denied to them by law (Sigona, 2015; Sardelić, 2017b). However, it also takes a step back to analyse the reasons why certain minorities end up as stateless in the first place. It recognises that there are limits to what non-citizens, especially stateless persons, can achieve with their acts of citizenship (Bloemraad *et al.*, 2017).

Instead of doctrinal legal research, I use the socio-legal approach of constitutional ethnography as developed by Kim Lane Scheppele (2004: 395): 'Constitutional ethnography is the study of the central legal elements of polities using methods that are capable of recovering the lived detail of the politico-legal landscape.' Citizenship (or the lack thereof) is one such 'central legal element of polities'. Using constitutional ethnography to analyse selected cases of minority statelessness, I claim that racialised citizenship regimes in contemporary contexts of statelessness embrace a much more fluid approach than the 'inalterability of belonging'. Instead racialized citizenship captures the 'reinterpretation of belonging'. It renders some minorities stateless by making a proxy connection between migration and race (De Genova, 2002; Bhambra, 2018). Racialised citizenship regimes recategorise previous minority citizens as 'illegal immigrants', and this leads to minority statelessness. The total infringement of citizenship occurs when this process is also coupled with the withdrawal of the wide array of rights associated with citizenship status.

Varieties of minority statelessness

According to Nicholas De Genova (2017: 18), the construction of a migrant status arises from the processes of unequal bordering, which assign uneven rights to different statuses:

> The juridical status and social condition that we conventionally designate as 'migrant' (or 'immigrant') in fact signifies what is always a rather variegated or heterogeneous spectrum of legal distinction and social inequalities and differences: there are many types of migrants, and it is precisely the work of immigration regimes and citizenship law to hierarchically sort them and rank them ... Nevertheless, it is the bordered definition of state territoriality that constitutes particular forms and expressions of human mobility as 'migration' and classifies specific kind of people who move as 'migrants'. To reiterate: borders make migrants.

The processes of bordering appear even in cases where those designated as migrants have never crossed any borders themselves, but the territorial borders or citizenship regime may have changed (De Genova, 2017: 28). Whilst migrant statuses are hierarchical and unequal, in most common understandings citizenship status should represent an equal status for all who possess it, with few legitimate exceptions (such as children who are semi-citizens: Cohen, 2009). Yet numerous studies have shown that citizens can be unequal in terms of rights even if they all possess the same citizenship status (Rigo, 2005; Cohen, 2009; Hepworth, 2014; Nyers, 2019). Some citizens are more vulnerable to arbitrary deprivation of citizenship, leading to statelessness: this illustrates the inequality among citizens to its extreme. Similar to how irregular migrants are constructed through the regular processes of bordering (De Genova, 2017), the practices which arbitrarily deprive some minorities of their citizenship are rarely random themselves but have a certain logic behind them: they show states' systematic denials of citizenship (Stevens, 2017a) and some common structural or administrative features of statelessness (Owen, 2018).

As newer studies critical of Arendt's conceptualisation of stateless-ness have argued (Swider 2017; Blitz, 2017; Stevens, 2017a), not all cases of statelessness necessarily lead to a loss of rights, nor do they necessarily arise from a totalitarian state. It is here that the concept of total infringement of citizenship can be introduced to represent (usually unrecognised) statelessness status coupled with the loss of human rights. This is where stateless people fall into the category that Arendt (1968: 299–300) called the 'abstract nakedness of being nothing but a human'. The total infringement of citizenship is ultimately linked to racialised citizenship regimes.

One of the predicaments that stateless minorities face is states' denial of their statelessness, where their *de jure* stateless status is often not recognised. States would usually categorise them as irregular, undocumented or illegal migrants who have come from somewhere else. Yet it is the states in question that construct these minorities as stateless by means of laws and policies that take their citizenship status away on the territory where they were previously citizens. The clearest example of such practices can be found in instances of state disintegration, such as the cases of Roma in the former Czechoslovakia and Yugoslavia and Russian-speaking minorities in the Baltic states.

Romani minorities

When discussing statelessness and the position of minorities, Arendt does not mention Romani minorities despite the fact they were subjected to similar citizenship deprivation practices to Jews before and during World War II (Sardelić, 2017c). Roma were not recognised as a minority in the Minority Treaties, and Arendt only examined the position of minorities mentioned in them. Romani minorities faced statelessness during the disintegration both of Czechoslovakia and of former Yugoslavia (Sardelić, 2015). The fact that both peaceful and violent disintegrations led to the most marginalised populations ending up at risk of statelessness shows that wars were not a decisive factor for the risk of statelessness. The most important factors were the redrawing of borders and the transforming of criteria as to who constitutes citizenry.

Around 150,000 Roma were required to acquire citizenship in the Czech Republic after its independence in 1993, and as many as

25,000 of them found themselves at risk of statelessness (Linde, 2006; Kochenov, 2007). The socialist Czechoslovak government relocated numerous Roma from the Slovak to the Czech part of the federation. The official reason given was the availability of employment in the more industrialised regions. Unofficially, the government applied this policy so that the Romani population would be evenly distributed in both parts of the federation and not concentrated in one part (Kochenov, 2007; see also Chapter 2). However, in many cases Romani individuals did not have their residence properly registered in the Czech part. After the fall of the Berlin Wall, most relocated Roma lost their previous employment through factory closures, and many were forced into informal work (Donert, 2017). This affected their citizenship status. Because all Czechoslovak citizens had held either Slovak or Czech republican citizenship since 1969 (Baršová, 2014), Roma who were relocated from Slovakia to Czechia were identified as Slovak republican citizens, as were their children, who might have never been in Slovakia (Kochenov, 2007).

In 1992 the Czech government introduced a new Citizenship Act (Baršová, 2014), which when applied in 1993 meant that all residents with Slovakian republican citizenship had to naturalise as Czech citizens after the 'velvet divorce'. There were no criteria that would directly target Roma, but the marginalisation and stereotypes of Roma left them in legal limbo and without the possibility of naturalisation. According to the provisions in Article 7 of the 1993 Citizenship Act, only residents with officially registered residence and with no criminal record for five years could naturalise. This rule disproportionally affected Roma who were either not officially registered or had criminal records due to misdemeanours (informal work or minor thefts, for example). According to Beata Struhárová (1999), Ľudovít Gorej, a Romani man with a Slovakian republican citizenship who was raised in an orphanage on Czech territory from infancy, was sentenced to expulsion in 1996 because he stole €4 worth of sugar beets. Between 1994 and 1997, 663 individuals designated as Slovak citizens were expelled. The vast majority were expelled for minor offences and were Roma (Struhárová, 1999). The state authorities treated many Roma as thieves or unsettled nomads and therefore as underserving of Czech citizenship. This was despite the fact that the former socialist government had relocated them and their unemployment was a consequence of broader transition processes.

Critical civil society reports showed that the inability to access citizenship according to new laws disproportionally affected Roma and stressed that the new Czech authorities designed these policies in a way to exclude Roma (Šklová and Miklušáková, 1998). In 1996 the Czech government amended the Citizenship Act, giving the Ministry of Interior discretion to overlook the clean record requirement for naturalisation. In 1998 Václav Havel gave an amnesty to all Slovak citizens who had been sentenced for less than five years (Struhárová, 1999). The Citizenship Act was again amended in 1999 so that citizens of the former federation could become Czech citizens by declaration (Baršová, 2014).

Roma who resided in the Czech territory were mostly entitled to Slovak citizenship and were therefore not considered to be *de jure* stateless. Czechia used this fact to retroactively irregularise their status and designate them as migrants, which made them deportable (De Genova, 2002), despite the fact that at the time they did not cross any international borders and many of them did not even cross the Czech republican border. Whilst the 1993 Citizenship Act did not create a statelessness situation *per se*, it left future generations of Roma at risk of administrative *de jure* statelessness (Owen, 2018) and without access to rights connected to citizenship and even residence. The provisions in the 1993 Citizenship Act targeted Roma as a racialised group: national authorities ascribed nomadism and criminalities as cultural traits of Roma. The initial Czech Citizenship Act, therefore, can be regarded as an outcome of a racialised citizenship regime as it made a great number of Roma unable to naturalise because of their belonging to a particular minority group.

Whilst most cases of hindered citizenship access after Czechoslovakia's disintegration were typically resolved with the amendments to the Citizenship Act by the turn of millennium, the issue remained a protracted and intergenerational problem for Romani minorities after the collapse of Yugoslavia. The statelessness of Romani minorities from the former Yugoslav space was a result of restrictive citizenship acts (similar to those in the Czech case), destruction of citizenship registries, forced displacement and overall discrimination against Roma (Cahn, 2012; Sardelić, 2015).

In the aftermath of the Yugoslav wars and multiple border re-drawings, many Romani individuals became forcedly displaced, particularly those who fled during the 1998–99 war in Kosovo (Perić and Demirovski, 2000) to North Macedonia and other parts of what was then the Federal Republic of Yugoslavia: Serbia and Montenegro. Roma who fled to North Macedonia crossed an international border and, in most cases, received a form of refugee status (Sardelić, 2015). By receiving refugee status, they fell under the 2010 *Prato Conclusions* definition of *de facto* statelessness. Yet Romani individuals who fled to Serbia and Montenegro did not cross any internationally recognised borders at the time, as Serbia, Montenegro and Kosovo were still one state (Sardelić, 2018). They were hence categorised as internally displaced persons. In subsequent years, Montenegro proclaimed its independence (in 2006, with wide international recognition), as did Kosovo (in 2008, with limited international recognition). In addition, many birth registries and other vital state records were destroyed or relocated during the war in Kosovo (UNHCR, 2011).

The emergence of new borders caused a conundrum in citizenship and migrant taxonomy in the post-Yugoslav states. Whilst previously being in the domain of a single state, the internally displaced persons found themselves in a new citizenship constellation (Bauböck, 2010) of three independent states (Sardelić, 2015). Montenegro's independence was internationally recognised, but in official documents the state authorities continued to refer to forced Romani migrants from Kosovo as internally displaced persons and not as refugees (Džankić, 2012; Sardelić, 2015), and hence they were not accorded rights as refugees. At the same time, they were not given the rights of citizens either. To paraphrase De Genova's (2017: 18) words, 'borders cross everyone, including those who never cross borders'.

Montenegro's parliament made amendments to the Law on Foreigners to include the definition of a stateless person (Article 2) in 2017 and statelessness determination procedure (Article 59) in 2018 after the Universal Periodic Review highlighted the absence of this procedure (UNHCR, 2018a). The law identified the right of temporary residence for stateless persons. Yet it left those Romani minorities, who were administratively *de jure* stateless because of a lack of documents, in legal limbo (Owen, 2018). According to the 2018 European Commission Montenegro report, a 'new law on foreigners adopted in February 2018 [and] a separate procedure for determining statelessness was introduced. So far, there are no officially recognised stateless persons, despite having an estimated number of 486 people who consider themselves stateless living in the country' (European Commission, 2018a: 29). A previous UNHCR report stated that the former Yugoslav states (excluding Slovenia), who were signatories of the 2011 Zagreb Declaration, estimated around 20,000 individuals without proper personal identification documents and who were hence at risk of becoming *de jure* statelessness (UNHCR, 2011: 3).

Many Romani individuals who crossed internal republican borders in socialist Yugoslavia still cannot regularise their citizenship status, not simply because of discrimination and socio-economic disadvantages, but because of the way legal acts of citizenship in the newly established states are set (Sardelić, 2015). In 2004 the Croatian Constitutional Court decided on a case where a Romani woman born in the territory of today's BIH wanted to naturalise as a Croatian citizen after living for decades in Croatia in a civil partnership with a man who was a Croatian citizen. One of the conditions of naturalisation is that the person wanting to acquire citizenship has to be proficient in the Croatian language and Latin script and be familiar with Croatian culture and social arrangements (see Croatian Citizenship Act of 1991). However, the applicant in question was illiterate and could not prove her knowledge of the Latin script. The judgement of the Constitutional Court (U-III/1918/2000) did not mention that she was of Romani origin or explain why this woman was illiterate (because of the enduring educational discrimination of Roma; see Chapter 3) (Constitutional Court of Croatia, 2003). However, in a dissenting opinion, one of the judges questioned whether the criterion of proficiency in Latin script should apply to former Yugoslav citizens in any event. The judgement also ignored the statelessness circle: the Constitutional Court noted that the Romani woman in question could not attain Croatian citizenship since she was not legally married to the Croatian citizen. This ignored the fact that individuals in post-Yugoslav countries cannot marry if they do not possess a birth certificate, and this is one of the main reasons for the reproduction of statelessness in the former Yugoslav countries (Kingston, 2017).

As in the Czech case, it was civil society actors in the region, such as the WeBLAN (Western Balkans Legal Aid Network),[3] and international NGOs, such as the ERRC, the European Network on Statelessness and the Institute for Statelessness and Inclusion, who highlighted the predicament of stateless Roma in the post-Yugoslav states most widely, through the #RomaBelong campaign (ERRC, 2017). In the case of the Yugoslav countries, it would be difficult to prove that the newly established definitions of citizenry were a direct attempt to exclude Roma since they were more noticeably targeted at others (Sardelić, 2015). However, Roma had more difficulties with regularising their status in the long run than other minorities who might have been initially targeted. Although states contributed to the position of Roma with historical racist practices (such as segregation and forced relocations), they did not acknowledge their position when constructing the new citizenship legislation.

The conflict in former Yugoslavia shaped Roma's risk of becoming stateless both within and beyond the borders of the post-Yugoslav states and had a spill-over effect on forced migrants who became at risk of statelessness in Italy. According to the *Statelessness Index Survey* of 2019, there were 732 persons in Italy with statelessness status. However, there were estimates of up to 15,000 people being stateless without their status being legally recognised, and 'most belong to the Roma community originating from former Yugoslavia' (European Network on Statelessness, 2019: 9). As Nando Sigona (2015) has pointed out, Italy passed a law at the beginning of the 1990s according to which any child of a stateless person can become an Italian citizen. However, there was a catch-22: for the child to become an Italian citizen, her or his parents had to have their legal status regulated in Italy with documented legal residence as well as proof that no other state has considered them their citizens. A clear majority of Romani forced migrants from Yugoslavia could not regulate their status, owing to the initial lack of documents when they fled their countries and their inability to retrieve these documents in the newly established countries. Additionally, whilst Italy has now a fee-free statelessness determination procedure, accessing statelessness status cannot only be valued in terms of monetary compensation. Besides access to rights with recognised citizenship status, the statelessness status would give the individuals in question the same access to social welfare and healthcare as any other 'lawfully resident foreigner' (European Network on Statelessness, 2019: 31). This shows that it is not merely citizenship that gives the 'rights to have rights': the right to have rights precedes citizenship and starts with any form of legal status, even that of a stateless person. Whilst initially Romani refugees were from former Yugoslavia, what thresholds would they now have to cross to become a recognised part of Italian citizenry? With states refusing to recognise these Roma as part of Italian society, and denying rights connected to this status, Romani refugees in Italy (mostly situated in so-called *campi nomadi*) remain on the fringes, where they depend on familial and other networks through which they gain rights denied by the state (Sigona, 2015). Racialised citizenship regimes are not a reality for either post-conflict or postsocialist contexts: they are a very real experience within the EU itself.

Russian-speaking minorities in the Baltic states

According to the 2017 UNHCR Global Trends report, the largest documented stateless populations in the EU live in two Baltic states: 233,571 in Latvia and 80,314 in Estonia (UNHCR, 2018a). These stateless populations mostly belong to Russian-speaking minorities who are not proficient in the majority languages (Estonian and Latvian):[4] in the Soviet period, Russian was also an official language. However, despite the fact that these populations fit the 1954 Statelessness Convention's definition of *de jure* statelessness, Estonia and Latvia do not consider them to be stateless in their national legislation. They are legally recognised in Latvia as 'non-citizens' by the former USSR Citizens' Act (Krūma, 2015: 8), and in Estonia as persons of 'undefined' (Järve and Poleshchuk, 2010: 1) or 'undetermined' (Semjonov *et al.*, 2015: 1) citizenship and, consequently, labelled as aliens.

Whilst Latvia distinguishes between stateless persons and non-citizens in its laws (Krūma, 2015: 7) and has signed and ratified 1954 and 1961 Statelessness Conventions, Estonia did not sign the Conventions and does not include statelessness as a category in its law (Semjonov *et al.*, 2015). International organisations, such as the CoE, the UN and the OSCE, refer to these populations as stateless in their reports (Kudaibergenova, 2020). Yet the state authorities in Latvia and Estonia do not recognise them as stateless. For example, the Latvian government states on its website: 'Latvia's non-citizens are not stateless persons. The protection provided to non-citizens in Latvia extends beyond that which is required by the 1954 Stateless-ness Convention. The fact that non-citizens cannot be considered stateless persons has been acknowledged by the United Nations High Commissioner for Refugees (UNHCR) – see UNHCR's Global Trends report (published on 19 June 2017)' (Government of Latvia, 2018). The Global Trends report, however, counts Latvian non-citizens as stateless, but concludes that they do not fall under the protection of the 1954 Statelessness Convention because their basic human rights are already protected by the Latvian state as they have guaranteed residence and diplomatic protection (UNHCR, 2017a: 69). The Estonian authorities have claimed they have not acceded to the Statelessness Conventions because 'in their assessment, there are no stateless persons in Estonia, just a number of *individuals with undefined citizenship*' (Semjonov et al., 2015: 15; emphasis added).

After the Soviet Union's disintegration in the 1990s, the official discourse of the three Baltic countries was that they were not declaring independence, but rather restoring it from the Soviet occupation. Unlike the two other Baltic states, Lithuania adopted the so-called zero option after the restoration of its independence in 1990: all residents either were automatically citizens (those who had citizenship before 1940 and their descendants) or had relatively unobstructed access to it (Kūris, 2010). The two main minorities, the Russians and the Poles, were relatively small in Lithuania and did not represent a threat to Lithuania's national identity (Kūris, 2010). Estonia and Latvia took a different approach: individuals who were Estonian and Latvian citizens before 16 June 1940 and their descendants were automatically Estonian and Latvian citizens, whilst those who migrated after this date had to naturalise. The naturalisation process included a test in the majority languages, Latvian and Estonian, the only two official languages after the collapse of the Soviet Union. At the beginning of the 1990s, the radical political discourse described the migrants who came to Estonia through the USSR's state-promoted relocation policy as illegal: 'During the autumn/winter of 1991–92, some Estonian politicians, including a number of representatives with the congress of Estonia, argued that all those who entered Estonia after 16 June 1940, did so illegally and therefore have no automatic right to citizenship' (Semjonov et al., 2015: 1). Subsequently, in 1992, around 500,000 people in Estonia (representing 32 per cent of the population) were deprived of their citizenship (UNHCR, 2016, 16) and 700,000 in Latvia (Ivlevs and King, 2012: 4).

The position of non-citizens in Latvia and aliens in Estonia represents a special conundrum in statelessness studies. As they are *in stricto sensu* not citizens of any state, they fit the definition of statelessness, but not that of the total infringement of citizenship. Their statelessness is unrecognised and is formulated as a different 'non-citizenship' status. At the same time, their rights are approximated to those of citizens: with the major exception of political rights (voting rights), non-citizens of Latvia and people with undetermined citizenship in Estonia possess other economic and social rights that most stateless populations do not (Swider, 2017). One of these rights is the possession of non-citizen and alien passports, which gives their holders a right to visa-free travel in the Schengen countries as well as the Russian Federation. Aliens in Estonia and non-citizens in Latvia are protected against deportation, and the states recognise their link with the territory. This is why Kochenov and Dimitrovs (2016: 64) conclude that they cannot be considered stateless in the same way as other populations:

> Non-citizenship of Latvia verges on a nationality without citizenship or political participation. To the bearers it brings a large array of rights traditionally associated with citizenship, including the unconditional right to enter Latvian territory, to remain, and to build a life there: work, non-discrimination and permanent residence are all included in the package. It definitely does not imply 'classical' statelessness in the sense of international law.

In subsequent years, both Latvia and Estonia amended their citizenship legislation so as to reduce childhood statelessness. The first reforms for facilitated access to citizenship in Estonia began in 1998 (Kudaibergenova, 2020) and culminated in 2015, when all children under fifteen born in Estonia to alien parents automatically became citizens (if their parents did not submit a written objection), whereas in 2013 they became citizens upon their parents' request (Semjonov *et al.*, 2015; Krūma, 2015).

Nevertheless, despite such appropriations, Russian speaking-minorities are discriminated against not only in the political domain, but also in terms of employment and access to education (Kudaibergenova, 2020). They are clearly unequal to those who hold

Estonian or Latvian citizenship because they are *in stricto sensu de jure* stateless. Yet the question is whether their statelessness can be connected to racialised citizenship and the total infringement of citizenship. The initial citizenship acts in Latvia and Estonia did make citizenship acquisition difficult, but the legislation introduced subsequently acknowledged that Russian-speaking minorities belonged to those territories, although their belonging was clearly unequal.

Haitians in the Dominican Republic

Kristy Belton (2011: 59) argues that the *in situ* statelessness of Haitians in the Dominican Republic represents a case of rooted displacement, and she calls this group 'non-citizen insiders'. Since the 1920s, Haitians have been crossing to the Dominican Republic as migrant workers (via an undefined border), especially in the then flourishing sugar industry after the US occupation of both Haiti and the Dominican Republic (Belton, 2015). Many Haitians were employed as undocumented workers. Until 2010, the Dominican Republic generally applied the *jus soli* principle granting citizenship on the basis of birth on its territory except for children of diplomats, who fell into the 'in transit' category. The children of undocumented migrants were entitled to Dominican citizenship if they were born on its territory. The deprivation of citizenship started with a systematic refusal by the Dominican authorities to issue birth certificates to children of undocumented Haitian migrants. In 2013 the Dominican Republic's Constitutional Court limited the *jus soli* principle by reinterpreting the 1929 Citizenship Act and associating the irregular migrant status with the 'in transit' status. With this reinterpretation, the authorities of the Dominican Republic retroactively deprived around 200,000 Dominican citizens of Haitian descent of their citizenship and made all who came to the Dominican Republic after 1929 stateless (IACHR, 2015: 21).

The IACHR report stated that the deprivation of citizenship was accompanied by discourses demanding that Haitians be deported from the country because they were portrayed in the Dominican media as criminals (IACHR, 2015). Although of Haitian descent, these former Dominican citizens had never known Haiti as their home country (Belton, 2015; Hayes de Kalaf, 2019). Racism towards Afro-descendants had historical roots in colonialism and slavery, but also in the nation-building of the Dominican Republic, which constructed its historical narratives from white Spanish heritage as distinct from black Haitians. Yet, according to the IACHR (2015: 144), there was also widespread denial of racism: 'For their part, at every meeting held with the State, all officials firmly denied the existence of racism or discriminatory practices in the country against Dominicans of Haitian descent, Haitians, or persons of African descent in general.' The deprivation of citizenship was not directly racist, but it targeted undocumented migrants, who were, according to the new interpretation, 'in transit'. However, most of the people 'in transit' were of Haitian descent, and the reinterpretation of the Constitutional Court did not give them any possible means of being naturalised. The decision of the Constitutional Court brought about a total infringement of citizenship, which took away both their citizenship status and any accompanying rights as part of a highlighted racialised (Hayes De Kalaf, 2019) citizenship regime.

Rohingya from Myanmar

The 2017 UNHCR Global Trends Report stated that there were 1.5 million stateless Rohingya in Myanmar and Bangladesh (UNHCR, 2018a). Rohingya minorities have been described as 'the world's most persecuted minority' (OHCHR, 2017). Many reports on statelessness have claimed that Rohingya became stateless through the 1982 Citizenship Law because they were not recognised under the 135 'national races' that were present in the country in 1823, that is, before the British colonial occupation of Burma (Kyaw, 2017; Cheesman, 2017). However, on the basis of primary sources in the Burmese language, some scholars have argued critically that the development of citizenship policies and practices has not been as straightforward as that portrayed by major international organisations (Cheesman, 2017; Kyaw, 2017; Parashar and Alam, 2018). These scholars have argued that the 1982 Citizenship Law did not itself deprive Rohingya of their citizenship, but the practices of the state authorities destroyed the documents of Rohingya proving their citizenship, or refused to register them according to the new Citizenship Act.

The first postcolonial Constitution of Burma (drafted in 1947) introduced the terms 'Indigenous races' and 'national races', but did not name Rohingya as one of the national races. However, the 1948 Citizenship Act recognised virtually all the inhabitants of Burma as citizens. Belonging to one of the pre-1823 Indigenous or national races was not the only possible way to be recognised as a citizen of Burma (Parashar and Alam, 2018). Although Rohingya were not explicitly recognised as belonging to one of the national races in the legislation, they were recognised as such in later parliamentary debate (Parashar and Alam, 2018). Tracing the genealogy of the concept of 'national races', Nick Cheesman (2017) argues that they emerged as a determinant of Burmese politics more recently, in 1964. At this point the political discourse in Burma started changing when General Ne Win gave centrality to the concept of 'national races' in his Union Day speech (Cheesman, 2017: 465). As the borders between Myanmar, Bangladesh and India were initially poorly defined, the discourse accompanying the concept of 'national races' was that there had been continuous 'illegal migration' to Myanmar from the neighbouring countries since the colonial period.

In the ensuing decades, the status of Rohingya also changed dramatically: previously thought of as one of the national races, they were increasingly perceived as foreign Bengalis who came to Myanmar as British-sponsored labour migrants, and as 'illegal migrants' who arrived after Burmese independence (Parashar and Alam, 2018). The 1982 Citizenship Law indeed gave primacy to 'national races', but it also included safeguards according to which those recognised as citizens in the 1948 Citizenship Law could not be automatically deprived of citizenship. Rather, the Rohingya were deprived of citizenship because the authorities refused to register them as citizens (Parashar and Alam, 2018) and instead gave them white temporary residence cards (Kyaw, 2017; Cheesman, 2017). The official Burmese explanation for this practice was that the Rohingya have dubious citizenship status and that it still needed to be determined whether or not they were citizens of Myanmar (Kyaw, 2017). It was the introduction of these cards that left Rohingya in legal limbo, as neither citizens nor foreigners in Myamar, and not the Citizenship Act itself, as is often wrongly stated (Kyaw, 2017; Cheesman, 2017). Since membership of the 'national races' is the most important political category in Myanmar, Rohingya activists argued that Rohingya too are a national race on the basis of historical sources (the government of Myanmar and Buddhist nationalists dispute this claim; see Cheesman, 2017). The practices of the state caused multiple forced displacements of people with ambiguous legal status both within Myanmar and in neighbouring countries, especially Bangladesh. Rohingya were the minority who were most hit by the irregularisation of their status and displacement as the practices and discourses transformed them from previous citizens to less than aliens (as they also did not have a clear foreigner status).

Children of the Windrush generation in the UK

The context of postcolonialism did not only affect statelessness outside Europe, but contributed to it also within Europe. Since 2012 the UK Home Office had been introducing 'hostile environment' immigration policies. The so-called Windrush generation scandal in 2018 demonstrated a product of this policy: the hostile environment did not simply address the situation of 'illegal immigrants', but also contributed to the 'production of illegality' (De Genova, 2002b) not only of migrants, but also of those with precarious citizenship. It transformed citizens into 'illegal migrants'. The term 'Windrush generation' refers to people who went to the UK from the British Caribbean colonies between 1948 and 1971, beginning with the *Empire Windrush*, the first ship that arrived with the new workers the UK needed because of the labour shortages after World War II (Pennant and Sigona, 2018). According to the 1948 UK Citizenship Act, they were citizens at the time of their arrival, not immigrants. When the status of colonial citizenship regime changed, the 1971 Immigration Act gave the Windrush generation automatic 'leave to remain' in the UK, which granted them access to the new British citizenship. Many of them did not regularise their status as citizens because the 'leave to remain' status already provided them with the right to work, education and access to healthcare (Sigona, 2018). Another reason was the inexplicably high citizenship registration fee (Harvey, 2018). The only proof that the Windrush generation had of their 'leave to remain' status were their landing cards, which the UK Home Office destroyed in 2010 (Sigona, 2018).

The Windrush generation were former UK citizens who became 'aliens who are citizens' (Stevens, 2017a: 217) and hence deportable to the Caribbean states of which they were never citizens. The 'evidentiary challenges' (Stevens, 2017b: 3) that the Windrush generation faced left their children born in the UK in an exemplary case of administrative statelessness (Owen, 2018). Their parents' inability to prove their citizenship and the 'leave to remain' status created a legal limbo for the next generation since they fell in the category of people 'who cannot prove what they are not, not a citizen of any state or "stateless", any more than they can prove who they are' (Stevens, 201b7: 3). The Home Office's destruction of landing cards left the Windrush generation and their children with no viable options to prove their citizenship or to provide a case against being deported. Without access to healthcare, work and housing, they felt the consequences of the hostile environment: when they were constructed as 'illegal immigrants', 'borders pervade everyday lives' (Tonkiss, 2018).

The denial of citizenship to the Windrush generation still needs to be researched further. At present, it is not possible to conclude that the destruction of the landing cards by the Home Office was a direct racist action. But the end product was the same: it was black UK citizens who had difficulties in proving their identity. As Tonkiss (2018) comments: 'The construction of nationality also intersects with other perceived markers of social diversity … It is predominantly these people, and not their white counterparts with similar family histories of migration, who are persistently required to prove their belonging.' The destruction of landing cards led to the total infringement of citizenship because racialised citizenship was embedded within British citizenship legislation and practices by the authorities. At the time when the Windrush generation arrived in the UK, they did not nominally cross any borders of the British Empire: yet it was the change in the citizenship regime and subsequent practices of the state that rendered them 'illegal immigrants' and caused the total infringement of citizenship.

Total infringement of citizenship: a conclusion

This chapter has analysed five cases of minority statelessness, two of them connected to postsocialist contexts (Romani minorities and Russian-speaking minorities) and three to postcolonial contexts (Dominicans of Haitian descent, Rohingya and the Windrush generation). The contexts within which the minority statelessness occurred are diverse, yet they all reveal one commonality: previous citizens were transformed into unwanted, undocumented or irregular aliens through the reinterpretation of their belonging and reconstruction of citizenry, which cemented the inclusion of most, but made the citizenship of some others precarious. In all the cases analysed, the states were (at least initially) unwilling to recognise minorities who were deprived of citizenship as being stateless, but rather described them as foreigners from somewhere else. In most cases, the transformation from citizens to aliens also meant a total infringement of citizenship (that is, deprivation of citizenship accompanied by deprivation of political, economic and social rights). The exceptional case was the Russian-speaking minorities in Estonia and Latvia: whilst they were clearly discriminated against in their everyday lives, the two Baltic states did not deny that the minorities belonged to the state and gave them residency rights and protection from deportation. They did, however, introduce a hierarchy of belonging, and whilst the minorities had most of the rights of full citizens, they lacked voting rights.

Aside from the Russian-speaking minorities in the Baltic states, each of the cases discussed can be categorised as a stateless minority with total infringement of citizenship: the deprivation of citizenship was accompanied by deprivation of political, social and economic rights. In addition, whilst the number of Russian-speaking minorities without citizenship is well documented, the numbers in other cases are only estimates. These cases also show that total infringement of citizenship was based on racialised citizenship regimes. According to citizenship laws, discourses and practices relating to citizenship and belonging, all these minorities were denied their belonging to the states in questions. They found themselves with in-between statuses (Sardelić, 2015; Lori, 2017), fitting neither the definition of citizens nor that of stateless persons. Nevertheless, racialised citizenship regimes are transformable and can, with time, be either fortified or abolished. The study of racialised citizenship regimes shows that whilst minority statelessness does often occur in postsocialist or postcolonial settings, it cannot be regarded as a simple straightforward result of the end of socialism or colonialism. Whilst these served as the background for previous discrimination, it is just as much the introduction of new legislation, discourses and practices by (officially democratic) states that deny citizenship and construct minority statelessness.

Notes

1 In an earlier report on stateless children, the UNHCR highlighted the predicament of stateless Romani children in Italy (UNHCR, 2015).
2 This chapter does not deal with the complex situation of stateless Palestinians, which is also omitted altogether from the UNHCR report on minority statelessness. The reason for the omission is that they have a different sort of claim for state recognition. For a discussion on the statelessness of Palestinians, see Molavi (2013) and Fiddian-Quasmiyeh (2015). The position of stateless Kurds in the EU has also been previously discussed (see Eliassi, 2016; Tas, 2017).
3 For more on WeBLAN, see: https://www.statelessness.eu/blog/addressing-statelessness-western-balkans-%E2%80%93-ens-and-weblan-joint-workshop (accessed: 1 December 2020).
4 As pointed out by Kudaibergenova (2020), Russian-speaking minorities are a problematic concept. In the former Soviet states, almost all residents spoke Russian. It is equally problematic to assume that Russian-speaking minorities all spoke Russian as their mother tongue.

5

Out of ignorance and despair? Sabotage as a citizenship enactment at the fringes

Introduction

In 2013, Nazif Mujić, a Bosnian citizen of Romani background, received a Silver Bear Award at the Berlin International Film Festival. He won the award for his leading role in a low-budget film, *An Episode in the Life of an Iron Picker*, directed by the acclaimed director Danis Tanović. The film showed the daily struggles stateless Roma face: in a role of a husband, playing out his life, Mujić destroys his car and sells it as scrap metal so that he can pay for his wife's urgent medical treatment. She has no health insurance because of to a lack of personal documents. After his success in Berlin, Mujić returned to Bosnia and Herzegovina (BIH) as a praised actor. Yet a year later he went back to Germany, this time as an asylum seeker. Fame and success in the film industry did not improve Mujić's socio-economic position, his legal status or the ethnic discrimination he faced in being identified as belonging to a Romani minority. His family remained on the margins both in BIH as citizens and as asylum seekers in Germany. His asylum application was rejected as Germany regarded BIH as a safe third country and recognised his asylum claim as based on socio-economic grievances rather than persecution. After Germany rejected his asylum application, he went back to BIH, where he sold his Silver Bear trophy for €4000 in an act of despair but also as a protest because the fame had not brought his family out of poverty. He died in February 2018 at the age of forty-seven; the headlines reporting his death read: 'Film Star's Death Highlights Plight of Bosnia's Roma' (Lekić, 2018).

The selling of the Silver Bear trophy and Mujić's untimely death seemed just like another episode from his film. Nevertheless, this chapter begins with the case of Mujić because it illustrates two broader issues connected to citizenship. First, it demonstrates the value of citizenship for minorities at the fringes. Building upon previous chapters in this book, this chapter claims that citizenship for marginalised minorities is often devalued or even value-less in view of its different dimensions, status and rights (Joppke, 2007). Citizenship status does not necessarily give rights, and having rights does not necessarily lead to life improvements for marginalised minorities. Second, unlike previous chapters, this chapter seeks to understand how Romani individuals at the fringes of citizenship respond to their citizenship being devalued, precarious (Lori, 2017) and/or irregularised (Sardelić, 2017b; Nyers, 2019). Following some previous research (see Vermeersch, 2006; McGarry, 2010; Sigona, 2015), this chapter confirms that Romani individuals are not merely passive observers of their predicament, but act in response to it. At the same time as the civil rights movement in the US, a similar movement developed in Europe as the struggle for the Romani rights continued (Vermeersch, 2006; Donert, 2017; Chang and Rucker-Chang, 2020; see also Chapter 1), and it continued to flourish after the pivotal transformations in Europe: from the fall of the Berlin Wall through to the present-day concluded and ongoing EU negotiations. However, this chapter also highlights a different kind of enactment of citizenship (Isin, 2017), which is more latent as it is not the activists who perform it. This type of enactment of citizenship is usually less visible as it is mundane or ordinary, and it seems at first glance to emerge only from an individual's desperation or ignorance. I argue that such acts are political as they carry the potential to create ruptures within citizenship (Isin, 2009). I name these acts 'citizenship sabotage'.

The case of Mujić is indicative, as Germany has assumed that the predicament of Roma is no longer connected to the Bosnian war but rather to the economic downfall of the postsocialist transition in the country. Yet as the ECtHR *Sejdić and Finci v. BIH* case (henceforth the *Sejdić and Finci* case) demonstrated, this is not the whole story. In 1995 the Dayton Peace Agreement legally cemented the position of minorities in BIH, including Roma, as second-class citizens (Cirković, 2014). According to the Bosnian Constitution based on the Dayton Agreement, only the Bosnian constitutive nations can fully be a part of BIH's political structure. As defined in the 2001 Election

Law, the BIH presidency consisted of three members who had to identify as Croat, Bosniak and Serbian (Cirković, 2014: 456–7). Jakob Finci and Dervo Sejdić, two Bosnian citizens of Jewish and Romani background who could not stand as candidates for the BIH presidency, challenged this structure on the basis of minority discrimination and won the case against Bosnia in 2009 at the ECtHR. This electoral policy, which was designed outside BIH to promote peace, later represented an obstacle for BIH in its EU negotiations. In 2013 the EU suspended Instrument for Pre-Accession (IPA) funds for Bosnia because of its failure to reform its citizenship policies (European Commission, 2013). Yet six years later, in 2019, the Dayton ethnic hierarchies and citizenship ambiguities it created remained intact. Because of the lack of progress in creating new anti-discrimination provisions in the Bosnian electoral system, on 22 December 2019, exactly ten years after the ECtHR judgement in *Sejdić and Finci*, a CoE press release marked this as a 'disturbing anniversary' (CoE, 2019).

BIH's political structure and its socio-economic downfall were the hierarchies in which Nazif Mujić, as a Bosnian citizen of Romani background, was embedded in his country. However, his acts of citizenship (Isin, 2009) showed that the hierarchies went beyond the borders of his country of citizenship. As a rejected asylum seeker in Germany, he found himself within the hierarchies of citizenship constellations (Bauböck, 2010) between BIH and Germany (Sardelić, 2018) when he was categorised as an 'illegitimate' asylum seeker. The decision to seek asylum in Germany as a response to the discrimination he faced in BIH showed that citizenship constellations materialise not by means of mere arrangements, but when someone enacts them (Isin, 2009) and when states use their acts of sovereignty (Nyers, 2006) to respond.

Mujić was a Bosnian citizen, and the post-conflict reality of this country did represent one of the determinants of his position. Besides the ambiguities of the unequal ethnic political power sharing, Romani children are almost three times as likely as their peers to live in poverty (UNICEF, 2017). Additionally, state disintegration contributed to minority statelessness. This was the case in both the former socialist Yugoslavia and Czechoslovakia (Sardelić, 2015, see also Chapter 4). However, whilst this political structure is specific to BIH, socio-economic disadvantage, ethnic discrimination and the civic marginalisation of Romani minorities exist throughout Europe and are reproduced beyond national borders. A broader look at the data from the FRA indicates that Roma face a similar socio-economic predicament in most EU Member States, where 80 per cent of Roma live below their country's specific poverty line (FRA, 2016). Roma do not face statelessness only in post-conflict and postsocialist societies, but also in the older EU Member States, such as Italy (Sigona, 2015). Romani minorities in various European locales have faced both severe socio-economic disadvantage and ethnic discrimination (FRA, 2016) and are also positioned at the fringes of citizenship, where discrimination is not embedded directly in law as it is in BIH. Whilst Roma have been a visible minority within the EU (Vermeersch, 2012) because of ethnic discrimination and socio-economic disadvantage, there is an aspect of their position as citizens that is being ignored: numerous struggles that Romani individuals, such as Mujić, face daily indicate not simply the predicament of a marginalised minority but the invisible edges within citizenship itself. The ways in which individuals who are (at least initially) not a part of the Romani movement and do not regard themselves as activists respond politically to unequal citizenship statuses remain under-addressed in citizenship studies.

This chapter explores how Romani individuals understand and respond to the devaluation of citizenship, that is, when citizenship is emptied of its substance and its rights (Isin, 2009). First, it addresses the value of acquiring citizenship for stateless Romani individuals following the Arendtian assumption that citizenship status corresponds to access to rights related to status (Arendt, 1968). Second, it discusses how some Romani individuals who have been granted or have citizenship but not corresponding rights reflect and act in accordance with such situations. Third, it shows the value of citizenship for Romani individuals who have both citizenship status and rights but no influence and how this manifests itself in terms of voting rights. Fourth, it presents excerpts from life history interviews undertaken with individuals who do not in any way fit the stereotypical image of Roma. Nevertheless, these interviews show how these individuals encountered the invisible edges of citizenship even when they managed to escape poverty and Roma self-identification. I argue that even though these strategies that Romani individuals employ in different situations cannot be considered to be activist or protest in the strict sense of the terms, they are still performative (Isin, 2017) and consequently political. They represent citizenship sabotage.

Defining sabotage as an enactment of citizenship

In 2009 Engin Isin argued for a pivotal turn in citizenship studies: he suggested that instead of studying 'who is a citizen' the studies of citizenship should move towards to the question 'what makes a citizen' (Isin, 2009: 383). In proposing this turn, he revealed citizenship's dynamic nature. Citizenship cannot be fully comprehended by studying the rules of who is entitled to have citizenship. According to Isin, we should look at the struggles around citizenship and the actors in these struggles who make claims to citizenship (rights or status) even though they do not possess it at the time (meaning that they are non-citizens). He distinguished between 'active' and 'activist' citizens. The first group follows the pre-written citizenship scenario: they are active in that they go to elections, participate in political parties and also stand in elections. Yet activist citizens do not follow the path that has previously been constructed for them. They create a 'rupture' in citizenship by claiming rights they currently do not have (Isin, 2009: 379). They claim these rights at various sites by protesting on the streets but also by taking their claims to the courts. Such acts of citizenship can, according to Isin, bring a transformation to citizenship by expanding rights to individuals and groups who previously have not possessed them.

The *Sejdić and Finci* case may be regarded as a paradigmatic example of what is means to be an activist citizen. When the constitutional order of their country prevented two citizens who did not identify with the 'constitutive nations' from standing as candidates in the presidential elections, they took their claim to the ECtHR. Similar to the Kurdish minority in Turkey who lack EU citizenship (Rumelili and Keyman, 2013), through the ECtHR, Sejdić and Finci enacted European citizenship to highlight the electoral discrimination of minorities in their non-EU country that was standing as a potential EU Member State. Whilst the Bosnian Constitution did not change, the *Sejdić and Finci* case created a rupture in a discriminatory citizenship policy: transforming this policy became one of the conditions for Bosnia's entry into the EU. Courts are one of the sites where struggles with citizenship take place (Isin, 2009: 368). The ECtHR had a number of cases, mostly represented by the ERRC, that through strategic litigation highlighted inequal treatment of Roma as citizens of their own countries, despite their having anti-discrimination legislation in place (see Chapter 3).

The Romani movement (Vermeersch, 2006) has, from the very start, been happening on multiple sites and beyond national borders and can be characterised in terms of activist citizenship. For example, from the early 1970s, the Romani movement created citizenship ruptures beyond European national as well as EU borders: from the activists advocating against the pejorative term 'Gypsy' in favour of the more inclusive term 'Roma' during the World Romani Congresses, to constructing an idea of Roma being a trans-border non-territorial nation with a flag and anthem as well as the first representative body, the International Romani Union (Klímová-Alexander, 2005; Rövid, 2011b). In a similar vein to the Indigenous movements, the Romani movement came to the international arena as a 'critique of the current political system based on nation-states and dominated by majority nations, calling for a revolution in international relations towards a non-territorial rule' (Klímová-Alexander, 2005: 146). This was followed by the later manifestations such as Roma Pride, which was formally based on LGBT Pride (McGarry, 2017: 171). Whilst some might argue that the Romani movement was simply the movement for Romani rights, it in fact created ruptures in citizenship and revealed minority inequalities that had previously been unseen (see Chapter 1). Similar insights occurred through the actions of the Romani women's movement, where Romani women activists were not simply addressing the intersection of male oppression with ethnic discrimination, but were highlighting broader issues of power relations in their own countries and beyond (Kóczé et al., 2018). Arts and culture have also been sites of activist citizenship culminating in the establishment of the European Roma Institute for Arts and Culture (ERIAC) in Berlin, which actively promotes Romani artists who fashion ruptures in citizenship in their artistic actions. Both the Romani women's movement and ERIAC emphasised the importance of Romani self-representation. Roma have been represented by non-Roma in all spheres of society, and this has developed an exoticised stereotype image: now, by highlighting the voice of Romani feminist activists as well as promoting Romani art and culture, the stereotyped image can be redrawn to create a new space for self-representation that also demonstrates the contribution of Romani culture to wider Europe (Connolly, 2017).

But what about actions that are less public, more individual, more mundane? What do they reveal about the fringes of citizenship and sites of citizenship struggle? Bhambra (2016) has questioned whether the non-citizens who do not make public claims could be considered apolitical. Catherine Neveu (2015: 151) has argued that ordinary citizens in their everyday situations are not necessarily non-political: 'approaching citizenship processes "from the ordinary" is a fruitful perspective from which the political dimensions of usually unseen and unheard practices and sites can be grasped, and unruly practices be treated not as inadequate or mismatched ones. Indeed, what is centrally at stake is the issue of visibility, or more exactly rendering visible (people, practices, processes) that often go unseen or unheard.'

Isin has highlighted the dichotomy between outstanding and invisible acts of citizenship as one of the puzzles that remains to be addressed within the theory of performative citizenship (Isin, 2017: 519–20). Do Roma who are not a part of the Romani movement contest discrimination they face in their everyday lives so that they create ruptures in citizenship? In 2016 the FRA published the *Second European Union Minorities and Discrimination Survey*, which found that almost a third of Romani respondents who were EU citizens indicated that they were not aware of anti-discrimination laws in their countries, only 12 per cent reported discrimination, and 82 per cent responded they did not know of any organisations that could support them if they were discriminated against; yet one in two Roma felt they were discriminated against on the basis of their ethnic origin (FRA, 2016: 11).

In order to analyse whether certain actions of Romani individuals in their everyday lives can be understood not merely as coping strategies but also as political acts, I suggest a new term for a type of citizenship enactment: citizenship sabotage. According to the *Oxford English Dictionary*, the word 'sabotage' means to 'deliberately destroy, damage, or obstruct (something), especially for political or military advantage'.[1] The concept of sabotage has been utilised particularly in relation to the workplace (Mars, 2001). For the anthropologist Gerald Mars, sabotage was not an easy phenomenon to investigate. It is often kept secret by employees or saboteurs as well as by employers: the first might face legal prosecution if identified, and the latter has a motivation to hide potential problems in the workplace. This is why there is a lack of quantifiable data on sabotage (Mars, 2001: xii). Mars states that sabotage is 'latent in any organization and its threat is always potent, if unspoken, factor in the balance of work place power. Its use, or at least the possibility of use, has a long history, and it is still the ultimate weapon of the formally powerless' (Mars, 2001: xi). Employers often interpret sabotage as irrational behaviour, but Mars suggests that it should be studied for its alternative rationalities that are about power relations: 'acts of sabotage – which may or may not be against the law – are always a reflection of a power struggle. They are about control and are therefore political acts at microlevel that are invariably linked with political implications on a macro level' (Mars, 2001: xiii).

   In light of Mars's understanding of workplace sabotage, I define citizenship sabotage as an act of citizenship that creates a rupture latently: it damages or obstructs the conventional script of citizenship, but this is noticeable only after the invisible act has already taken place. It is a deliberate act at the micro-level and has political implications for citizenship regimes, but it is not always clear in advance what these will be. The act itself might not appear as a rupture, yet it is an unconventional intervention into citizenship. Citizenship sabotage is not considered an extraordinary or heroic act as other enactments of citizenship frequently are. It is a seemingly mundane and often hidden act by an individual at the citizenship fringes, and it is repeatedly described as only an act of despair rather than a political act. However, like other citizenship enactments, even such acts of despair can have broader political implications and substantively redefine what it means to be a citizen. Most importantly, like other citizenship acts, citizenship sabotage is about (re)claiming rights.[2]

Citizenship sabotage and the Romani minorities at the fringes

The story of Nazif Mujić and his family can be understood as a different kind of enactment of citizenship. So too can that of Sejdić and Finci as they enacted their citizenship in the court. However, most struggles that individual Romani face do not reach the highest courts, nor do they receive particular attention even from the national authorities. The film about Mujić's life was entitled *An Episode in the Life of an Iron Picker* to demonstrate the ordinariness and repetitiveness of the struggles many Romani individuals face when their citizenship is devalued: because Mujić could not access the formal labour market, collecting scrap metal was his main source of income to support his family. However, the film also shows how fringe citizens act when faced with an extraordinary situation. As Mujić's wife was without personal documents and consequently did not have health insurance, the couple initially accessed health facilities by borrowing a health insurance card from another woman. The legal NGO Our Rights[3] observed this as a widespread practice in BIH, and the 2011 UNHCR *Report on Statelessness in South Eastern Europe* registered it as present throughout the region, especially among stateless women who wanted to give birth in hospital:

> The fear of being charged a hospital fee for giving birth without health insurance is an incentive for some women to give birth at home. Some women without documents borrow the health booklet of a friend or relative to avoid fees for giving birth in a hospital. This happens throughout the region. The child is consequently legally registered with a different family and it is very difficult to correct the erroneous registration later on (UNHCR, 2011: 28–9)

Such an act contributes to the intergenerational reproduction of legal invisibility and statelessness (Sardelić, 2015; see also Chapter 4). The UNHCR report presented this simply as an act of fear and despair to address an individual situation that a minority woman at the fringes of citizenship finds herself in. However, it also demonstrates something much more significant: that is, how individuals at the fringes claim rights when they lack citizenship status. Stateless Roma, despite being on the fringes and lacking citizenship, do not necessarily embody Arendt's notion of lacking rights here, and stateless people search for ways to claim the rights that the states deny as well (Sigona, 2015). With a mundane act, such as borrowing health insurance cards, stateless Romani women at the fringes claim citizenship status and ensure access to rights that create a rupture in citizenship. Borrowing health cards is not a prescribed way to be an 'active citizen' but it is one of the few possible acts that legally invisible persons have left in order to claim rights. Perhaps it is an act of despair, but it is also a political act which is noticed by the state authorities. It questions the legitimacy of healthcare access provided only to people (be they citizens, stateless people or people with a different immigrant status) who can prove their identity. It was citizenship sabotage, an incognito act of lending and borrowing health insurance cards, that revealed this problem.

Through the efforts of legal NGOs and advocacy groups, statelessness came to the agenda of international organisations such as the UNHCR. As part of the #IBelong campaign, the UNHCR published a short video on the predicament of Romani individuals who face statelessness in the former Yugoslavian country of North Macedonia. The initial caption of the video read: 'The Roma are the largest stateless minority in the country. Most have not had their births registered making it difficult for them to access Macedonian citizenship and basic rights' (UNHCR, 2017b). The video then featured the story of Mitar Rustemov, whose six children were still unregistered. In the video, Rustemov comments: 'Without documents, you are like a dead man.' Yet when asked why he wants his children to be registered, his initial response is the following: 'The boy wants to go to Belgrade and Germany to play football. How can the club take him without a birth certificate, ID card or passport?' (UNHCR, 2017b). It is only in the second instance that Rustemov mentions that having identity documents gives one the right to work and the right to education. His first response is that by acquiring citizenship, his children could enact citizenship sabotage, that is, move to another country.

At first glance, it might seem that Romani individuals such as Rustemov are unaware of what rights they can access in their own country with having legal identity and documents. However, if Rustemov's story is connected to Mujić's, another perspective is possible: it is not due to 'ignorance' that Romani individuals decide upon citizenship sabotage instead of being 'active citizens'. After Mujić's death, Deutsche Welle television interviewed his widow. She commented that after her husband became a famous actor, various authorities promised that the family's life would improve: 'Everything was beautiful at the recording [of the film], but we were hoping this will bring better opportunities for our children, for better life, that we will be able to send our children to school. They promised us they will give us some apartment, that we will have a better standard of life. But nothing was ever better' (Deutsche Welle, 2018). During the visa liberalisation processes in Serbia and North Macedonia, one of the benchmarks for visa-free travel into the Schengen zone was providing access to identity documents for minorities (Kacarska, 2015; see also Chapter 2). In this period, legal aid NGOs (such as WeBLAN),[4] with the assistance of the UNHCR, consciously started the registration processes of legally invisible people, of whom most were displaced Romani individuals (Praxis, 2016). Through the work of mobile teams and acts by determined individuals who worked in Romani communities, many legally invisible individuals were reached even in the most remote areas and their status was regularised. However, whilst the main objective of such registrations was to increase minority protection through general citizenship and, in particular, minority rights, some Romani individuals commented directly to the NGO representatives that their main motive in acquiring citizenship was to gain the ability to travel beyond the country of citizenship. This stems not simply from ignorance of the rights one gains with citizenship, but from the awareness that such rights remain unattainable. The *Sejdić and Finci* case demonstrates the rights that are unattainable legally. However, numerous Romani individuals, as testified by Mujić's widow, are aware that simply having a status and legally guaranteed rights does not necessarily translate into having rights in practice. As Chapter 3 showed, despite the fact that discrimination is prohibited legally, it continues to be an everyday reality for Romani children in accessing equal, non-segregated education, as well as for adults who want to access the labour market.

The value of acquiring identity documents, especially passports, became connected to new migration possibilities, and with them possibilities of accessing rights elsewhere. As research shows (Kummrow, 2015), in the years following visa liberalisation, the number of asylum seekers from North Macedonia and Serbia increased from 6,390 in 2009 (before the visa-free regime was been established) to 41,140 in 2014. Most of these asylum seekers made their applications in Germany, and a large majority claimed that they were persecuted because they belonged to Romani communities. Only a few asylum requests were granted. The rise was noticed by the EU

Parliament, which, in the years following visa liberalisation, voted in favour of visa-free suspension mechanisms for the Western Balkan countries in question, should the number of asylum seekers continue to increase (Sardelić, 2018). The response of the EU Member States was not new or unique in this case: similar examples had appeared before the 2004 enlargement (Clark and Campbell, 2000). Before the Czech Republic joined the EU in 2004, a special immigration regime operated by the UK prevented potential asylum seekers from boarding planes: the UK's House of Lords determined that this was based on racial profiling of Roma, who were disproportionally prevented from entering the UK (*Regina v. Immigration Officer at Prague Airport and Another, ex parte European Roma Rights Centre and Others*, 2004). In the case of the Western Balkans, however, the EU Parliament threatened all citizens of the respective countries with removal of the rights to visa-free travel if the number of asylum requests was not contained (Sardelić, 2018). The response of the North Macedonian and Serbian governments was similar to that of the UK previously: they did not allow individuals who were deemed as potential asylum seekers to leave their own country. The Serbian authorities put up posters at Belgrade airport in the Romani, Albanian and Serbian languages to discourage their minority citizens from travelling to the EU in order to seek asylum (see Chapter 2).

The explanations of why Romani individuals, as citizens of Western Balkan non-EU countries, sought asylum in the EU were usually limited to their devastating socio-economic position and ethnic discrimination. However, no study could confirm that those who sought asylum were the 'poorest of the poor'. Some studies on the migration of Romani individuals in general disputed that poverty was the main factor (Pantea, 2013; Sardelić, 2019c). Migration and asylum seeking could also be interpreted not just as an act of desperation, but also as an act of claiming rights that were inaccessible in the country of citizenship. This was also a protest against inaccessible rights. The outcome – that is, the endangering of mobility rights for all citizens – indicated that there was an instance of citizenship sabotage in the place. It created a rupture in the discriminatory citizenship regime, which also affected all citizens in broader citizenship constellations.

The third act of citizenship sabotage involved the efforts to make Romani minorities become active citizens. Roma have been largely invisible as citizens of their own countries (see Chapter 1), even when having both status and rights. This is especially the case in electoral processes, both for people voting and for those standing as candidates (McGarry, 2010). In its research on the 2019 European Parliament Elections, the European Roma Information Office concluded that only three candidates who identified as Roma were elected as MEPs: however, given that there are 6 million Roma who are citizens of the EU, it determined that there should be at least fifteen Romani MEPs in the European Parliament (European Roma Information Office, 2019). The significant obstacles Roma face in formal political participation (especially electoral processes) remain intact not only in EU Member States (McGarry, 2010) and candidate countries, but also across the broader OSCE Area. International organisations, among them especially OSCE, have been highlighting the need for Roma to become active citizens since the early 2000s. In 2003 OSCE published an *Action Plan on Improving the Situation of Roma within the OSCE Area*. One of the main focuses in this plan was to move beyond the classic scopes of addressing discrimination in education, housing, healthcare and the labour market to focus on 'enhancing participation in public and political life' (OSCE, 2003: 12). Whilst other international initiatives focused more on the first of these areas of action, OSCE became particularly interested in mobilising the political participation of Roma. One of the earliest projects based on the action plan was 'Roma Use Your Ballot Wisely', a project designed to 'empower Roma to become protagonists in the decisions involving and affecting themselves' (Krause, 2007: 1). One of the main factors listed as obstacles for the effective electoral participation of Roma was the 'vulnerability of Roma voters with regard to election-related practices of corruption and other irregularities (vote buying, pressure on voters, group and proxy voting)' (Krause, 2007: 3). Vote buying and other electoral malpractices are not limited to Romani communities. However, as some of the authors and policymakers have argued (OSCE, 2018), it is particularly because of political illiteracy and weak socio-economic status that Romani minorities are especially vulnerable to electoral malpractice. Vote-buying practice by parties was not present in the non-EU states, but was found in Slovakia, Romania, Hungary, the Czech Republic and Bulgaria (Centre for Policy Studies, 2018). Despite the long-standing efforts of organisations such as OSCE to enable Roma become 'empowered' voters and candidates, there has been little change. The question that needs to be asked is whether the international organisations should not approach the electoral challenges without presupposing that ignorance and political illiteracy are the main reason for Romani individuals to sell votes, but rather investigate the broader context of these. Some of the context does depend on the negative socio-economic conditions (Jovanović, 2014).

However, as Aidan McGarry and Timofey Agarin (2014) have shown, the question of political participation and representation is multi-layered: Roma can be present in political structures but this does not guarantee either a possibility of voicing concerns or influence in the matters that concern Romani minorities. Because the OSCE and other organisations have focused on making an informed decision whilst casting the vote, some Romani NGOs have commented: 'Romani people, too, have the right to cast their vote "badly"' (Romea.cz, 2018). Even though such actions have been represented as self-sabotage, it should also be investigated why some Roma decide to sell their own votes. It can be understood as an act of despair to address devastating economic situations. But it could also be reinterpreted in a different manner: if being an active citizen does not improve your position, selling votes could be understood also as citizenship sabotage as a protest against devalued rights.

All the cases described above concern Romani individuals who are socio-economically disadvantaged, and this condition is entwined with ethnic discrimination. A number of Romani-related policy papers have concluded that if Roma are educated and (formally) employed they will not face ethnic discrimination and civic marginalisation. As Vermeersch (2006: 230) notes, if this is really the case, there is a danger that 'if ethnically framed programs do not lead to any palpable changes, they run the risk of reinforcing the idea that there is something wrong in the ethnicity of the target group from being successful'. As has been pointed out throughout this book, a wide variety of politicians (such as Salvini, Fico and Božinović) claim that Roma are a special case among citizens and seek to justify why their position remains the same. One of such politicians was the third Czech President, Miloš Zeman, who in late 2017 proclaimed that 90 per cent of unadaptable citizens in the Czech Republic were

Roma (see Donert, 2018). These are citizens who are understood as socially problematic because they do not want to work and are uneducated. (There was no basis for Zeman's claims, and his statement was not historically contextualised within the Romani holocaust or the negative policies that targeted Roma in the Czech Republic after World War II (Donert, 2017; see also Chapters 3 and 4.) However, what was interesting was the response of 'ordinary' Romani citizens of the Czech Republic, who started posting photos on social media of themselves working in a wide variety of jobs: from nurses to bakers, from construction workers to kindergarten teachers (Gotev, 2018). Such protest was extraordinary since it was the Roma, the invisible 'ordinary citizens', who sabotaged the Czech president's unsubstantiated claim.

But do Roma fit the definition of 'ordinary citizens' – that is, do they manage to obtain education and secure formal and decent employment? Can they escape socio-economic disadvantage, ethnic discrimination and also civic marginalisation? How do Roma who would be described as ordinary citizens contemplate their own position? Among the numerous Romani individuals whom I interviewed for my previous research,[5] were some whose present positions would be considered 'success stories'.

Many of these interviewees moved across borders not because they were nomads, as the popular representation of Roma dictates, but because of employment opportunities in other counties (Sardelić, 2019a). One of the interviewees, Teša, was a Romani woman in her early forties who had migrated from one postsocialist EU Member State to another. Whilst she managed to secure formal employment later in life, as a schoolchild she was allocated to a Roma-only class. Teša described her memory of her schooling:

> I remember the time when we moved from the old school to the new one. There Roma had a separate entrance and there were even separate bathrooms for showering in the gym locker room. They did not see me as others and they told me I could use the gym locker room of non-Roma. But I've decided to be with our Roma because it would be humiliating for them. (Quoted in Sardelić, 2012b: 340)

Teša decided not to be in a mixed class despite given the option. She 'sabotaged' this option since she did not want it only for herself, but for all of her Romani peers. Roni, a man in his forties, went to school in a different country and did not manage to obtain an education because the school placement assessors decided he should be in a special school:

> When my parents took me to those examinations before school, I remember I had to take some tests and then I went into a normal school. My sister was put in a special school right away as she peed herself out of fear of taking those tests. I went to a normal school for less than a year. But then that changed. The family was problematic, there was poverty, we did not have electricity or water and I was doing to school dirty. I think they saw this and decided that I am not capable for this school and they put me into special school ... And what does anyone care if I can now speak several languages, I still have a stamp that I was in that special school. (Quoted in Sardelić, 2012b: 340)

Whilst his wife was employed, Roni was unable to secure formal employment, officially because of his low-level 'special' education. As he explained in the interview, he later worked as a migrant smuggler and was sentenced to prison for this. But because of the 'stamp' of the special school, he had no choice but to engage in citizenship sabotage.

Another interviewee, Sini, a PhD student, remembered her school years in the following way:

> This happened just before I was registered with my primary school. I had one of those pre-school examinations which are completely normal before children go to school. During this examination the doctor recommended that I should attend the school with a special programme. My relatives of course did not agree with this. And when I visited that doctor later on we told her that I went to a mainstream school as all other children and we all agreed that it was good that my relatives did not follow this opinion because this would mean a great damage. (Interview, 2018)

Sini's relatives intervened and sabotaged the decision of the state representative to place her in a school for children with special needs. This interview also shows that it is problematic to assume that none of the guardians of Romani children were able or willing to give legal consent (or dispute it) regarding school admissions (see Chapter 3). However, Sini commented that she saw that a number of her peers who did obtain education still had difficulties in getting employment:

> Even when Roma get education, they are not invited to job interviews because of their last names, which are considered typical Romani. And those who changed their last names to get to the interview were not offered employment when the potential employee found out they were Roma. The main problem remains how to get employment. (Interview, 2018)

Mary, a Romani woman in her early thirties, commented that she moved from a postsocialist EU Member State to another state within the EU to avoid precarious employment in her country of citizenship:

> When I was working in [country of citizenship], I was at first working on a project, and then the project was over, I got a job on another project … But there were some complications there, I did not get regular payment. And then I was unemployed for some time … But I am now so old that I did not want to be dependent on my parents. I decided to go to [another EU Member State]. (Interview, 2017, see also Sardelić, 2019a)

Another interviewee, Tania, a woman in her early thirties with a university degree, also decided to sabotage her citizenship by leaving her country when she could not get regular employment, but only employment on projects for Romani integration:

> In my opinion, there are not many jobs available. But this is not the main reason. I think it is still true that no matter if you have education they would rather take someone else, not Roma. The only exception is if the job requires knowledge of the Romani language or is in any way connected to Roma. I still remember when I was at the Employment Office, the employment advisor there was shocked that I wanted to write in my employment profile that I can speak Romani. She told me between the lines that she was afraid this would be a reason why I would not get a job. (Interview, 2017; see also Chapter 1 and Sardelić, 2019a)

Tania decided to sabotage her citizenship because she could only be recognised as belonging to the Romani minority and hence given precarious project employment on Romani integration action even though she had a higher level of education than the average population. It was the multicultural policies for the special employment of Roma that prevented her from securing a permanent employment position: she was not perceived as an ordinary citizen even though she did not want to be a Romani activist any more.

Ina, a woman in her late twenties with a postgraduate degree, decided to become a Romani activist when as a child she was not protected by the state in a situation of domestic violence as other children would be:

> My main inspiration for what I wanted to be in the future was the past I had with the domestic violence in my family ... Because for the longer period of time my mum was trying to address authorities to make the police react and to protect us, but every time, she was going to the local police station reporting, police officers were making just the police statement they never came to check what is happening ... So later I understood the main reason why this was happening was that actually the police in that period and even nowadays have strong stereotypes about Romani families. [The police said] the domestic violence in Romani families is a normal thing, this is how conflicts are settled and many times women have to prove they were not wrong in a situation. (Interview, 2018)

In this case, as the interviewee reflects, the problem was that the police did not protect her family as ordinary citizens of her country, but rather decided not to intervene on the basis of their interpretation of what Romani culture entails. This was not based on facts but on their racist 'multicultural vision'.

Dani, a university-educated Romani man in his late twenties, was born into a family with refugee status in Germany. His parents had come to Germany from different parts of the former Yugoslav republics because of the war:

> What I remember in Germany is basically nice things mostly. We had a really good apartment and a car, my parents were both employed, I was raised in a household where we only spoke German. None of my siblings spoke to me in any other language nor did they speak with each other in any other language. And I think it was my parents' plan to raise me as a German citizen, to feel more German, to integrate or assimilate, as I would say better into the society. We lived in very good conditions ... I had no knowledge of the fact that I was Roma or [a citizen of a post-Yugoslav country]. So for me my whole life was that I am German. When we were moved from Germany to [a post-Yugoslav country], all this was new to me: why are the police

taking us away? These are the things that I found out later. My family moved as refugees during the Yugoslav wars, which was dangerous for them as my Mum was a [citizen of a post-Yugoslav country] and my dad was a [citizen of another post-Yugoslav country]. So it was not very welcoming for them to stay in [a post-Yugoslav country]. … We got deported in 1997, I think, or 1998 because Germany claimed it was safe to go back to [a post-Yugoslav country]. … What I found out afterwards was that my Dad overstayed the visa on purpose knowing it was not allowed: he stayed and continued to work under the table. And when Germany found that out, we got deported. My father got deported to [another post-Yugoslav country] … and my mother and my siblings, we were all deported to [a post-Yugoslav country]. … But the first impression when we were deported with an aeroplane and got to [a post-Yugoslav country], I did not know where I was, I felt this was not my country. (Interview, 2018)

In this paradoxical case, the interviewee's father sabotaged the family's citizenship by acting as an ordinary citizen rather than a person with a temporary protection status. The very act of performing as an ordinary citizen was political. But from the perspective of the German state, it created a rupture, and this was the reason why the family was deported.

Conclusion

This chapter has highlighted the varied ways individuals at the fringes perform citizenship. As the last case shows, in some instances being an ordinary citizen is performative as it goes against the preconceived script of how a citizen and a rejected asylum seeker should act. Many Roma are vulnerable and act out of despair. Yet that does not make them powerless or apolitical, even when they are not part of formal activist movement. The acts I have described in this chapter do not fit the usual understanding of performative citizenship (that is, claiming rights in protests and through strategic litigation), but this does not mean that Romani individuals at the fringes of citizenship do not claim their rights in alternative ways. These acts were quiet and mundane, but created a rupture within citizenship. I have called them citizenship sabotage. The chapter has also showed that citizenship fringes are not a site framed only by socio-economic disadvantage and ethnic discrimination. The citizenship fringes are based on assumptions that citizenship is as universally inclusive as it can be, but this endeavour to 'cover all' can work to exclude certain populations.

Notes

1 See https://www.lexico.com/definition/sabotage (accessed: 7 December 2020).
2 The term 'citizenship sabotage' can, to a certain extent, be connected to what Spivak (2012) called 'affirmative sabotage'. However, the complex relationship between the two terms will have to be researched in more detail in the future.
3 I interviewed the representative of the NGO Our Rights in late 2012 as a part of a wider research project on statelessness in South-East Europe.
4 I interviewed all the representatives of WebLAN in late 2012. The initial network consisted of the NGO Praxis from Serbia, Our Rights from BIH, Civil Rights Programme from Kosovo, Macedonian Young Lawyers from North Macedonia and the Information Legal Centre from Croatia (Kostić, 2013). In 2017 most of the NGOs from WebLAN joined with ERRC, Institute for Statelessness and Inclusion and the European Network on Statelessness in a #RomaBelong Campaign mirroring the UNHCR's #IBelong Campaign.
5 Whilst I conducted fifty life-history interviews during my (post)doctoral research with individuals who identified as Roma, to comply with the GDPR Regulation and to fully protect the safety of the individuals interviewed, I have decided to present only a small number of anonymised excerpts from the interviews in this book (the pseudonyms I use do not have identification keys attached to them and cannot be traced back to personal data). Most of these interviews were conducted during my postdoctoral research, and two excerpts are from my doctoral research. The aim of this is not to represent 'typical' Romani experiences but rather to hint at the variety of experiences under this broad umbrella term. In addition, interviews took place in a variety of languages that both the interviewees and I were fluent in. In order to protect their identity, I give only English translations of the interviews.

Conclusion: reflecting on citizenship from the fringe

This book has contemplated the position of Roma as citizens in Europe. Whilst acknowledging ethnic discrimination and anti-Roma racism, as well as the socio-economic disadvantage that Roma face in some of world's most developed states,[1] it has explored the position of Romani minorities from the perspective of citizenship studies. Through a socio-legal analysis of (inter)national legislation and policies, it has focused on civic marginalisation: it has examined how states and international organisations have contributed to making the citizenship of Romani individuals devalued, precarious and irregularised. Despite usually possessing EU citizenship (for a discussion of statelessness, see Chapter 4), Roma as marginalised minorities are often grouped together with non-European migrants. This reveals the complexities of bordering processes in Europe which not only work against newcomers (van Baar, 2016) but also create hierarchies within its own citizenry. The chapters have discussed how legislation and policies create invisible edges of citizenship. Despite manifestly benevolent attempts to include all citizens – be it by means of universal inclusion or nuanced, group-targeted rights – it is because of these invisible edges that Roma end up as marginalised citizens. The invisible edges of citizenship illustrate the dynamic nature of citizenship and minority rights legislation: legislation and policies are never just prescribed rules of conduct but are also enacted arrangements. Marginalisation does not arise solely through a failure to implement distinctly well-meaning legislation: it can, in fact, be the very implementation that creates the fringes of citizenship. The fringes of citizenship are not merely a location – that is, they are not simply 'out there' – but can be understood as a dynamic relationship, almost a power struggle, between states' authorities enacting legislation on one side and those who have this legislation enacted upon them on the other.

I chose the perspective of citizenship studies to reflect upon the position of Roma because focusing only on ethnic discrimination and socio-economic disadvantage can imply that Romani minorities are an isolated European case and an exception to the otherwise universally inclusive citizenship (Vermeersch, 2006). It could also lend support to a simplistic inference that the civic marginalisation of Roma arises only because of socio-economic disadvantage. This is not the whole story. Using connected sociologies (Bhambra, 2014), I argued that whilst Romani identity can be considered unique (van Baar and Kóczé, 2020), states' approaches towards Roma as citizens are not: these approaches have been used with other marginalised minorities around the globe. In each chapter, when discussing the fringes of citizenship with respect to Roma, I have also drawn parallels with other cases (from Indigenous people to African Americans) of how states treat marginalised minorities on their territory. The aim of this book was not to create another ideal typology where Roma would fit 'better' but rather to unveil how current approaches have contributed to Roma not fitting within citizenry and hence becoming unequal. This is not because of their particular position *per se*, but because of the ways in which states have scrutinised and addressed this position through the invisible edges of citizenship.

In the Introduction I presented two concepts – the invisible edges of citizenship and the fringes of citizenship – as relevant to an understanding of both the position of Romani minorities in Europe and global citizenship studies more broadly. I claimed that the discussion of civic marginalisation should not only address how to improve the current position of marginalised citizens, but also should rethink what mechanisms led to such marginalisation. Civil marginalisation is not simply out there, but has been reproduced in the past and will continue to be produced if the assumptions underpinning the core of citizenship (such as who can be a citizen and what rights citizens have based on such status) are not addressed.

Chapter 1 maintained that Roma are visible as minorities but invisible as citizens. The chapter first looked at discussions of the naming and counting of Roma themselves. While derogatory names can lead to marginalisation, the chapter showed that opting for the more neutral names does not necessarily defeat marginalisation if it is not substantiated by more profound changes. Furthermore, both scholarly and policy debates argue that without reliable data on how many Roma live in Europe, there can be no substantive policy change. However, more data do not necessarily lead to better policies and legislation against marginalisation. Both neutral names and more data on the position of Roma can still be a part of the invisible edges of citizenship that contribute to the civic marginalisation of Roma. The chapter argued that whilst many states in Europe have developed multicultural laws and policies for Romani integration, the very same states have continued to violate the basic rights that Roma should have, like all other citizens. Special group rights can coexist with fundamental rights violations for marginalised minorities. In some cases, the special group rights act as an invisible edge of citizenship to steer the view away from the violations of fundamental rights that marginalised minorities experience. Some profound violations of human rights, such as coerced sterilisation, have happened both to Native Americans in Canada and to Roma in Europe. The procedures behind such occurrences were strikingly similar despite their happening across different geographical and historical contexts. Moreover, for both Roma and Indigenous people, different international organisations have applied developmental and project-based logic (such as designated decades) to improve their position. Such logic had two adverse effects. First, it portrayed marginalised minorities as backward, frozen in time and having incompatible cultural traits with liberal democracies, leading to an assumption that they could participate as full citizens only when they were 'developed enough'. Second, the emphasis that European international organisations gave to Roma also created a specific backlash within the countries where Roma were citizens. Local politicians portrayed Roma as being a minority that international organisations favoured over other citizens (Vermeersch, 2012). The way in which the Copenhagen criteria (and overall EU conditionality) were established implied that the human rights of Roma were violated only in the postsocialist EU Member States. However, as the chapter demonstrated, this was not the case, as it became clear that even in Western Europe and the older Member States Romani minorities experienced a similar predicament. The invisible edges of citizenship that marginalised Romani minorities were present in both the newer and the older EU Member States.

One of the often-cited reasons why EU conditionality focused on the position of Roma in Central and Eastern Europe was the possible prospect of *en masse* migration towards the Western Europe (Guglielmo and Waters, 2005). While such massive Westward migration of Roma never happened, Romani migrants were in the spotlight in public debates especially after the so-called *l'affaire des Roms* in France. However, in Chapter 2, I called for a reconsideration of how we discuss Roma who are mobile within the EU. Instead of discussing migration as a particular trait of Romani culture, we need to consider why states restrict from Roma those citizenship rights that should be possessed by all EU citizens. In other words, the position of Roma should be primarily discussed as citizens and not as migrants. According to available data, very few Roma are migrants: most do not move beyond their country of citizenship. However, the overwhelming media discussion (and arguably the academic debate too) on 'Romani migration' gave the impression that Roma were more likely to migrate than any other majority citizens. Whilst Chapter 1 looked at how states create special targeted rights for Roma (which do not often work), Chapter 2 focused on how states hinder access to universal rights for those marginalised citizens whom they deem problematic. Here I drew a parallel between Roma in Europe and Aboriginal people in Australia by scrutinising the 2007 Northern Territory National Emergency Response Act. I argued that in both cases the states applied invisible edges of citizenship by constructing alleged specific cultural features of marginalised minorities as a justification for actively impeding the rights these minorities should have enjoyed as part of the wider citizenry. By not granting marginalised minorities the rights they were entitled to, they positioned them on the fringes of citizenship.

Chapter 3 focused on 'citizens in the making' and how the education system can contribute to inequality of opportunity rather than mitigating it. It scrutinised court cases that dealt with the school segregation of African American and Romani children. The strategic litigation on Romani school segregation took inspiration from the earlier American cases. The *D.H. v. the Czech Republic* case has been referred to as the 'European *Brown v. Board of Education* case' (Chang and Rucker-Chang, 2020). However, there were also significant differences. The American cases dealt with the segregation embedded within *law*, while the European cases looked at the *practices* of school segregation. Whilst the *Brown* case concluded that spatial separation always constitutes discrimination, the European cases pondered whether spatial separation of an ethnic group was in fact discrimination at all (Arabadjieva, 2016). As such, the European cases took a step back from the earlier desegregation cases in the US (such as the *Brown* case), resembling more closely the outcomes of later cases like 1974 *Milliken v. Bradley*.

Chapter 3 was particularly interested in what justification state authorities gave for spatially separating Roma from other children. In all the cases discussed (*D.H.*, 2008 *Sampanis, Oršuš* and 2012 *Sampani*), the state authorities argued that there was no ethnic segregation and that the separation of Romani children was done with their best interests in mind. In the Czech Republic, Roma children were disproportionally represented in schools for children with special needs. The authorities argued that such classification was not undertaken according to ethnicity or race, but according to the children's intellectual abilities. Yet Roma were significantly and exponentially more likely to be classified as having learning disabilities than majority children. In the Greek cases, the authorities argued that they separated Romani children in order to protect them from the protests of non-Romani parents who did not want their children to attend school with their Romani peers. Instead of punishing the protesters, the authorities decided to grant their wishes by removing Romani children and placing them in separate school facilities. In the Croatian case, many Romani children were consigned into Roma-only classes. The reasoning of the authorities was that these were 'catch-up' classes for children who did not have a sufficient command of the Croatian language. However, it was only Romani children having these 'catch-up' classes, and there were no transfers into mixed classes despite some of the children's progress with the language. The authorities in this case even argued that they were taking a benevolent approach towards Romani children as they had celebrated International Romani Day in their schools. The discourse of the governments in question indicated how invisible edges of citizenship persist within the education system. Instead of offering equality of opportunity, it further cements the position of Roma at the fringes of citizenship. In all of these cases, the ECtHR decided there was ethnic discrimination in education.

In discussing these court cases, it is important to highlight the broader contexts within which they occurred. The US cases were decisively affected by the Cold War context, as racial segregation was damaging the US's international reputation and its geo-political goals (especially on the African continent; see Dudziak, 2011). Whilst some Roma segregation cases were related to postsocialist EU accession, the connection was not as straightforward: the segregation of Romani children was not simply a legacy of socialism, for it had occurred in older EU Member States too. Furthermore, EU conditionality did not end the segregation of Romani children in schools, and even now it continues to be a widespread practice across the EU. Even the court's decision to compensate the children who were segregated is facing a backlash: the Hungarian Prime Minister Orbán is suggesting that there should be a referendum to decide whether these children should even be compensated (Rorke, 2020).

Chapter 4 focused on the total infringement of citizenship: that is, the loss of citizenship status and (unrecognised) statelessness status coupled with the complete denial of rights associated with citizenship. UNHCR documents maintain that marginalised minorities are particularly vulnerable to statelessness around the globe. The most often cited reason for minorities ending up stateless is ethnic discrimination. I argued that it was not simply ethnic discrimination but racialised citizenship regimes that deprive certain minorities of both citizenship and the basic rights attached to it. I compared how Roma in different European countries and beyond have become stateless, discussing the Russian-speakers in the Baltic countries, the Dominicans of Haitian descent in the Dominican Republic, the Rohingya in Myanmar and the children of the Windrush generation in the UK. All of these cases were from different postsocialist and postcolonial contexts, yet they shared a common mechanism: states reinterpreted the belonging of these unwanted traditional minorities as if they were foreigners rather than co-citizens. In most cases (except for the Russian-speaking minorities in the Baltic states), this was accompanied by the loss of rights and any kinds of status, as statelessness status was commonly unrecognised.

Chapter 5 moved on to citizenship sabotage. As I explained in the Introduction, I did not intend to examine Roma as my 'research subjects' in this book, as some scholars have done in the past with a wide variety of marginalised minorities (Tuhiwai Smith, 2012).

The book also does not speak on behalf of Roma. There are many extraordinary academic and activist texts written by Romani activists and scholars (see Chapter 1). My interest was in the structures that position Roma as marginalised citizens. However, in Chapter 5 I showed that even Romani individuals who are not part of organised civil society movements and do not consider themselves activists can enact and create ruptures in those citizenship structures. The way Romani individuals claim rights that they are denied in their everyday lives is problematic for authorities, who often interpret these actions as destructive behaviour. However, by highlighting some examples where Romani individuals have claimed denied rights, I argued that such behaviour could be interpreted as a special kind of citizenship enactment (Isin, 2009): that is, citizenship sabotage. Similar to workplace sabotage, citizenship sabotage is also a small individual act seemingly arising from despair, yet it can have broader political consequences. Scholarly thinking about citizenship sabotage is needed to stop the patronising and paternalistic approach towards Roma as ignorant (non-)citizens who are absolutely unable to understand their own position. This perspective also renders the notion of empowerment problematic as it usually entails empowerment, so that Romani minorities would become complicit in the very systems that are structurally creating their civic marginalisation.

This book has sought to provide some additional theoretical perspectives on how to contemplate civic marginalisation vis-à-vis Romani experience. It has promoted four concepts: the fringes of citizenship, the invisible edges of citizenship, the total infringement of citizenship and citizenship sabotage. These concepts have helped me to analyse the civic marginalisation of Roma and some other minorities around the globe. I hope that in the future the book's notions will be applied to other situations where civic marginalisation occurs for specific groups.

It is perhaps obvious that different marginalised minorities face a common struggle and should therefore fight on a common front at the fringes of citizenship. Minority activists are already very aware of this (Matache and West, 2018; Cortés Gómez, 2019), and it was not the intention of this book to instruct their future activism. Rather, the intention was to attempt to make state authorities and international organisations aware of the invisible edges of citizenship they engage and the fringes of citizenship they create. As the EU

NRIS Framework comes to an end in 2020, it should not be replaced by another developmental and project-oriented approach towards Romani minorities in Europe. Such approaches do not acknowledge the depth of civic marginalisation. Future policies addressing the position of Roma should first reflect not only on antigypsyism but also on the assumptions they are built on. Can citizenship in liberal democratic societies claim to be fully inclusive if certain populations are systematically positioned on its fringes? The structures of citizenship need to be re-addressed so that they prevent the production of any new marginalisation, and we should also think about why marginalisation of certain citizens has a negative effect on the wider citizenry as a whole. This should not stop at economic shortcuts, as some previous policy recommendations have stated, but should show that inclusiveness of citizenship has value in itself. The fringes of citizenship are not exceptions but are at the very core of what citizenship itself entails.

Notes

1 All the states where Roma live that are discussed in this book have been categorised as having a very high human development index (HDI) (Serbia, Bosnia and Herzegovina North Macedonia and Kosovo each have just a high HDI: United Nations Development Programme, 2019).

References

Acosta Arcarazo, D. (2015) 'Civic Citizenship Reintroduced? The Long-Term Residence Directive as a Post-National Form of Membership', *European Law Journal*, 21(2): 200–19.

Act LXXVII on the Rights of National and Ethnic Minorities 1993 (Hungary). Available at: https://www.refworld.org/docid/4c3476272.html (accessed: 14 September 2020).

Act CLXXIX on the Rights of Nationalities of Hungary 2011 (Hungary). Available at: https://www.venice.coe.int/WebForms/documents/default.aspx?pdffile=CDL-REF(2012)014-e (accessed: 14 September 2020).

Act on National and Ethnic Minorities and on Regional Languages 2005 (Poland). Available at: http://ksng.gugik.gov.pl/english/files/act_on_national_minorities.pdf (accessed: 14 September 2020).

Act on Rights of Members of National Minorities 2001 (273) (Czech Republic). Available at: https://www.legislationline.org/download/id/7669/file/Czech_Act_rights_national_minorities_2001_en.pdf (accessed: 14 September 2020).

Albert, G. (2019) 'Children are the Future – and What Will It Look Like?' In M. Kaleja, E. Nyklová and M. Vítková (eds.) *Rodina, škola a přátelé na cestě ke kvalitnímu společnému vzdělávání: recenzovaný sborník příspěvků z mezinárodní vědecké a odborné conference*, pp. 43–6. Available at: https://www.slu.cz/file/cul/94ac4d0f-0294-4158-8df6-5e480c35c323 (accessed: 1 December 2020).

Alderson, P., Hawthorne, J. and Killen, M. (2005) 'Are Premature Babies Citizens with Rights? Provision Rights and the Edges of Citizenship', *Journal of Social Sciences*, 9: 71–81.

Alliance Against Antigypsyism (2017) *Antigypsyism: A Reference Paper*. Available at: http://antigypsyism.eu/ (accessed: 22 September 2020).

Althusser, L. (1971) *Lenin and Philosophy and Other Essays*. London: Nlb.

Altman, J. C. and Hinkson, M. (2007) *Coercive Reconciliation: Stabilise, Normalise, Exit Aboriginal Australia*. North Carlton, Victoria: Arena Publications.

Anderson, B. (2016) 'Why the EU–Turkey Migrant Deal is a Moral Disaster', *Fortune*, 17 March. Available at: https://fortune.com/2016/03/17/eu-turkey-migrant-crisis-deal-disaster/ (accessed: 22 September 2020).

Arabadjieva, K. (2016) 'Challenging the School Segregation of Roma Children in Central and Eastern Europe', *The International Journal of Human Rights*, 20(1): 33–54.

Aradau, C., Huysmans, J., Macioti, P. G. and Squire, V. (2013) 'Mobility Interrogating Free Movement: Roma Acts of European Citizenship'. In E. F. Isin and M. Saward (eds.) *Enacting European Citizenship*. Cambridge: Cambridge University Press, pp. 132–54.

Arendt, H. (1968) *The Origins of Totalitarianism*. New York: Harcourt, Brace & World.

Armillei, R. and Lobo, M. (2017) '"Parallel Emergencies" in Italy and Australia: Marginalised and Racialised Romani and Aboriginal "Camp Dwellers"', *Journal of Intercultural Studies*, 38(5): 560–75.

Bader Ginsburg, R. (2005) 'Brown v. Board of Education in International Context', *Columbia Human Rights Law Review*, 36 (3): 493–502.

Baehr, E. and Schmidt-Haberkamp, B. (2017) *'And There'll Be No Dancing': Perspectives on Policies Impacting Indigenous Australia since 2007*. Newcastle upon Tyne: Cambridge Scholars Publishing.

Baker, C. (2018) *Race and the Yugoslav Region: Postsocialist, Post-Conflict, Postcolonial?* Manchester: Manchester University Press.

Balch, A., Balabanova, E. and Trandafoiu. R. (2013) 'A Europe of Rights and Values? Public Debates on Sarkozy's Roma Affair in France, Bulgaria and Romania', *Journal of Ethnic and Migration Studies*, 40(8): 1154–74.

Baldwin, L., Leroux, M., Torrisi, C. and Vergine, S. (2019) 'How Pope Francis Became a Hate Figure for the Far Right', *OpenDemocracy*. 13 April. Available at: www.opendemocracy.net/en/5050/how-pope-francis-became-hate-figure-far-right/ (accessed: 9 March 2020).

Balibar, É. and Wallerstein, I. M. (1991) *Race, Nation, Class*. London: Verso.

Barany, Z. D. (2002) *The East European Gypsies: Regime Change, Marginality and Ethnopolitics*. Cambridge: Cambridge University Press.

Baršová, A. (2014) *Country Report: Czech Republic*. Available at: http://cadmus.eui.eu/handle/1814/33840.

Barta, T. (2008) 'Sorry, and Not Sorry, in Australia: How the Apology to the Stolen Generations Buried a History of Genocide', *Journal of Genocide Research*, 10(2): 201–14.

Bauböck, R. (2010) 'Studying Citizenship Constellations', *Journal of Ethnic and Migration Studies*, 36(5): 847–59.

Bauer, E. (2018) 'Racialised Citizenship, Respectability and Mothering among Caribbean Mothers in Britain', *Ethnic and Racial Studies*, 41(1): 151–69.

BBC (2010) 'Q&A: France Roma Expulsions', *BBC News*, 19 October. Available at: www.bbc.com/news/world-europe-11027288 (accessed: 9 March 2020).

Beck, S. and Ivasiuc, A. (2018) *Roma Activism: Reimagining Power and Knowledge*. New York: Berghahn Books.

Belton, K. A. (2011) 'The Neglected Non-Citizen: Statelessness and Liberal Political Theory', *Journal of Global Ethics*, 7(1): 59–71.

—— (2015) 'Rooted Displacement: The Paradox of Belonging among Stateless People', *Citizenship Studies*, 19(8): 907–21.

Benhabib, S. (2000) *The Rights of Others: Aliens, Residents and Citizens.* Cambridge: Cambridge University Press.

Bentley, P. (2014) 'Elisabeta Dano Tracked to Germany after Finding Herself at Centre of Welfare Case', *Daily Mail*, 15 November. Available at: www.dailymail.co.uk/news/article-2835442/The-Roma-gipsy-sparked-crackdown-benefit-tourism-Elisabeta-Dano-25-tracked-German-city-finding-centre-landmark-welfare-case.html (accessed: 9 March 2020).

Bhabha, J. (2017) 'The Politics of Evidence: Roma Citizenship Deficits in Europe'. In B. HN. Lawrance and J. Stevens (eds.) *Citizenship in Question: Evidentiary Birthright and Statelessness.* Durham, NC, and London: Duke University Press, pp. 48–59.

Bhambra, G. K. (2014) *Connected Sociologies.* London: Bloomsbury.

—— (2015) 'Citizens and Others: The Constitution of Citizenship through Exclusion', *Alternatives: Global, Local, Political*, 40(2): 102–14.

—— (2016) 'Whither Europe? Postcolonial versus Neocolonial Cosmopolitanism', *Interventions*, 18(2): 187–202. DOI: https://doi.org/10.108 0/1369801x.2015.1106964.

—— (2017a) 'Brexit, Trump, and "Methodological Whiteness": On the Misrecognition of Race and Class', *The British Journal of Sociology*, 68(1): 214–32.

—— (2017b) 'Methodological Whiteness', *Global Social Theory*. Available at: https://globalsocialtheory.org/concepts/methodological-whiteness/ (accessed: 26 November 2020).

—— (2018) *Turning Citizens into Migrants.* Available at: https://www. redpepper.org.uk/talking-about-migrants-is-a-dogwhistle-way-of-talking-about-race/ (accessed: 7 December 2020).

Blitz, B. K. (2013) 'Evaluating Transitions: Human Rights and Qualitative Democracy in Central and Eastern Europe', *Europe-Asia Studies*, 63(9): 1745–70.

—— (2017) 'The State and the Stateless: The Legacy of Hannah Arendt Reconsidered'. In T. Bloom, K. Tonkiss and P. Cole (eds.) *Understanding Statelessness.* London and New York: Routledge, pp. 70–83.

Blitz, B. K. and Lynch, M. (2011) *Statelessness and the Deprivation of Nationality: A Comparative Study on the Benefits of Nationality.* Cheltenham: Edward Elgar.

Bloemraad, I., Sarabia, H. and Fillingim, A. E. (2017) 'Citizenship Acts: Legality Power and the Limits of Political Action'. In R. G. Gonzales and N. Sigona (eds.) *Within and beyond Citizenship: Borders Membership and Belonging.* London and New York: Routledge, pp. 81–95.

Bloom, T., Tonkiss, K., and Cole, P. (eds.) (2017) *Understanding Statelessness.* London and New York: Routledge.

Bosniak, L. (2007) 'Being Here: Ethical Territoriality and the Rights of Immigrants', *Theoretical Inquiries in Law*, 8(2): 389–410.

Bračič, A. (2016) 'Reaching the Individual: EU Accession, NGOs, and Human Rights', *American Political Science Review*, 110(3): 530–46.

Brooks, E. (2018) *Europe Is Ours: A Manifesto by Dr. Ethel Brooks*. Available at: www.romaniarts.co.uk/europe-is-ours-a-manifesto-by-dr-ethel-brooks/ (accessed: 9 March 2020).

Brown, P., Martin, P. and Scullion, L. (2014) 'Migrant Roma in the United Kingdom and the Need to Estimate Population Size', *People Place and Policy Online* 8: 19–33. Available at: https://extra.shu.ac.uk/ppp-online/migrant-roma-in-the-united-kingdom-and-the-need-to-estimate-population-size/ (accessed: 26 November 2020).

Brown v. the Board of Education of Topeka 347 U.S. 483 (US Supreme Court, 1954). Available at: https://supreme.justia.com/cases/federal/us/347/483/ (accessed: 22 September 2020).

Brubaker, R. (2012) *Ethnicity without Groups*. Cambridge, MA, and London: Harvard University Press.

Brüggemann, C. and Friedman, E. (2017) 'The Decade of Roma Inclusion: Origins, Actors, and Legacies', *European Education*, 49(1): 1–9.

Çağlar, A. and Mehling, S. (2013) 'Sites and the Scales of the Law: Third-Country Nationals and EU Roma Citizens'. In E. F. Isin and M. Saward (eds.) *Enacting European Citizenship*. Cambridge: Cambridge University Press, pp. 155–77.

Cahn, C. (2012) 'Minorities, Citizenship and Statelessness in Europe', *European Journal of Migration and Law*, 14(3): 297–316.

Cahn, C. and Guild, E. (2010) *Recent Migration of Roma in Europe*, 2nd edn. Available at: www.osce.org/hcnm/78034?download=true (accessed: 6 March 2020).

Calma, T. (2009) 'The Northern Territory Intervention – It's Not our Dream', *Law in Context: A Socio-Legal Journal*, 27(2): 14–41.

Carrera, S. (2005) 'What Does Free Movement Mean in Theory and Practice in an Enlarged EU?', *European Law Journal*, 11(6): 699–721.

Carrera, S. and Faure Atger, A. (2010) *L'affaire des Roms: A Challenge to the EU's Area of Freedom, Security and Justice*. Available at: www.files.ethz.ch/isn/121924/10–09-Carrera%20&%20Faure%20Atger%20on%20Roma%20Affair.pdf (accessed: 9 March 2020).

Carrera, S., Rostas, I. and Vosyliūtė, L. (2017) 'Combating Institutional Anti-Gypsyism: Responses and Promising Practices in the EU and Selected Member States', *CEPS Research Paper*. Available at: www.ceps.eu/ceps-publications/combating-institutional-anti-gypsyism-responses-and-promising-practices-eu-and-selected/ (accessed: 9 March 2020).

Carrera, S., Vosyliūtė, L., Rostas, I., Danova-Roussinova, S., Guerin, J. and Smialowski, S. B. (2019) 'Scaling Up Roma Inclusion Strategies: Truth, Reconciliation and Justice for Addressing Antigypsyism'. Available at: https://www.europarl.europa.eu/RegData/etudes/STUD/2019/608859/IPOL_STU(2019)608859_EN.pdf (accessed: 22 September 2020).

Case C–333/13 *Dano v. Jobcenter Leipzig*, ECLI:EU:C:2014:2358 (CJEU, 2014) Available at: https://eur-lex.europa.eu/legal-content/EN/TXT/?uri=CELEX%3A62013CJ0333 (accessed: 22 September 2020).

Centre for Policy Studies (2018) *Roma Civil Monitor Pilot Project: A Synthesis Report on Implementation of National Roma Integration Strategies in Bulgaria, Czech Republic, Hungary Romania and Slovakia.* Available at: https://cps.ceu.edu/sites/cps.ceu.edu/files/attachment/basicpage/3034/rcm-civil-society-monitoring-report-1-synthesis-cluster-1–2017-eprint-fin.pdf (accessed: 9 March 2020).

Chang, F. B. and Rucker-Chang, S. T. (2020) *Roma Rights and Civil Rights: A Transatlantic Comparison.* Cambridge: Cambridge University Press.

Chapman v. the United Kingdom Application no. 27238/95 (ECtHR, 18 January 2001). Available at: https://hudoc.echr.coe.int/eng#{%22ite mid%22:[%22001–59154%22]} (accessed: 22 September 2020).

Cheesman, N. (2017) 'How in Myanmar "National Races" Came to Surpass Citizenship and Exclude Rohingya', *Journal of Contemporary Asia*, 47(3): 461–83.

Chopin, I., Germaine, C. and Tanczos, J. (2017) *Roma and the Enforcement of Anti-Discrimination Law.* Brussels: European Commission; Luxemburg: Publications Office of the European Union.

Cirković, E. (2014) 'Contested Citizenship in Bosnia and Herzegovina'. In E. F. Isin and P. Nyers (eds.) *Routledge Handbook of Global Citizenship Studies.* London and New York: Routledge, pp. 455–65.

Ciulinaru, D. (2018) 'When "Inclusion" Means "Exclusion": Discourses on the Eviction and Repatriations of Roma Migrants, at National and European Union Level', *Journal of International Migration and Integration*, 19(4): 1059–73.

Clark, C. and Campbell, E. (2000) '"Gypsy Invasion": A Critical Analysis of Newspaper Reaction to Czech and Slovak Romani Asylum-Seekers in Britain, 1997', *Romani Studies*, 10(1): 23–47.

Clements, L. (2001) 'An Emerging Consensus on the Special Needs of Minorities: The Lessons of Chapman v. UK', *European Roma Rights Centre*. Available at: www.errc.org/roma-rights-journal/an-emerging-consensus-on-the-special-needs-of-minorities-the-lessons-of-chapman-v.-uk (accessed: 9 March 2020).

CoE (Council of Europe) (1993) *Recommendation 1203 (1993): Gypsies in Europe.* Available at: http://assembly.coe.int/nw/xml/XRef/Xref-XML2HTML-EN.asp?fileid=15237&lang=en (accessed: 22 September 2020).

—— (2016) *Resolution 403 (2016): The Situation of Roma and Travellers in the Context of Rising Extremism, Xenophobia and the Refugee Crisis in Europe.* Available at: https://rm.coe.int/1680718bfd (accessed: 22 September 2020).

—— (2019) 'Sejdić and Finci – after 10 Years of Absence of Progress, New Hopes for a Solution for the 2022 Elections', press release, 22 December. Available at: www.coe.int/en/web/execution/-/sejdic-and-finci-after10-years-of-absence-of-progress-new-hopes-for-a-solution-for-the-2022-elections (accessed: 22 September 2020).

Cohen, E. F. (2009) *Semi-Citizenship in Democratic Politics*. New York: Cambridge University Press.

Connolly, K. (2017) '"A Place to Call our Own": Europe's First Roma Cultural Centre Opens in Berlin', *The Guardian*, 8 June. Available at: www.theguardian.com/world/2017/jun/08/roma-artists-launch-art-cultural-centre-institute-berlin (accessed: 9 March 2020).

Constantin, S. (2010) 'The Legal and Institutional Framework for National Minorities in Slovakia', *Treatises and Documents: Journal of Ethnic Studies*, 63: 8–53.

Constitutional Court of Croatia (2003) Odluka Ustavnog suda Republike Hrvatske broj U-III-1918/2000. Available at: https://narodne-novine.nn.hr/clanci/sluzbeni/2004_01_2_50.html (accessed: 26 November 2020).

Constitutional Court of Croatia (2011) Odluka U-I-3597/2010. Available at: https://narodne-novine.nn.hr/clanci/sluzbeni/full/2011_08_93_1981.html (accessed: 26 November 2020).

Constitutional Law on the Right of National Minorities 2002 (Croatia). Available at: http://www.vsrh.hr/CustomPages/Static/HRV/Files/Legislation__Constitutional-Law-on-the-Rights-NM.pdf and http://www.propisi.hr/print.php?id=5270 (accessed: 14 September 2020).

The Constitution of Finland 1999. Available at: https://www.eduskunta.fi/FI/naineduskuntatoimii/julkaisut/Documents/ekj_3+2013.pdf (accessed: 14 September 2020)

The Constitution of the Republic of Poland 1997. Available at: https://www.sejm.gov.pl/prawo/konst/angielski/kon1.htm (accessed: 14 September 2020).

The Constitution of the Republic of Slovenia 1991. Available at: https://www.us-rs.si/media/constitution.pdf (accessed: 14 September 2020).

The Constitution of the Slovak Republic 1992. Available at: https://www.prezident.sk/upload-files/46422.pdf (accessed: 14 September 2020).

Cooke, M., Mitrou, F., Lawrence, D., Guimond, E. and Beavon, D. (2007) 'Indigenous Well-Being in Four Countries: An Application of the UNDP'S Human Development Index to Indigenous Peoples in Australia, Canada, New Zealand, and the United States', *BMC International Health and Human Rights*, 7(1). DOI: https://doi.org/10.1186/1472-698x-7-9.

Cooper v. Aaron 358 U.S. 1 (US Supreme Court, 1958). Available at: https://supreme.justia.com/cases/federal/us/358/1/ (accessed: 22 September 2020).

Corradi, L. (2018) *Gypsy Feminism: Intersectional Politics, Alliances, Gender and Queer Activism*. London and New York: Routledge, Taylor & Francis Group.

Cortés Gómez, I. (2019) 'Escaping the Labyrinth of Roma Political Representation: Reflections on Common Citizenship'. In I. Cortés Gómez and M. End (eds.) *Dimensions of Antigypsyism in Europe*. Brussels: European Network against Racism and Central Council of German Sinti and Roma, pp. 366–86.

Cortés Gómez, I. and End, M. (eds.) (2019) *Dimensions of Antigypsyism in Europe*. Brussels: European Network Against Racism and Central

Council of German Sinti and Roma. Available at: www.enar-eu.org/
IMG/pdf/20116_book_roma_final.pdf (accessed: 14 September 2020).

Costache, I. (2018) 'Reclaiming Romani-ness', *Critical Romani Studies*,
1(1): 30–43. DOI: https://doi.org/10.29098/crs.v1i1.11.

Cownie, F. and Bradney, A. (2013) 'Socio-Legal Studies: A Challenge to
the Doctrinal Approach'. In D. Watkins and M. Burton (eds.) *Research
Methods in Law*. Abingdon and New York: Routledge, pp. 34–55.

Croatian Citizenship Act 1991 Available at: www.refworld.org/
pdfid/3ae6b4dc14.pdf (accessed: 7 December 2020).

Crowe, D. (2007) *A History of the Gypsies of Eastern Europe and Russia*.
New York: Palgrave Macmillan.

Dawar, A. (2013) 'Roma Surge Threatens to Add to Estimated 200,000
Population Already in UK', *The Express*, 31 October. Available at:
https://www.express.co.uk/news/uk/440204/Roma-surge-threatens-to-
add-to-estimated-200–000-population-already-in-UK (accessed: 9 March
2020).

De Blois, J., R. Celikates and Y. Jansen (eds.) (2015) *The Irregularization of
Migration in Contemporary Europe: Detention, Deportation, Drowning*.
London: Rowman & Littlefield International.

De Genova, N. P. (2002) 'Migrant "Illegality" and Deportability in Everyday
Life', *Annual Review of Anthropology*, 31(1): 419–47.

—— (2017) 'Citizenship's Shadow: Obscene Inclusion, Abject Belonging,
or the Regularities of "Migrant Irregularity"'. In R. G. Gonzales and N.
Sigona (eds.) *Within and beyond Citizenship: Borders Membership and
Belonging*. London and New York: Routledge, pp. 17–35.

Deutsche Welle (2018) 'Život poslije kratkotrajne slave'. *Deutsche Welle*,
December. Available at: https://www.dw.com/bs/%C5%BEivot-poslije-
kratkotrajne-slave/av-51832674 (accessed: 14 December 2020).

D.H. and Others v. the Czech Republic Application no. 57325/00 (ECtHR,
11 November 2007). Available at: https://hudoc.echr.coe.int/fre#{%22it
emid%22:[%22001-83256%22]} (accessed: 9 March 2020).

Donert, C. (2017) *The Rights of the Roma: The Struggle for Citizenship
in Postwar Czechoslovakia*. Cambridge: Cambridge University Press.

—— (2018) 'Anti-Roma Stigma of Czech President Miloš Zeman Threatens
Progress over Romani Rights', *The Conversation*, 24 January. Available
at: https://theconversation.com/anti-roma-stigma-of-czech-president-
milos-zeman-threatens-progress-over-romani-rights-88437 (accessed:
22 September 2020).

Dudziak, M. L. (2004) 'Brown as a Cold War Case', *Journal of American
History*, 91(1): 32–42.

—— (2011) *Cold War Civil Rights: Race and the Image of American
Democracy*. Princeton, NJ, and Oxford: Princeton University Press.

Duhaček, G. (2019) 'Nazovimo prosvjed protiv Roma u Čakovcu pravim
imenom: to je čisti rasizam', *Index.Hr*, 1 June. Available at: www.index.hr/
vijesti/clanak/nazovimo-prosvjed-protiv-roma-u-cakovcu-pravim-imenom-
to-je-cisti-rasizam/2089889.aspx (accessed: 9 March 2020).

Durst, J. and Nagy, V. (2018) 'Transnational Roma Mobilities', *Intersections*, 4(2): 3–16. DOI: https://10.17356/ieejsp.v4i2.466.

Durst, J. and Nyírő, Z. (2018) 'Soul Work and Giving Back. Ethnic Support Groups and the Hidden Costs of Social Mobility', *Intersections*, 4(1): 88–108. DOI: https://doi.org/10.17356/ieejsp.v4i1.406.

Dyck, E. (2013) *Facing Eugenics: Reproduction, Sterilization and the Politics of Choice*. Toronto and London: University of Toronto Press.

Džankić, J. (2012) 'Understanding Montenegrin Citizenship', *Citizenship Studies*, 16(3–4): 337–51.

Eliassi, B. (2016) 'Statelessness in a World of Nation-States: The Cases of Kurdish Diasporas in Sweden and the UK', *Journal of Ethnic and Migration Studies*, 42(9): 1403–19.

Employment Equity Act 1995, c. 44 (Canada). Available at: https://laws-lois.justice.gc.ca/eng/acts/E-5.401/ (accessed: 14 September 2020).

Epperson, L. (2014) 'Brown's Dream Deferred: Lessons on Democracy and Identity from Cooper v. Aaron to the School-to-Prison Pipeline Essays', *Wake Forest Law Review*, 49(3): 687–702.

Equality Act 2010, c. 15 (UK). Available at: https://www.legislation.gov.uk/ukpga/2010/15/contents (accessed: 14 September 2020).

Erel, U. and Reynolds, T. (2018) 'Introduction: Migrant Mothers Challenging Racialized Citizenship', *Ethnic and Racial Studies*, 41(1): 55–72.

ERGO (European Grassroots Organizations Network) (2020) 'ERGO Network Feedback on Commission Roadmap', 27 March. Available at: https://ergonetwork.org/2020/03/ergo-network-feedback-on-commission-roadmap/ (accessed: 22 September 2020).

ERRC (European Roma Rights Centre) (1999) *Borders, Visas and Asylum*, 15 July. Available at: http://www.errc.org/roma-rights-journal/borders-visas-and-asylum (accessed: 22 September 2020).

—— (2001) *Roma Rights Violations by Authorities in Croatia*, 15 August. Available at: www.errc.org/roma-rights-journal/roma-rights-violations-by-authorities-in-croatia (accessed: 22 September 2020).

—— (2012) *Slovakia: A Report by the European Roma Rights Centre*. Available at: www.errc.org/uploads/upload_en/file/slovakia-country-profile-2011–2012.pdf (accessed: 22 September 2020).

—— (2014) *Highest Court in Macedonia Upholds Freedom of Movement for All Macedonians, Including Roma*, 15 July. Available at: www.errc.org/press-releases/highest-court-in-macedonia-upholds-freedom-of-movement-for-all-macedonians-including-roma (accessed: 22 September 2020).

—— (2016) *Coercive and Cruel: Sterilisation and its Consequences for Romani Women in the Czech Republic (1966–2016)*, 28 November. Available at: www.errc.org/reports-and-submissions/coercive-and-cruel-sterilisation-and-its-consequences-for-romani-women-in-the-czech-republic-1966–2016 (accessed: 22 September 2020).

—— (2017) *Roma Belong: Discrimination, Statelessness and Marginalisation of Roma in the Western Balkans and Ukraine*. Available at: www.errc.org/reports-and-submissions/roma-belong–discrimination-statelessness-

and-marginalisation-of-roma-in-the-western-balkans-and-ukraine (accessed: 7 December 2020).

—— (2019) *Our Story – European Roma Rights Centre*. Available at: www.errc.org/who-we-are/our-story (accessed: 22 September 2020).

EU (European Union) (2004) *Directive 2004/38/EC of the European Parliament and the Council of 29 April 2004 on the Right of Citizens of the Union and their Family Members to Move and Reside Freely within the Territory of the Member States Amending Regulation (EEC) No 1612/68 and Repealing Directives 64/221/EEC, 68/360/EEC, 72/194/EEC, 73/148/ EEC, 75/34/EEC, 75/35/EEC, 90/364/EEC, 90/365/EEC and 93/96/ EEC, 29 April 2004, 2004/38/EC*. Available at: https://www.refworld.org/ docid/4a54bbb00.html (accessed: 22 September 2020).

—— (2012) Charter of Fundamental Rights of the European Union, 26 October 2012, 2012/C 326/02. Available at: https://www.refworld.org/ docid/3ae6b3b70.html (accessed: 22 September 2020).

—— (2013) *Regulation (EU) No 1289/2013 of the European Parliament and the Council of 11 December 2013 Amending Council Regulation (EC) No 539/2001 Listing the Third Countries Whose Nationals Must be in Possession of Visas when Crossing the External Borders and Those Whose Nationals are Exempt from That Requirement*. Available at: https://eur-lex.europa.eu/LexUriServ/LexUriServ.do?uri=OJ:L:2013 :347:0074:0080:EN:PDF#:~:text=This%20Regulation%20should%20 provide%20a,not%20intergovernmental%20inter%20national%20 organisations (accessed: 22 September 2020).

Euractiv (2012) 'France, Romania Sign Roma Repatriation Deal', *Euractiv*, 13 September. Available at: www.euractiv.com/section/social-europe-jobs/ news/france-romania-sign-roma-repatriation-deal (accessed: 22 September 2020).

—— (2014) 'EU Judges Rule against "Welfare Tourists" in Nod to Cameron', *Euractiv*, 12 November. Available at: www.euractiv.com/section/justice-home-affairs/news/eu-judges-rule-against-welfare-tourists-in-nod-to-cameron (accessed: 22 September 2020).

European Commission (2000) *Council Directive 2000/43/EC of 29 June 2000 Implementing the Principle of Equal Treatment between Persons Irrespective of Racial or Ethnic Origin*. Available at: https:// eur-lex.europa.eu/legal-content/EN/TXT/?uri=CELEX%3A32000L0043 (accessed: 1 December 2020).

—— (2001) *Council Directive 20 01/55/EC of 20 July 2001 on Minimum Standards for Giving Temporary Protection in the Event of a Mass Influx of Displaced Persons and on Measures Promoting a Balance of Efforts between Member States in Receiving Such Persons and Bearing the Consequences Thereof*, 7 August 2001, OJ L.212/12–212/23; 7.8.2001, 2001/55/EC. Available at: https://www.refworld.org/docid/3ddcee2e4.html (accessed: 22 September 2020).

—— (2011a) *Commission Staff Working Paper: Croatia 2011 Progress Report (Accompanying the Document Communication from the Commission* to the European Parliament and the Council) *Enlargement Strategy and Main Challenges 2011–2012.* Available at: https://ec.europa.eu/neighbourhood-enlargement/sites/near/files/pdf/key_documents/2011/package/hr_rapport_2011_en.pdf (accessed: 9 March 2020).

—— (2011b) *Communication from the Commission to the European Parliament, the Council, the European Economic and Social Committee and the Committee of the Regions: An EU Framework for National Roma Integration Strategies up to 2020,* COM/2011/0173 final, Brussels, 5 April 2011. Available at: https://eur-lex.europa.eu/legal-content/en/ALL /?uri=CELEX%3A52011DC0173 (accessed: 21 September 2020).

—— (2011c) *Interim Report from the Commission to the Council and the European Parliament on Reforms in Croatia in the Field of Judiciary and Fundamental Rights (Negotiation Chapter 13).* Available at: https://ec.europa.eu/neighbourhood-enlargement/sites/near/files/pdf/hp/interim_report_hr_ch23_en.pdf (accessed: 9 March 2020).

—— (2011d) *Voluntary Return.* Available at: https://ec.europa.eu/home-affairs/financing/fundings/projects/project_example_022_en (accessed: 9 March 2020).

—— (2013) 'EU-BiH: After the 3rd Round of High Level Dialogue on Accession Process Corner', press release, 10 October. Available at: https://ec.europa.eu/commission/presscorner/detail/en/MEMO_13_874. (accessed: 9 March 2020).

—— (2018a) *Commission Staff Working Document: Montenegro 2018 Report.* Available at: https://ec.europa.eu/neighbourhood-enlargement/sites/near/files/20180417-montenegro-report.pdf (accessed: 9 March 2020).

—— (2018b) *Report on the Evaluation of the EU Framework for National Roma Integration Strategies up to 2020.* Available at: https://eur-lex.europa.eu/legal-content/EN/TXT/?qid=1544112037077&uri=CELEX:52018DC0785 (accessed: 9 March 2020).

—— (2018c) *Roma Integration by County.* Available at: https://ec.europa.eu/info/policies/justice-and-fundamental-rights/combatting-discrimination/roma-and-eu/roma-integration-eu-country_en (accessed: 22 September).

European Council (2009) 'The Stockholm Programme – an Open and Secure Europe Serving and Protecting Citizens' (2010/C 115/01). Available at: https://eur-lex.europa.eu/LexUriServ/LexUriServ.do?uri=OJ:C:2010:115:0001:0038:EN:PDF (accessed: 22 September 2020).

European Migration Network (2018) 'Impact of visa liberalisation on countries of destination'. Available at: https://ec.europa.eu/home-affairs/sites/homeaffairs/files/13a_hungary_visa_liberalisation_2018_en.pdf (accessed: 26 November 2020).

European Network on Statelessness (2019) *Statelessness Index Survey 2019: Italy.* Available at: https://index.statelessness.eu/sites/default/files/ENS_Statelessness_Index_Survey-Italy-2019_1.pdf (accessed: 7 December 2020).

European Parliament (2017) *European Parliament Resolution of 25 October 2017 on Fundamental Rights Aspects in Roma Integration in the EU: Fighting Anti-Gypsyism* (2017/2038(INI)). Available at: https://www.europarl.europa.eu/doceo/document/TA-8–2017–0413_EN.html (accessed: 22 September 2020).

—— (2019) *European Parliament Resolution of 12 February 2019 on the Need for a Strengthened post-2020 Strategic EU Framework for National Roma Inclusion Strategies and Stepping Up the Fight against Anti-Gypsyism* (2019/2509(RSP)). Available at: https://www.europarl.europa.eu/doceo/document/TA-8–2019–0075_EN.html (accessed: 22 September 2020).

European Parliament Anti-Racism and Diversity Intergroup (2017) 'Lack of Birth Certificates Leaves Roma Children in Europe at Risk of Statelessness and without Healthcare or Education'. Available at: https://www.ardi-ep.eu/lack-of-birth-certificates-leaves-roma-children-in-europe-at-risk-of-statelessness-and-without-healthcare-or-education/ (accessed: 1 December 2020).

European Roma Information Office (2019) *Roma Political Participation at the 2019 European Elections*. Available at: www.erionet.eu/blog/2019/07/03/roma-political-participation-at-the-2019-european-elections (accessed: 9 March 2020).

EUROPOL (European Union Agency for Law Enforcement Cooperation) (2016) *Trafficking in Human Beings in the EU*. Available at: https://ec.europa.eu/anti-trafficking/sites/antitrafficking/files/situational_report_trafficking_in_human_beings-_europol.pdf (accessed: 22 September 2020).

Farkas, L. (2014) *Report on Discrimination of Roma Children in Education Justice*. Brussels: European Commission. Available at: https://tandis.odihr.pl/bitstream/20.500.12389/21933/1/08101.pdf (accessed: 6 March 2020).

Faure Atger, A. (2013) 'European Citizenship Revealed: Sites, Actors and Roma Access to Justice in the EU'. In E. F. Isin and M. Saward (eds.) *Enacting European Citizenship*. Cambridge: Cambridge University Press, pp. 178–94.

FCNM (Framework Convention for the Protection of National Minorities) (1999) 'Report Submitted by the United Kingdom Pursuant to Article 25, Paragraph 25 of the Framework Convention for the Protection of National Minorities'. Available at: https://rm.coe.int/CoERMPublicCommonSearchServices/DisplayDCTMContent?documentId=090000168008b194 (accessed: 22 September 2020).

—— (2002a) 'Advisory Committee on the Framework Convention for the Protection of National Minorities: Opinion on Austria Adopted on 16 May 2002'. Available at: https://rm.coe.int/CoERMPublicCommonSearchServices/DisplayDCTMContent?documentId=090000168008bd35 (accessed: 22 September 2020).

—— (2002b) 'Advisory Committee on the Framework Convention for the Protection of National Minorities. Opinion on Germany Adopted on 1 March 2002'. Available at: https://rm.coe.int/CoERMPublicCommonSearchServices/DisplayDCTMContent?documentId=090000168008bd59 (accessed: 22 September 2020).

—— (2014a) 'Advisory Committee on the Framework Convention for the Protection of National Minorities: Opinion on Spain Adopted on 3 December 2014'. Available at: https://rm.coe.int/CoERMPublicCommon SearchServices/DisplayDCTMContent?documentId=0900001680307ecc (accessed: 22 September 2020).

—— (2014b) 'Fourth Report Submitted by Croatia Pursuant to Article 25, Paragraph 25 of the Framework Convention for the Protection of National Minorities Received on 11 September 2014'. Available at: https://rm.coe.int/CoERMPublicCommonSearchServices/DisplayDCTMContent?documentId=0900001680094aa8 (accessed: 22 September 2020).

—— (2014c) 'Fourth Report Submitted by Italy Pursuant to Article 25, Paragraph 25 of the Framework Convention for the Protection of National Minorities Received on 14 March 2014'. Available at: https://rm.coe.int/CoERMPublicCommonSearchServices/DisplayDCTMContent?documentId=0900001680090310 (accessed: 22 September 2020).

—— (2014d) 'Fourth Report Submitted by the United Kingdom Pursuant to Article 25, Paragraph 25 of the Framework Convention for the Protection of National Minorities Received on 26 March 2014'. Available at: https://rm.coe.int/CoERMPublicCommonSearchServices/DisplayDCTMContent?documentId=09000016805a8c52 (accessed: 22 September 2020).

—— (2016a) 'Advisory Committee on the Framework Convention for the Protection of National Minorities: Fourth Opinion on Austria Adopted on 16 October 2016'. Available at: https://rm.coe.int/168070f1e3 (accessed: 22 September 2020).

—— (2016b) 'Advisory Committee on the Framework Convention for the Protection of National Minorities: Fourth Opinion on Croatia Adopted on 18 November 2015'. Available at: https://rm.coe.int/CoERMPublicCommonSearchServices/DisplayDCTMContent?documentId=09000016806c268b (accessed: 9 March 2020).

—— (2017) 'Fourth Report Submitted by Ireland Pursuant to Article 25, Paragraph 25 of the Framework Convention for the Protection of National Minorities Received on 7 July 2014'. Available at: https://rm.coe.int/fourth-report-submitted-by-ireland-pursuant-to-article-25-paragraph-2-/168072f704 (accessed: 22 September 2020).

Ferreira, N. (2019) 'A Roma European Crisis Road-Map: A Holistic Answer to a Complex Problem'. In T. Magazzini and S. Piemontese (eds.) *Constructing Roma Migrants: European Narratives and Local Governance*. Cham: Springer, pp. 31–50.

Fiddian-Qasmiyeh, E. (2015) '(Re)conceptualising "Stateless Diasporas" in the European Union'. In: R. Cohen, J. Story and N. Moon (eds.) *The Impact of Diasporas*. Oxford: Oxford Diasporas Programme and The Impact of Diasporas in the Making of Britain, pp. 38–43.

FitzGerald, D. (2017) 'History of Racialized Citizenship'. In A. Shachar, R. Bauböck, I. Bloemraad and M. Vink (eds.) *The Oxford Handbook of Citizenship*. Oxford: Oxford University Press, pp. 129–50.

Foster, M. and Lambert, H. (2019) *International Refugee Law and the Protection of Stateless Persons*. Oxford: Oxford University Press.

FRA (Fundamental Rights Agency) (2016) *Second European Union Minorities and Discrimination Survey Roma – Selected Findings*. Available at: https://fra.europa.eu/en/publication/2016/eumidis-ii-roma-selected-findings (accessed: 9 March 2020).

—— (2018) 'Many EU Roma Face Life Like People in the World's Poorer Countries', press release, 20 March. Available at: https://fra.europa.eu/en/press-release/2018/many-eu-roma-face-life-people-worlds-poorer-countries (accessed: 9 March 2020).

Gándara, P. (2005) 'Addressing Educational Inequities for Latino Students: The Politics of "Forgetting"', *Journal of Hispanic Higher Education*, 4(3): 295–313.

Ganje, L. A. (2011) 'Marketing the Sacred: Commodifying Native-American Cultural Images'. In S. D. Ross and P. M. Lester (eds.) *Images that Injure: Pictorial Stereotypes in the Media*. Santa Barbara: Pranger, pp. 91–106.

Gatti, R., Karacsony, S., Kosuke, A., Ferré, C., Carmen, D. and Nieves, P. (2016) *Being Fair, Faring Better: Promoting Equality of Opportunity for Marginalized Roma*. Washington, DC: World Bank Group.

Geddes, A. and Hadj-Abdou, L. (2016) 'An Unstable Equilibrium: Freedom of Movement and the Welfare State in the European Union'. In G. P. Freeman and N. Mirilovic (eds.) *Handbook on Migration and Social Policy*. Cheltenham: Edward Elgar, pp. 222–38.

Gerald, J.M. (2019) '"Hounded by the Terrible Threat": Illness at the Edges of Citizenship in Carlos Bulosan's America is in the Heart', *MFS Modern Fiction Studies*, 65(4): 599–617. DOI: https://doi.org/10.1353/mfs.2019.0046.

Gibney, M. J. (2019) 'Denationalisation and Discrimination', *Journal of Ethnic and Migration Studies*, 46(12): 2551–68.

Gillet, K. and Horowitz, J. (2019) 'Pope Francis Apologizes to Roma for Mistreatment and Urges European Unity', *The New York Times*, 2 June. Available at: www.nytimes.com/2019/06/02/world/europe/pope-francis-romania.html (accessed: 22 September 2020).

Gilroy, P. (1987) *There Ain't No Black in the Union Jack: The Cultural Politics of Race and Nation*. Chicago: University of Chicago Press.

Goldston, J. A. (2010) 'The Struggle for Roma Rights: Arguments that have Worked', *Human Rights Quarterly*, 32(2): 311–25.

—— (2017) 'The Unfulfilled Promise of Educational Opportunity in the United States and Europe: From Brown to D.H. and Beyond'. In J. Bhabha, A. Mirga and M. Matache (eds.) *Realizing Roma Rights*. Philadelphia: University of Pennsylvania Press, pp. 163–84.

Gonzales, R. G. and Sigona, N. (eds.) (2017) *Within and beyond Citizenship: Borders, Membership and Belonging*. London and New York: Routledge.

Goodwin, M. (2009) 'Taking on Racial Segregation: The European Court of Human Rights at a Brown v. Board of Education Moment?', *Rechtsgeleerd Magazijn THEMIS*, 3. *SSRN*. DOI: https://doi.org/10.2139/ssrn.1623163.

Goodwin, M. and Buijs, R. (2013) 'Making Good European Citizens of the Roma: A Closer Look at the EU Framework for National Roma Integration Strategies', *German Law Journal*, 14(10): 2041–56.

Gotev, G. (2018) 'Czech President Defends Assertion that Most Roma don't Work', *Euractiv*, 8 October. Available at: www.euractiv.com/section/languages-culture/news/czech-president-defends-assertion-that-most-roma-dont-work/ (accessed: 22 September 2020).

Government of Croatia (2019) 'Ministar Božinović: Ključ rješenja romske problematike u Međimurju je obrazovanje'. *Vlada Republike Hrvatske*, 4 June. Available at: https://vlada.gov.hr/vijesti/ministar-bozinovic-kljucrjesenja-romske-problematike-u-medjimurju-je-obrazovanje/26110 (accessed: 22 September 2020).

Government of Latvia (2018) *Citizenship Policy in Latvia*. Available at: www.mfa.gov.lv/en/policy/society-integration/citizenship/citizenship-policy-in-latvia (accessed: 7 December 2020).

Greenberg, J. (2010) 'Report on Roma Education Today: From Slavery to Segregation and Beyond', *Columbia Law Review*, 110(4): 919–1001.

Guglielmo, R. and Waters, T. W. (2005) 'Migrating towards Minority Status: Shifting European Policy towards Roma', *Journal of Common Market Studies*, 43(4): 763–85.

Gunther, C. T. (2013) 'France's Repatriation of Roma: Violation of Fundamental Freedoms', *Cornell International Law Journal*, 45: 206–25. Available at: https://www.lawschool.cornell.edu/research/ILJ/upload/Gunther-final.pdf (accessed: 6 March 2020).

Hall, S. (1996) 'New Ethnicities'. In D. Morley and K-H Chen (eds.) *Critical Dialogues in Cultural Studies*. London: Routledge, pp. 442–51.

Harrington, J. (2014) 'Navigating Global Citizenship Studies'. In E. F. Isin and P. Nyers (eds.) *Routledge Handbook of Global Citizenship Studies*. London and New York: Routledge, pp. 12–20.

Harrington, J. and Manji, A. (2017) 'The Limits of Socio-Legal Radicalism', *Social & Legal Studies*, 26(6): 700–15.

Harvey, A. (2018) *In Praise of the 1961 Statelessness Convention*. Available at: www.statelessness.eu/updates/blog/praise-1961-statelessness-convention (accessed: 7 December 2020)

Hayden, R. M. (1992) 'Constitutional Nationalism in the Formerly Yugoslav Republics', *Slavic Review*, 51(4): 654–73.

Hayes de Kalaf, E. (2019) 'Making Foreign: Legal Identity, Social Policy and the Contours of Belonging in the Contemporary Dominican Republic'. Unpublished PhD dissertation, University of Aberdeen.

Hepple, B. (2006) 'The European Legacy of Brown v. Board of Education', *University of Illinois Law Review*, 3: 605–24.

Hepworth, K. (2012) 'Abject Citizens: Italian "Nomad Emergencies" and the Deportability of Romanian Roma', *Citizenship Studies*, 16(3–4): 431–49.

—— (2014) 'Topologies of Citizenship'. In E. F. Isin and P. Nyers (eds.) *Routledge Handbook of Global Citizenship Studies*. London and New York: Routledge, pp. 110–18.

—— (2015) *At the Edges of Citizenship: Security and the Constitution of Non-Citizen Subjects*. London: Routledge.

Holley-Walker, D. (2004) 'Is Brown Dying? Exploring the Resegregation Trend in our Public Schools', *New York Law School Law Review*, 49: 1085. *SSRN*. Available at: https://ssrn.com/abstract=922098 (accessed: 22 September 2020).

Horváth and Kiss v. Hungary Application no. 11146/11 (ECtHR, 23 January 2013). Available at: https://hudoc.echr.coe.int/eng#{%22ite mid%22:[%22001-109467%22]} (accessed: 22 September 2020).

Hughes, J. and Sasse, G. (2003) 'Monitoring the Monitors: EU Enlargement Conditionality and Minority Protection in the CEECs EU Enlargement and Minority Rights', *Journal on Ethnopolitics and Minority Issues in Europe*, 14(4): 26–59.

Humphris, R. (2019) *Home-Land: Romanian Roma, Domestic Spaces and the State*. Bristol: Bristol University Press.

IACHR (Inter-American Commission on Human Rights) (2015) *Situation of Human Rights in the Dominican Republic*. Available at: www.oas.org/en/iachr/reports/pdfs/DominicanRepublic-2015.pdf (accessed: 22 September 2020).

Isin, E. F. (2009) 'Citizenship in Flux: The Figure of the Activist Citizen', *Subjectivity*, 29(1): 367–88.

—— (2012) 'Citizens without Nations', *Environment and Planning D: Society and Space*, 30(3): 450–67.

—— (2017) 'Performative Citizenship'. In A. Shachar, R. Bauböck, I. Bloemraad and M. Vink (eds.) *The Oxford Handbook of Citizenship*. Oxford: Oxford University Press, pp. 500–26.

Isin, E. F. and Nyers, P. (eds.) (2014) *Routledge Handbook of Global Citizenship Studies*. London and New York: Routledge.

Iusmen, I. (2018) '"Non multa, sed multum": EU Roma Policy and the Challenges of Roma Inclusion', *Journal of European Integration*, 40(4): 427–41.

Ivļevs, A. and King, R. M. (2012) 'From Migrants to (Non-)Citizens: Political Economy of Naturalisations in Latvia', *IZA Journal of Migration*, 1(1):14.

Janko Spreizer, A. (2004) '"Avtohtoni" in "Neavtohtoni" Romi v Sloveniji: socialna konstrukcija teritorialnega razmejevanja identitet', *Treatises and Documents: Journal of Ethnic Studies*, 45: 202–25.

Järve, P. and Poleshchuk, V. (2010) *Country Report: Estonia. EUDO Citizenship Obvervatory*. Available at: https://cadmus.eui.eu/bitstream/handle/1814/19611/Estonia2010.pdf?sequence=1&isAllowed=y.

Jenkins, C. (2013) 'UK Roma Population One of Biggest in Europe', *Channel 4 News*, 30 October. Available at: www.channel4.com/news/immigration-roma-migrants-bulgaria-romania-slovakia-uk (accessed: 9 March 2020).

Jenne, E. (2000) 'The Roma of Central and Eastern Europe: Constructing a Stateless Nation'. In J. Stein (ed.) *The Politics of National Minority Participation in Post-Communist Societies: State-Building, Democracy and Ethnic Mobilization*. Abingdon and New York: Routledge, pp. 189–212.

Joppke, C. (2007) 'Transformation of Citizenship: Status, Rights, Identity', *Citizenship Studies*, 11(1): 37–48.

Jovanović, J. (2017) *Lack of Birth Certificates Leaves Roma Children in Europe at Risk of Statelessness and without Healthcare or Education*. Available at: https://www.ardi-ep.eu/lack-of-birth-certificates-leaves-roma-children-in-europe-at-risk-of-statelessness-and-without-healthcare-or-education/ (accessed: 22 September 2020).

Jovanović, Ž. (2014) 'There are 6 Million Roma in the EU. What if their Voices were Heard?' *Open Society Foundations: Voices*, 22 May. Available at: www.opensocietyfoundations.org/voices/power-ballot-box-roma-europe (accessed: 22 September 2020).

—— (2015) 'Why Europe's "Roma Decade" didn't Lead to Inclusion', *Open Society Foundations: Voices*, 21 September. Available at: www.opensocietyfoundations.org/voices/why-europe-s-roma-decade-didn-t-lead-inclusion (accessed: 22 September 2020).

Jovanović, Ž. and Daragiu. M. (2010) 'European Roma Learn from African American Rights Struggle'. *Open Society Foundations: Voices*, 13 June. Available at: www.opensocietyfoundations.org/voices/european-roma-learn-african-american-rights-struggle (accessed: 22 September 2020).

Jutarnji (2010) 'Romska lekcija za Hrvate koja nas je stajala sramote i 560 tisuća kuna', *Jutarnji*, 18 March. Available at: https://www.jutarnji.hr/vijesti/hrvatska/romska-lekcija-za-hrvate-koja-nas-je-stajala-sramote-i-560-tisuca-kuna/2236481/ (accessed: 22 September 2020).

Kacarska, S. (2015) 'Losing the Rights along the Way: The EU–Western Balkans Visa Liberalisation', *European Politics and Society*, 16(3): 363–78.

Kallius, A., Monterescu, D. and Rajaram, P. K. (2016) 'Immobilizing Mobility: Border Ethnography, Illiberal Democracy, and the Politics of the "Refugee Crisis" in Hungary', *American Ethnologist*, 43(1): 1–13.

Kamm, H. (1993) 'Havel Calls the Gypsies "Litmus Test"', *The New York Times*, 10 December. Available at: www.nytimes.com/1993/12/10/world/havel-calls-the-gypsies-litmus-test.html (accessed: 22 September 2020).

Keating, M. (2001) *Plurinational Democracy : Stateless Nations in a Post-Sovereignty Era*. Oxford: Oxford University Press.

Kingston, L. N. (2017) 'Worthy of Rights: Statelessness as a Cause and Symptom of Marginalisation'. In T. Bloom, K. Tonkiss and P. Cole (eds.) *Understanding Statelessness*. London and New York: Routledge, pp. 17–34.

Kirchgaessner, S. (2018) 'Far-Right Italy Minister Vows "Action" to Expel Thousands of Roma', *The Guardian*, 19 June. Available at: www.theguardian.com/world/2018/jun/19/italy-coalition-rift-roma-register-matteo-salvini (accessed: 6 March 2020).

Klímová-Alexander, I. (2005) *The Romani Voice in World Politics: The United Nations and Non-State Actors*. Aldershot and Burlington: Ashgate.

—— (2007) 'Transnational Romani and Indigenous Non-Territorial Self-Determination Claims', *Ethnopolitics*, 6(3): 395–416.

Kochenov, D. (2007) 'EU Influence on the Citizenship Policies of the Candidate Countries: The Case of the Roma Exclusion in the Czech Republic', *Journal of Contemporary European Research*, 3(2): 124–40.

Kochenov, D. and Dimitrovs, A. (2016) 'EU Citizenship for Latvian "Non-Citizens"': A Concrete Proposal', *Houston Journal of International Law*, 38(1): 55–97.

Kóczé, A. (2009) 'The Limits of Rights-Based Discourse in Romani Women's Activism: The Gender Dimension in Romani Politics'. In N. Sigona and N. Trehan (eds.) *Romani Politics in Contemporary Europe Poverty, Ethnic Mobilization and the Neoliberal Order*. Basingstoke: Palgrave Macmillan, pp. 135–55.

—— (2018) 'Race, Migration and Neoliberalism: Distorted Notions of Romani Migration in European Public Discourses', *Social Identities*, 24(4): 459–73. DOI: https://doi.org/10.1080/13504630.2017.1335827.

Kóczé, A. and Rövid. M. (2017) 'Roma and the Politics of Double Discourse in Contemporary Europe', *Identities*, 24(6): 684–700.

Kóczé, A., Vincze, E., Zentai, V. and Jovanović, J. (eds.) (2018) *The Romani Women's Movement: Struggles and Debates in Central and Eastern Europe*. Abingdon and New York: Routledge.

Kostakopoulou, T. (2008) *The Future Governance of Citizenship*. Cambridge: Cambridge University Press.

Kostić, I. (2013) 'Addressing Statelessness in the Western Balkans – ENS and WeBLAN Joint Workshop', *European Network on Statelessness*. Available at: www.statelessness.eu/blog/addressing-statelessness-western-balkans-%E2%80%93-ens-and-weblan-joint-workshop (accessed: 9 May 2019).

Kostka, J. (2018) *Financing Roma Inclusion with European Structural Funds: Why Good Intentions Fail*. Abingdon and New York: Routledge.

Krause, S. (2007) 'Mapping the Electoral Participation of Roma in South-Eastern Europe'. Expert paper, Contact Point for Roma and Sinti Issues, ODIHR–European Commission Joint Project 'Roma Use Your Ballot Wisely!' Available at: www.osce.org/odihr/23693?download=true (accessed: 9 May 2019).

Krūma, K. (2015) 'Country Report on Citizenship Law: Latvia'. Global Citizenship Observatory. Available at: http://cadmus.eui.eu/handle/1814/34481.

Kudaibergenova, D. T. (2020) *Towards Nationalizing Regimes: Conceptualizing Power and Identity in the Post-Soviet Realm*. Pittsburgh, PA: University of Pittsburgh Press.

Kummrow, L. (2015) 'To What Extent has the EU Visa Liberalization Process Contributed to Further Discrimination of Roma Community in Serbia and Macedonia?' Unpublished MA thesis, University College London.

Kūris, E. (2010) *Country Report: Lithuania* [GLOBALCIT], EUDO Citizenship Observatory, 2010/29, Country Reports. Cadmus, European University Institute Research Repository. Available at: http://hdl.handle.net/1814/19622.

Kurtić, V. and Jovanović, J. (2018) 'Romani Women's Friendship, Empowerment, and Politics: Views on Romani Feminism in Serbia and Beyond'. in A. Kóczé et al. (eds.) *The Romani Women's Movement: Struggles and Debates in Central and Eastern Europe*. Abingdon and New York: Routledge, pp. 135–58.

Kyaw, N. N. (2017) 'Unpacking the Presumed Statelessness of Rohingyas', *Journal of Immigrant and Refugee Studies*, 15(3): 269–86.

Kymlicka, W. (1995) *Multicultural Citizenship*. Oxford: Oxford University Press.

—— (2002a) *Contemporary Political Philosophy: An Introduction*. Oxford: Oxford University Press.

—— (2002b) 'Western Political Theory and Ethnic Relations in Eastern Europe'. In W. Kymlicka and M. Opalski (eds.) *Can Liberal Pluralism be Exported? Western Political Theory and Ethnic Relations in Eastern Europe*. Oxford: Oxford University Press, pp. 16–116.

La croix (2010) 'Discours de Nicolas Sarkozy à Grenoble', *La croix*, 2 August. Available at: www.la-croix.com/Actualite/Monde/Discours-de-Nicolas-Sarkozy-a-Grenoble-_NG_-2010–08–02–555076 (accessed: 6 March 2020).

Ladányi, J. and Szelényi, I. (2006) *Patterns of Exclusion: Constructing Gypsy Ethnicity and the Making of an Underclass in Transitional Societies of Europe*. New York: Columbia University Press.

Lakić, M. (2019) 'Pope Backs Bosnian Roma Family against Italian rightists', *BalkanInsight*, 10 May. Available at: https://balkaninsight.com/2019/05/10/bosnian-roma-family-defy-italian-rightist-protests/ (accessed: 1 December 2020).

Lavida and Others v. Greece Application no. 7973/10 (ECtHR, 20 May 2013). Available at: https://hudoc.echr.coe.int/eng#{%22itemid%22: [%22001-109467%22]} (accessed: 22 September 2020).

Lawrance, B. N. and Stevens, J. (eds.) (2017) *Citizenship in Question: Evidentiary Birthright and Statelessness*. Durham, NC, and London: Duke University Press.

Leavitt, P. A., Covarrubias, R., Perez, Y. A. and Fryberg, S. A. (2015) '"Frozen in Time": The Impact of Native American Media Representations on Identity and Self-Understanding', *Journal of Social Issues*, 71(1): 39–53.

Leggio, D. V. (2019) '"Modern-Day Fagins", "Gaudy Mansions" and "Increasing Numbers": Narratives on Roma Migrants in the Build-Up to the British EU Referendum'. In T. Magazzini and S. Piemontese (eds.) *Constructing Roma Migrants European Narratives and Local Governance*. Cham: Springer, pp. 69–90.

Lekić, M. (2018) 'Film Star's Death Highlights Plight of Bosnia's Roma', *Balkan Insight*, 21 February. Available at: https://balkaninsight.com/2018/02/21/death-of-famous-bosnian-roma-shows-hard-life-02–19–2018/ (accessed: 6 March 2020).

Lentin, A. (2004) *Racism and Anti-Racism in Europe*. London: Pluto Press.

—— (2020) *Why Race Still Matters*. Cambridge and Medford, MA: Polity Press.

Lichnofsky, C. (2013) 'Ashkali and Egyptians in Kosovo: New Ethnic Identifications as a Result of Exclusion during Nationalist Violence from 1990 till 2010', *Romani Studies*, 23(1): 29–60.

Liégeois, J.-P. (2007) *Roma in Europe*. Strasbourg: Council of Europe Publishing.

Lightfoot, S. R. (2012) 'Selective Endorsement without Intent to Implement: Indigenous Rights and the Anglosphere', *The International Journal of Human Rights*, 16(1): 100–22.

Linde, R. (2006) 'Statelessness and Roma Communities in the Czech Republic: Competing Theories of State Compliance', *International Journal on Minority and Group Rights*, 13(4): 341–65.

Lori, N. A. (2017) 'Statelessness, "In-Between" Statuses, and Precarious Citizenship'. In A. Shachar, R. Bauböck, I. Bloemraad and M. Vink (eds.) *The Oxford Handbook of Citizenship*. Oxford: Oxford University Press, pp. 743–66.

Lucassen, L., Willems, W. and Cottaar, A. (1998) *Gypsies and Other Itinerant Groups: A Socio-Historical Approach*. Houndmills, Basingstoke: Palgrave.

Lynch, M. and Cook, T. (2006) 'Citizens of Nowhere: Stateless Biharis of Bangladesh'. Washington, DC: Refugees International. Available at: https://www.refworld.org/pdfid/47a6eba70.pdf (accessed: 22 September 2020).

Maas, W. (2013) *Democratic Citizenship and the Free Movement of People*. Leiden: Martinus Nijhoff.

Macoun, A. (2011) 'Aboriginality and the Northern Territory Intervention', *Australian Journal of Political Science*, 46(3): 519–34.

Magazzini, T. (2017) 'Redistribution, Recognition or Representation? EU Roma Integration Policies as a Test for Social Justice'. Unpublished PhD thesis, University of Deusto.

Magazzini, T. and Piemontese, S. (eds.) (2019) *Constructing Roma Migrants: European Narratives and Local Governance*. Cham: Springer.

Manby, B. (2015) *Nationality, Migration and Statelessness in West Africa*. Available at: www.unhcr.org/ecowas2015/Nationality-Migration-and-Statelessness-in-West-Africa-REPORT-EN.pdf (accessed: 7 December 2020).

Mars, G. (ed.) (2001) *Work Place Sabotage*. Dartmouth: Ashgate.

Marshall, T. H. (1949) *Citizenship and Social Class*. London: Pluto.

Matache, M. (2018) 'Introduction: Roma in a Time of Paradigm Shift and Chaos', *Journal of Poverty and Social Justice*, 26(1): 51–7.

Matache, M. and West, C. (2018) 'Roma and African Americans Share a Common Struggle', *The Guardian*, 20 February. Available at: www.theguardian.com/commentisfree/2018/feb/20/roma-african-americans-common-struggle (accessed: 9 March 2020).

Matras, Y. (2004) 'The Role of Language in Mystifying and De-Mystifying Gypsy Identity'. In N. Saul and S. Tebbutt (eds.) *Role of the Romanies*

Images and Counter Images of 'Gypsies'/Romanies in European Cultures. Liverpool: Liverpool University Press, pp. 53–78.

Matras, Y. and Leggio, D. V. (eds.) (2018) *Open Borders, Unlocked Cultures: Romanian Roma Migrants in Western Europe.* Abingdon and New York: Routledge, Taylor & Francis Group.

McGarry, A. (2010) *Who Speaks for Roma? Political Representation of a Transnational Minority Community.* New York: Continuum International Publishing Group.

—— (2017) *Romaphobia: The Last Acceptable Form of Racism.* London: Zed Books.

McGarry, A. and Agarin, T. (2014) 'Unpacking the Roma Participation Puzzle: Presence, Voice and Influence', *Journal of Ethnic and Migration Studies*, 40(12): 1972–90.

Međimurje (2010) 'Nije segregacija, nego romski teror!' *Medjimurje*, 17 June. Available at: https://medjimurje.hr/aktualno/kolumne/osobni-pogled-2365/ (accessed: 22 September 2020).

Medimurjepress (2019) 'Mirni prosvjed u Čakovcu "Želim normalan život"', *Medjimurjepress*, June. Available at: https://medjimurjepress.net/gradovi/ grad-cakovec/mirni-prosvjed-u-cakovcu-zelim-normalan-zivot/ (accessed: 22 September 2020).

Messing, V. (2014) 'Methodological Puzzles of Surveying Roma/Gypsy Populations', *Ethnicities*, 14(6): 811–29.

—— (2019) 'Conceptual and Methodological Considerations in Researching "Roma Migration"'. In T. Magazzini and S. Piemontese (eds.) *Constructing Roma Migrants: European Narratives and Local Governance.* Cham: Springer, pp. 17–30.

Mezzadra, S. and Neilson, B. (2013) *Border as Method or the Multiplication of Labor.* Durham, NC: Duke University Press.

Milevska, T. (2013) 'Legal Wrangling Looms over EU Plan to Suspend Visa-Free Travel', *Euractiv*, 16 September. Available at: https:// www.euractiv.com/section/justice-home-affairs/news/legal-wrangling-looms-over-eu-plan-to-suspend-visa-free-travel/. (accessed: 20 September 2020).

Milliken v. Bradley 418 U.S. 717 (US Supreme Court, 1974). Available at: https://supreme.justia.com/cases/federal/us/418/717/ (accessed: 22 September 2020).

Minority Rights Group International (2017) *Denial and Denigration: How Racism Feeds Statelessness – Minority Stories.* Available at: https:// stories.minorityrights.org/statelessness/ (accessed: 22 September 2020).

Minow, M. (2012) *In Brown's Wake: Legacies of America's Educational Landmark.* New York and Oxford: Oxford University Press.

Mirga, A. (2009) 'The Extreme Right and Roma and Sinti in Europe: A New Phase in the Use of Hate Speech and Violence?', *Roma Rights*, 1: 5–9. Available at: www.errc.org/uploads/upload_en/file/04/10/m00000410.pdf (accessed: 22 September 2020).

Mirga-Kruszelnicka, A. (2018) 'Challenging Anti-Gypsyism in Academia', *Critical Romani Studies*, 1(1): 8–28. DOI: https://doi.org/10.29098/ crs.v1i1.5.

Molavi, S. C. (2013) *Stateless Citizenship: The Palestinian-Arab Citizens of Israel*. Leiden and Boston: Brill.

Moreton-Robinson, A. (2011) 'Virtuous Racial States: The Possessive Logic of Patriarchal White Sovereignty and the United Nations Declaration on the Rights of Indigenous Peoples', *Griffith Law Review*, 20(3): 641–58.

Moses, A. D. (2011) 'Official Apologies, Reconciliation, and Settler Colonialism: Australian Indigenous Alterity and Political Agency', *Citizenship Studies*, 15(2): 145–59.

National Minorities and Minority Languages Act 2009 (724) (Sweden). Available at: http://notisum.se/rnp/sls/sfs/20090724.pdf (accessed: 14 September 2020).

Neveu, C. (2015) 'Of Ordinariness and Citizenship Processes', *Citizenship Studies*, 19(2): 141–54.

Nirenberg, J. (2009) 'Romani Political Mobilization from the First International Romani Union Congress to the European Roma, Sinti and Travellers Forum'. In N. Sigona and N. Trehan (eds.) *Romani Politics in Contemporary Europe: Poverty, Ethnic Mobilization, and the Neoliberal Order*. Basingstoke: Palgrave Macmillan, pp. 94–115.

Northern Territory National Emergency Response Act 2007, no. 129 (Australia). Available at: https://www.legislation.gov.au/Series/C2007A00129 (accessed: 22 September 2020).

Nozick, R. (1974) *Anarchy, State and Utopia*. New York: Basic Books, Cop.

Nteta, T. M., Sharrow, E. A. and Tarsi, M. R. (2018) 'Burying the Hatchet? Elite Influence and White Opinion on the Washington Redskins Controversy', *Social Science Quarterly*, 99(2): 473–89.

Nyers, P. (2006) 'The Accidental Citizen: Acts of Sovereignty and (Un) Making Citizenship', *Economy and Society*, 35(1): 22–41.

—— (2019) *Irregular Citizenship, Immigration, and Deportation*. London and New York: Routledge.

OHCHR (Office of the United Nations High Commissioner for Human Rights) (2004) *Report of the Secretary-General on the Preliminary Review by the Coordinator of the International Decade of the World's Indigenous People on the Activities of the United Nations System in Relation to the Decade*. Available at: https://documents-dds-ny.un.org/doc/UNDOC/GEN/N04/405/51/PDF/N0440551.pdf?OpenElement (accessed: 22 September 2020).

—— (2017) *Human Rights Council Opens Special Session on the Situation of Human Rights of the Rohingya and Other Minorities in Rakhine State in Myanmar*. Available at: https://www.ohchr.org/EN/NewsEvents/Pages/DisplayNews.aspx?NewsID=22491&LangID=E (accessed: 22 September 2020).

Okely, J. (1994) 'Constructing Difference: Gypsies as "Other"', *Anthropological Journal on European Cultures*, 3(2): 55–73.

Okin, S. M. (1999) 'Feminism and Multiculturalism: Some Tensions', *Ethics*, 108(4): 661–84.

Olivera, M. (2012) 'The Gypsies as Indigenous Groups: The Gabori Roma Case in Romania', *Romani Studies*, 22(1): 19–33.

O'Nions, H. (2010) 'Divide and Teach: Educational Inequality and the Roma', *The International Journal of Human Rights*, 14(3): 464–89.

—— (2011) 'Roma Expulsions and Discrimination: The Elephant in Brussels', *European Journal of Migration and Law*, 13(4): 361–88.

—— (2015) 'Narratives of Social Inclusion in the Context of Roma School Segregation', *Social Inclusion*, 3(5): 103–14.

Open Society Foundation (2010) *No Data – No Progress: Country Findings*. Available at: www.opensocietyfoundations.org/publications/no-data-no-progress-country-findings (accessed: 6 March 2020).

Orfield, G. Schley, S., Glass, D. and Reardon, S. (1994) 'The Growth of Segregation in American Schools: Changing Patterns of Separation and Poverty since 1968', *Equity & Excellence in Education*, 27(1): 5–8.

Oršuš and Others v. Croatia Application no. 15766/03 (ECtHR, 16 March 2010). Available at: https://hudoc.exec.coe.int/ENG#{%22EXECIdentif ier%22:[%22004-10085%22]} (accessed: 9 March 2020).

OSCE (Organization for Security and Co-operation in Europe) (2003) *Action Plan on Improving the Situation of Roma within the OSCE Area*. Available at: https://www.osce.org/odihr/17554 (accessed: 14 December 2020).

—— (2018) *Third Status Report: Implementation of the Action Plan on Improving the Situation of Roma and Sinti within the OSCE Area*. Available at: www.osce.org/odihr/roma-sinti-action-plan-2018-status-report (accessed: 9 March 2020).

—— (2020) *Action Plan on Improving the Situation of Roma and Sinti within the OSCE Area*. Available at: www.osce.org/odihr/17554 (accessed: 9 March 2020).

Österle, A., P. Balázs and J. Delgado (2009) 'Travelling for Teeth: Character-istics and Perspectives of Dental Care Tourism in Hungary', *British Dental Journal*, 206(8): 425–8. DOI: https://doi.org/10.1038/sj.bdj.2009.308 (accessed: 6 March 2020).

O'Sullivan, D. (2020) '*We Are All Here to Stay*' : *Citizenship, Sovereignty and the UN Declaration on the Rights of Indigenous Peoples*. Canberra, ACT: Australian National University Press.

Owen, D. (2013) 'Citizenship and the Marginalities of Migrants', *Critical Review of International Social and Political Philosophy*, 16(3): 326–43.

—— (2018) 'On the Right to Have Nationality Rights: Statelessness, Citizen-ship and Human Rights', *Netherlands International Law Review*, 65(3): 299–317.

Pantea, M.-C. (2013) 'From "Making a Living" to "Getting Ahead": Roma Women's Experiences of Migration', *Journal of Ethnic and Migration Studies*, 38(8): 1251–68.

Parashar, A. and Alam. J. (2018) 'The National Laws of Myanmar: Making of Statelessness for the Rohingya', *International Migration*, 57(1): 94–108.

Parker, O. (2012) 'Roma and the Politics of EU Citizenship in France: Everyday Security and Resistance', *JCMS: Journal of Common Market Studies*, 50(3): 475–91.

Parker, O. and Catalán, O. L. (2014) 'Free Movement for Whom, Where, When? Roma EU Citizens in France and Spain', *International Political Sociology*, 8(4): 379–95.

Parker, O. and Toke, D. (2013) 'The Politics of a Multi-Level Citizenship: French Republicanism, Roma Mobility and the EU', *Global Society*, 27(3): 360–78.

Parker, W. (2000) 'The Color of Choice: Race and Charter Schools', *Tulane Law Review*, 75(3): 563–630.

Pennant, A. and Sigona, N. (2018) 'Black History is Still Largely Ignored, 70 Years after *Empire Windrush* Reached Britain', *The Conversation*, 22 June. Available at: https://theconversation.com/black-history-is-still-largely-ignored-70-years-after-empire-windrush-reached-britain-98431 (accessed: 7 December 2020).

Perche, D. (2017) 'Ten Years on, it's Time we Learned the Lessons from the Failed Northern Territory Intervention', *The Conversation*, 25 June. Available at: https://theconversation.com/ten-years-on-its-time-we-learned-the-lessons-from-the-failed-northern-territory-intervention-79198 (accessed: 9 March 2020).

Perič, T. and Demirovski, M. (2000) 'Unwanted: The Exodus of Kosovo Roma (1998–2000)', *Cambridge Review of International Affairs*, 13(2): 83–96.

Perica, V. (2006) 'The Most Catholic Country in Europe? Church, State, and Society in Contemporary Croatia', *Religion, State and Society*, 34(4): 311–46.

Perkins, H. (2013) 'Roma Army: 200,000 are Already Here with MORE on the Way', *Daily Star*, November. Available at: https://www.dailystar.co.uk/news/latest-news/roma-army-200–000-already-18631969 (accessed: 9 March 2020).

Pettigrew, T. F. (2004) 'Justice Deferred a Half Century after Brown v. Board of Education', *American Psychologist*, 59(6): 521–9.

Phillips, V. F. (2017) 'Beyond Trademark: The Washington Redskins Case and the Search for Dignity', *Chicago-Kent Law Review*, 92: 1061–86. Available at: https://scholarship.kentlaw.iit.edu/cklawreview/vol92/iss3/17/ (accessed: 22 September 2020).

Plaut, S. (2016) 'Follow the Money: International Donors, External Homelands and their Effect on Romani Media and Advocacy', *Ethnic and Racial Studies*, 40(7): 1058–76.

Plessy v. Fergusson 163 U.S. 537 (US Supreme Court, 1896). Available at: https://supreme.justia.com/cases/federal/us/163/537/ (accessed: 22 September 2020).

Pogány, I. (2004) *The Roma Cafe*. London: Pluto Press.

—— (2006) 'Minority Rights and the Roma of Central and Eastern Europe'. *Human Rights Law Review* 6(1): 1–25. DOI: https://doi.org/10.1093/hrlr/ngi034.

—— (2012) 'Pariah Peoples: Roma and the Multiple Failures of Law in Central and Eastern Europe', *Social & Legal Studies*, 21(3): 375–93.

Powell, R. and Lever, J. (2015) 'Europe's Perennial "Outsiders": A Processual Approach to Roma Stigmatization and Ghettoization', *Current Sociology*, 65(5): 680–99.

Praxis (2016) 'Praxis in the Show Good Afternoon: About Legally Invisible People – Pink', *Praxis*. Available at: www.praxis.org.rs/index.php/en/praxis-in-media/item/1130-praxis-u-emisiji-dobar-dan-o-pravno-nevidljivim-licima-pink/1130-praxis-u-emisiji-dobar-dan-o-pravno-nevidljivim-licima-pink (accessed: 9 March 2020).

Pusca, A. M. (2012) *Eastern European Roma in the EU: Mobility, Discrimination, Solutions*. New York: International Debate Education Association.

Race Relations Act 1976, c. 74 (UK). Available at: https://www.legislation.gov.uk/ukpga/1976/74/enacted (accessed: 14 September 2020).

Racial Discrimination Act 1975 (Australia), no. 52 c. 17. Available at: https://www.legislation.gov.au/Details/C2016C00089 (accessed: 26 November 2020).

Ram, M. (2014a) 'European Integration, Migration and Representation: The Case of Roma in France', *Ethnopolitics*, 13(3): 203–24.

—— (2014b) 'Europeanized Hypocrisy: Roma Inclusion and Exclusion in Central and Eastern Europe', *Journal on Ethnopolitics and Minority Issues in Europe*, 13(3): 15–44.

Ramos, H. (2006) 'What Causes Canadian Aboriginal Protest? Examining Resources, Opportunities and Identity, 1951–2000', *Canadian Journal of Sociology*, 31(2): 211–34.

Rawls, J. (1971) *A Theory of Justice: Revised Edition*. Cambridge, MA: Belknap Press of Harvard University Press.

Reding, V. (2010a) 'Statement by Viviane Reding, Vice-President of the European Commission and EU Commissioner for Justice, Fundamental Rights and Citizenship, on the Roma Situation in Europe', European Commission press release. Available at: https://ec.europa.eu/commission/presscorner/detail/en/MEMO_10_384 (accessed: 9 March 2020).

—— (2010b) 'Statement by Viviane Reding, Vice-President of the European Commission, EU Commissioner for Justice, Fundamental Rights and Citizenship, on the Recent Developments Concerning the Respect for EU Law as Regards the Situation of Roma in France', European Commission press release. Available at: https://ec.europa.eu/commission/presscorner/detail/en/MEMO_10_502 (accessed: 9 March 2020).

Regina v. Immigration Officer at Prague Airport and Another, ex parte European Roma Rights Centre and Others (2004) UKHL 55, United Kingdom: House of Lords (Judicial Committee), 9 December 2004. Available at: https://www.refworld.org/cases,GBR_HL,41c17ebf4.html (accessed: 3 December 2020).

Rigo, E. (2005) 'Citizenship at Europe's Borders: Some Reflections on the Post-Colonial Condition of Europe in the Context of EU Enlargement'. *Citizenship Studies*, 9(1): 3–22.

Roma Community in the Republic of Slovenia Act 2007 (Republic of Slovenia). Available at: http://www.pisrs.si/Pis.web/pregledPredpisa?id =ZAKO4405 (accessed: 14 September 2020).

Romea.cz (2010) 'Gypsy Rock against Sarkozy!' *Romea.cz*, 8 November. Available at: www.romea.cz/en/entertainment/gypsy-rock-against-sarkozy (accessed: 9 March 2020).

—— (2015) 'Slovak PM: We can't Integrate "our Own" Roma, to Say Nothing of Refugees', *Romea.cz*, 2 September. Available at: www.romea.cz/en/ news/world/slovak-pm-we-can-t-integrate-our-own-roma-to-say-nothing-of-refugees (accessed: 14 September 2020).

—— (2018) 'Slovakia Has 41 Romani Mayors – 39 Male and Two Female – a Record High', *Romea.cz*, 3 November. Available at: www.romea.cz/en/ news/world/slovakia-has-41-romani-mayors-39-male-and-two-female-a-record-high (accessed: 14 September 2020).

Rorke, B. (2020) *Orban Weighs in against Court Ruling and Calls for Justice for Segregationists*. ERRC, 10 January. Available at: http:// www.errc.org/news/orban-weighs-in-against-court-ruling-and-calls-for-justice-for-segregationists (accessed: 14 September 2020).

Rorke, B. and Szilvasi, M. (2017) 'Racism's Cruelest Cut: Coercive Sterilisation of Romani Women and their Fight for Justice in the Czech Republic (1966–2016)', *OpenDemocracy*, 24 January. Available at: www.opendemocracy.net/en/can-europe-make-it/racisms-cruelest-cut-coercive-sterilization-of-roman/ (accessed: 14 September 2020).

Rostas, I. (2012) *Ten Years After: A History of Roma School Desegregation in Central and Eastern Europe*. Budapest: Roma Education Fund.

—— (2019) *A Task for Sisyphus: Why Europe's Roma Policies Fail*. Budapest and New York: Central European University Press.

Rostas, I. and Kostka, J. (2014) 'Structural Dimensions of Roma School Desegregation Policies in Central and Eastern Europe', *European Educational Research Journal*, 13(3): 268–81.

Rövid, M. (2011a) 'Cosmopolitanism and Exclusion: On the Limits of Transnational Democracy in Light of the Case of Roma'. Unpublished PhD thesis, Central European University.

—— (2011b) 'One-Size-Fits-All Roma? On the Normative Dilemmas of the Emerging European Roma Policy', *Romani Studies*, 21(1): 1–22.

Rucker-Chang, S. (2018) 'Challenging Americanism and Europeanism: African-Americans and Roma in the American South and European Union "South"', *Journal of Transatlantic Studies*, 16(2): 181–99.

Rumelili, B. and Keyman, F. (2013) 'Enacting European Citizenship beyond the EU: Turkish Citizens and their European Political Practices'. In E. F. Isin and M. Saward (eds.) *Enacting European Citizenship*. Cambridge: Cambridge University Press, pp. 66–83.

S&D (2015) 'Until Robert Fico Shows he is a Progressive he does not Deserve Place in the Party of European Socialists', Socialists and Democrats, press release, 28 September. Available at: www.socialistsanddemocrats.eu/

newsroom/until-robert-fico-shows-he-progressive-he-does-not-deserve-place-party-european-socialists (accessed: 22 September 2020).

Sampani and Others v. Greece Application no. 59608/09 (ECtHR, 11 December 2012). Available at: https://hudoc.echr.coe.int/fre?i=001-115166 (accessed: 22 September 2020).

Sampanis and Others v. Greece Application no. 32526/05 (ECtHR, 5 June 2008). Available at: https://hudoc.echr.coe.int/eng-press#{%22ite mid%22:[%22003-2378798-2552166%22]} (accessed: 22 September 2020).

Sardelić, J. (2011) 'Constructing or Repositioning Roma in Postsocialist Slovenia and Croatia?' Unpublished master's thesis, Central European University.

—— (2012a) 'Constructing "New" Minorities: An Evaluation of Approaches to Minority Protection in Postsocialist Slovenia from the Perspective of Liberal Multiculturalism', *Treatises and Documents: Journal of Ethnic Studies*, 67: 100–22.

—— (2012b) 'Kulturne reprezentacije manjšin'. Unpublished PhD thesis, University of Ljubljana.

—— (2013a) 'The Roma Community Act in the Republic of Slovenia: Legal Implementation of Romani Non-Territorial Autonomy?' In E. Nimni, A. Osipov and D. Smith (eds.) *The Challenge of Non-Territorial Autonomy: Theory and Practice*. Oxford: Peter Lang, pp. 197–211.

—— (2013b) 'Romani Minorities on the Margins of Post-Yugoslav Citizenship Regimes', CITSEE Working Paper no. 2013/31. *SSRN*. DOI: https://doi.org/10.2139/ssrn.2388859.

—— (2015) 'Romani Minorities and Uneven Citizenship Access in the Post-Yugoslav Space', *Ethnopolitics*, 14(2): 159–79.

—— (2016) 'Roma between Ethnic Group and an "Underclass" as Portrayed through Media Discourses in Socialist Slovenia'. In R. Archer, I. Duda and P. Stubbs (eds.) *Social Inequalities and Discontent in Yugoslav Socialism*. London and New York: Routledge, pp. 95–111.

—— (2017a) 'From Temporary Protection to Transit Migration: Responses to Refugee Crises along the Western Balkan Route', *Robert Schuman Centre for Advanced Studies Global Governance Programme*, European University Institute. Available at: https://cadmus.eui.eu/handle/1814/47168.

—— (2017b) 'The Position and Agency of the "Irregularized": Romani Migrants as European Semi-Citizens', *Politics*, 37(3): 332–46.

—— (2017c) 'The Vulnerability of Roma Minorities to Statelessness in Europe'. *Minority Rights Group International*. Available at: https://stories.minorityrights.org/statelessness/chapter/the-vulnerability-of-roma-minorities-to-statelessness-in-europe/ (accessed: 15 December 2020).

—— (2018) 'In and Out from the European Margins: Reshuffling Mobilities and Legal Statuses of Romani Minorities between the Post-Yugoslav Space and the European Union', *Social Identities*, 24(4): 489–504.

—— (2019a) 'Differing Romani Mobilities? The Case of Cross-Border Migration of Roma Between Slovenia and Austria'. In T. Magazzini and

S. Piemontese (eds.) *Constructing Roma Migrants: European Narratives and Local Govern.* Cham: Springer, pp. 227–42.

—— (2019b) 'The Politics around Romani Migration: European and National Perspectives'. In S. M. Croucher, J. R. Caetano and E. A. Campbell (eds.) *The Routledge Companion to Migration, Communication, and Politics.* Abingdon and New York: Routledge, pp. 296–306.

—— (2019c) 'Roma in Times of Territorial Rescaling: An Inquiry into the Margins of European Citizenship', *Ethnopolitics*, 18(4): 325–39.

Sardelić, J. and McGarry, A. (2017) 'How the Refugee Crisis is Dealing Another Blow to Europe's Roma', *The Conversation*, 20 March. Available at: http://theconversation.com/how-the-refugee-crisis-is-dealing-another-blow-to-europes-roma-74000 (accessed: 22 September 2020).

Sawyer, C. and Blitz, B. K. (2011) *Statelessness in the European Union.* Cambridge: Cambridge University Press.

Scheppele, K. L. (2004) 'Constitutional Ethnography: An Introduction', *Law & Society Review*, 38(3): 389–406.

Schlager, E. (2017) 'Policy and Practice: A Case Study of U.S. Foreign Policy Regarding the Situation of Roma in Europe'. In J. Bhabha, A. Mirga and M. Matache (eds.) *Realizing Roma Rights.* Philadelphia: University of Pennsylvania Press, pp. 59–75.

Sejdić and Finci v. BIH Application nos. 27996/06 and 34836/06 (ECtHR, 22 December 2009). Available at: http://hudoc.echr.coe.int/app/conversion/pdf/?library=ECHR&id=001-96491&filename=001-96491.pdf&TID=igauxmghdq (accessed: 14 December 2020).

Sejmonov, A., Karzetskaja, J. and Ezhova, E. (2015) 'Ending Childhood Statelessness: A Study on Estonia', *European Network on Statelessness*. Available at: https://www.statelessness.eu/sites/www.statelessness.eu/files/Estonia_2.pdf (accessed: 22 September 2020).

Shachar, A., Bauböck, R., Bloemraad, I., and Vink, M. P. (eds.) (2017) *The Oxford Handbook of Citizenship.* Oxford: Oxford University Press.

Sharkey, A. and Shields, R. (2008) 'Abject Citizenship: Rethinking Exclusion and Inclusion: Participation, Criminality and Community at a Small Town Youth Centre', *Children's Geographies*, 6(3): 239–56.

Shaw, J. and Štiks, I., 2010. 'The Europeanisation of Citizenship in the Successor States of the Former Yugoslavia: An Introduction'. CITSEE Working Paper 2010/01, School of Law, University of Edinburgh. Available at: https://www.law.ed.ac.uk/sites/default/files/2020-02/178_theeuropeanisationofcitizenshipinthesuccessorstatesoftheformeryugoslaviaanintrod.pdf (accessed: 7 December 2020).

Shmidt, V. R. and Jaworsky, B. N. (2020) *Historicizing Roma in Central Europe: Between Critical Whiteness and Epistemic Injustice.* Abingdon and New York: Routledge.

Sigona, N. (2003) 'How can a "Nomad" Be a "Refugee"?', *Sociology*, 37(1): 69–79.

—— (2015) 'Everyday Statelessness in Italy: Status, Rights, and Camps', *Ethnic and Racial Studies*, 39(2): 263–79.

—— (2018) 'The Contested Politics of Naming in Europe's "Refugee Crisis"', *Ethnic and Racial Studies*, 41(3): 456–60.

Sigona, N. and Vermeersch, P. (2012) 'Editors' Introduction. The Roma in the New EU: Policies, Frames and Everyday Experiences', *Journal of Ethnic and Migration Studies*, 38(8): 1189–93.

Silverman, C. (2018) 'From Reflexivity to Collaboration', *Critical Romani Studies*, 1(2): 76–97.

Silverstein, P. (2008) 'Kabyle Immigrant Politics and Racialised Citizenship in France'. In D. Reed-Danahay and C. B. Brettel (eds.) *Citizenship, Political Engagement, and Belonging: Immigrants in Europe and the United States*. New Brunswick: Rogers University Press, pp. 23–42.

Simhandl, K. (2009) 'Beyond Boundaries? Comparing the Construction of the Political Categories "Gypsies" and "Roma" before and after EU Enlargement'. In N. Sigona and N. Trehan (eds.) *Romani Politics in Contemporary Europe: Poverty, Ethnic Mobilization, and the Neoliberal Order*. Basingstoke and New York: Palgrave Macmillan, pp. 72–92.

Šklová, J. and Miklušáková, M. (1998) 'Citizenship of Roma after the Split of Czechoslovakia: A Social Problem to be Faced by Other Multinational States', *European Journal of Social Work*, 1(2): 177–87.

Šlezak, H. (2009) 'Spatial Segregation of the Roma Population in Međimurje County', *Hrvatski geografski glasnik/Croatian Geographical Bulletin*, 71(2): 65–81.

Sokolová, V. (2008) *Cultural Politics of Ethnicity: Discourses on Roma in Communist Czechoslovakia*. Stuttgart: Ibidem.

Soysal, Y. N. (1997) *Limits of Citizenship: Migrants and Postnational Membership in Europe*. Chicago: University of Chicago Press.

Spivak, G. C. (1988) 'Can the Subaltern Speak?' In N. Cary and L. Grossberg (eds.) *Marxism and the Interpretation of Culture*. Basingstoke: Macmillan, pp. 271–313.

—— (2012) *An Aesthetic Education in the Era of Globalization*. Cambridge, MA: Harvard University Press.

Staples, K. (2012) *Retheorising Statelessness*. Edinburgh: Edinburgh University Press.

Stegman, E. and Phillips, V. F. (2014) 'Missing the Point – the Real Impact of Native Mascots and Team Names on American Indian and Alaska Native Youth', Center for American Progress, July. *SSRN*. Available at: https://papers.ssrn.com/sol3/papers.cfm?abstract_id=2472075 (accessed: 22 September 2020).

Stevens, J. (2017a) 'The Alien who is a Citizen'. In B. N. Lawrance and J. Stevens (eds.) *Citizenship in Question: Evidentiary Birthright and Statelessness*. Durham, NC, and London: Duke University Press, pp. 217–40.

—— (2017b) 'Introduction'. In B. N. Lawrance and J. Stevens (eds.) *Citizenship in Question: Evidentiary Birthright and Statelessness*, Durham, NC, and London: Duke University Press, pp. 1–24.

Stewart, M. (2002) 'Deprivation, the Roma and "the Underclass"'. In C. M. Hann (ed.) *Postsocialism: Ideals, Ideologies, and Practices in Eurasia*. London and New York: Routledge, pp. 133–55.

—— (ed.) (2012) *The Gypsy 'Menace': Populism and the New Anti-Gypsy Politics*. London: Hurst.

Stote, K. (2015) *An Act of Genocide: Colonialism and the Sterilization of Aboriginal Women*. Halifax: Fernwood Publishing.

Stout, K. (2019) 'Sterilization of Indigenous Women in Canada', *The Canadian Encyclopedia*. Available at: www.thecanadianencyclopedia.ca/en/article/sterilization-of-Indigenous-women-in-canada (accessed: 22 September 2020).

Stronger Futures in the Northern Territory Act 2012, (no. 100 Australia). Available at: https://www.legislation.gov.au/Details/C2012A00100/Controls/ (accessed: 22 September 2020).

Struhárová, B. (1999) 'Disparate Impact: Removing Roma from the Czech Republic', *European Roma Rights Centre*. Available at: www.errc.org/roma-rights-journal/disparate-impact-removing-roma-from-the-czech-republic (accessed: 6 March 2020).

Stupp, C. (2017) 'Commission to Review Funds for Anti-Roma Discrimination', *Euractiv*, 30 August. Available at: www.euractiv.com/section/eu-priorities-2020/news/commission-to-review-funds-for-anti-roma-discrimination/ (accessed: 6 March 2020).

Surdu, M. (2017) *Those Who Count: Expert Practices of Roma Classification*. Budapest: Central European University Press.

Swider, K. (2017) 'Why End Statelessness?' In T. Bloom, K. Tonkiss and P. Cole (eds.) *Understanding Statelessness*. London and New York: Routledge, pp. 191–210.

Szalai, J. and Schiff, C. (2014) *Migrant, Roma and Post-Colonial Youth in Education across Europe: Being 'Visibly Different'*. Houndmills, Basingstoke: Palgrave Macmillan.

Takacs, B. (2017) 'Māori and Romani and Juvenile Justice – Approaches and Responses from Different Justice Systems'. Unpublished PhD thesis, Auckland University of Technology.

Tas, Latif (2017) 'The Influence of Diaspora Politics on Conflict and Peace: Transnational Activism of Stateless Kurds'. In David Cament and Ariane Sadjed (eds.) *Diaspora as Cultures of Cooperation*. Basingstoke: Palgrave Macmillan, pp. 171–98.

Taylor, A., Tátrai, P. and Erőss, A. (2018) 'Visible Minorities in Remote Areas: A Comparative Study of Roma in Hungary and Indigenous People in Australia', *Hungarian Geographical Bulletin*, 67(1): 43–60.

Taylor, C. (1994) *Multiculturalism: Examining the Politics of Recognition*. Edited by Amy Gutmann. Princeton, NJ: Princeton University Press.

Telegram (2019) 'Ljudi u Čakovcu prosvjedovali protiv Roma; okupilo ih se oko 1000, u jednom trenu došlo je i do malog sukoba', *Telegram*, June. Available at: www.telegram.hr/politika-kriminal/ljudi-u-cakovcuprosvjeduju-protiv-roma-okupilo-se-oko-200-ljudi-u-jednom-trenu-je-doslo-i-do-malog-sukoba/ (accessed: 20 September 2020).

Tonkiss, K. (2018) 'The Windrush Scandal and the Incoherence of Liberal Exclusion', *Discover Society*, June. Available at: https://discoversociety.org/2018/06/05/the-windrush-scandal-and-the-incoherence-of-liberal-exclusion/ (accessed: 7 December 2020).

Tonkiss, K. and Bloom, T. (2015) 'Theorising Noncitizenship: Concepts, Debates and Challenges', *Citizenship Studies*, 19(8): 837–52.

Torres-Ríos, N. (2018) 'Limitations of the Jones Act: Racialised Citizenship and Territorial Status', *Rutgers Race and the Law Review*, 19(1): 1–24.

The Treaty of Lisbon 2009. Available at: https://eur-lex.europa.eu/legal-content/EN/TXT/?uri=LEGISSUM%3Aai0033 (accessed: 22 September 2020).

The Treaty of Rome 1957. Available at: https://eur-lex.europa.eu/legal-content/EN/TXT/?uri=LEGISSUM%3Axy0023 (accessed: 22 September 2020).

Trehan, N. and Kóczé, A. (2009) 'Racism, (Neo-)Colonialism and Social Justice: The Struggle for the Soul of the Romani Movement in Postsocialist Europe'. In G. Huggan and I. Law (eds.) *Racism Postcolonialism Europe*. Liverpool: Liverpool University Press, pp. 50–73.

Tremlett, A. (2013) '"Here Are the Gypsies!" The Importance of Self-Representations and How to Question Prominent Images of Gypsy Minorities', *Ethnic and Racial Studies*, 36(11): 1706–25.

—— (2014) 'Making a Difference without Creating a Difference: Super-Diversity as a New Direction for Research on Roma Minorities', *Ethnicities*, 14(6): 830–48.

Tuhiwai Smith, Linda (2012) *Decolonizing Methodologies: Research and Indigenous Peoples*. London: Zed.

UN (United Nations) (1969) International Convention on the Elimination of All Forms of Racial Discrimination OHCHR. Available at: https://www.ohchr.org/en/professionalinterest/pages/cerd.aspx (accessed: 26 November 2020).

—— (2013) *The Role of the United Nations in Advancing Roma Inclusion*. Available at: https://europe.ohchr.org/Documents/Publications/RomaInclusion.pdf (accessed: 22 September 2020).

United Nations Development Programme (2019) *2019 Human Development Index Ranking*. Available at: http://hdr.undp.org/en/content/2019-human-development-index-ranking (accessed: 14 December 2020).

UNHCR (United Nations High Commissioner for Refugees) (1954) *Convention Relation to the Status of Stateless Persons*. Available at: https://www.unhcr.org/ibelong/wp-content/uploads/1954-Convention-relating-to-the-Status-of-Stateless-Persons_ENG.pdf (accessed: 7 December 2020).

—— (2010) *Expert Meeting: The Concept of Stateless Persons under International Law ('Prato Conclusions')*. Available at: www.refworld.org/docid/4ca1ae002.html (accessed: 7 December 2020).

—— (2011) *Report on Statelessness in South Eastern Europe UNHCR Offices in Bosnia & Herzegovina, Croatia, Former Yugoslav Republic* of Macedonia, Montenegro, Serbia (and Kosovo: SCR 1244) – Bureau for Europe*. Available at: https://www.refworld.org/pdfid/514d715f2.pdf (accessed: 22 September 2020).

—— (2014a) *Global Action Plan to End Statelessness 2014–2024*. Available at: https://www.refworld.org/docid/545b47d64.html (accessed: 22 September 2020).

—— (2014b) *Handbook on Protection of Stateless Persons*. Available at: https://www.unhcr.org/dach/wp-content/uploads/sites/27/2017/04/CH-UNHCR_Handbook-on-Protection-of-Stateless-Persons.pdf (accessed: 15 December 2020).

—— (2015) *I Am Here, I Belong: The Urgent Need to End Childhood Statelessness*. Available at: www.unhcr.org/ibelong/wp-content/uploads/2015-10-StatelessReport_ENG16.pdf (accessed: 17 December 2020).

—— (2016) *Mapping Statelessness in Estonia*. Available at: www.refworld.org/pdfid/5a338b5c4.pdf (accessed: 7 December 2020).

—— (2017a) *Global Trends: Forced Displacement 2016*. Available at: https://www.unhcr.org/5943e8a34.pdf (accessed: 17 December 2020).

—— (2017b) 'Stateless Minorities: Ethnic Minorities of the Former Yugoslav Republic of Macedonia'. Video, *YouTube*. Available at: www.youtube.com/watch?v=hsfzOVfO3M4&t=104s (accessed: 22 September 2020).

—— (2017c) *'This is Our Home': Stateless Minorities in the Search of Citizenship*. Available at: https://www.unhcr.org/ibelong/wp-content/uploads/UNHCR_EN2_2017IBELONG_Report_ePub.pdf (accessed: 17 December 2020).

—— (2018a) *Global Trends: Forced Displacement in 2017*. Available at: https://reliefweb.int/report/world/global-trends-forced-displacement-2017 (accessed: 7 December 2020).

—— (2018b) *UNHCR Submission on Montenegro: 29th UPR Session*. Available at: www.refworld.org/country,,,,MNE,,5b0819d54,0.html (accessed: 7 December 2020).

—— (2020) *Ending Statelessness*. Available at: https://www.unhcr.org/ending-statelessness.html (accessed: 17 December 2020).

UNICEF (United Nations Children's Fund (2017) *Roma Children*. Available at: www.unicef.org/bih/en/roma-children (accessed: 22 September 2020).

United Nations Declaration on the Rights of Indigenous Peoples (2007) Available at: https://www.un.org/development/desa/indigenouspeoples/wp-content/uploads/sites/19/2018/11/UNDRIP_E_web.pdf (accessed: 22 September 2020).

Universal Declaration of Human Rights 1948. Available at: https://www.un.org/en/universal-declaration-human-rights/ (accessed: 22 September 2020).

Vajda, V. (2015) 'Towards "Critical Whiteness" in Romani Studies', *Roma Rights*, 2: 47–56. Available at: http://www.errc.org/roma-rights-journal/roma-rights-2–2015-nothing-about-us-without-us-roma-participation-in-policy-making-and-knowledge-production (accessed: 22 September 2020).

van Baar, H. (2011) 'Europe's Romaphobia: Problematization, Securitization, Nomadization', *Environment and Planning D: Society and Space*, 29(2): 203–12.

—— (2015) 'The Perpetual Mobile Machine of Forced Mobility: Europe's Roma and the Institutionalization of Rootlessness'. In J. de Blois, R. Celikates and Y. Jansen (eds.) *The Irregularization of Migration in Contemporary Europe: Detention, Deportation, Drowning*. London: Rowman & Littlefield International, pp. 71–86.

—— (2016) 'Evictability and the Biopolitical Bordering of Europe', *Antipode*, 49(1): 212–30.

—— (2017) 'Boundary Practices of Citizenship: Europe's Roma at the Securitization and Citizenship Nexus'. In R. G. Gonzales and N. Sigona (eds.) *Within and beyond Citizenship Borders, Membership and Belonging*. London and New York: Routledge, pp. 143–58.

—— (2019) 'From "Lagging Behind" to "Being Beneath"? The De-Developmentalization of Time and Social Order in Contemporary Europe'. In H. van Baar, A. Ivasiuc and R. Kreide (eds.) *The Securitization of the Roma in Europe*. Cham: Palgrave Macmillan, pp. 159–82.

Van Baar, H. and A. Kóczé (2020) *The Roma and their Struggle for Identity in Contemporary Europe*. New York: Berghahn.

Van Baar. H. and Vermeersch, P. (2018) 'The Limits of Operational Representations: Ways of Seeing Roma beyond the Recognition-Redistribution Paradigm', *Intersections*, 3(4): 120–39.

Van Den Bogaert, S. (2018) *Segregation of Roma Children in Education: Addressing Structural Discrimination through the Framework Convention for the Protection of National Minorities and the Racial Equality Directive 2000/43/EC*. Leiden: Brill.

Van de Port, M. (1998) *Gypsies, Wars and Other Instances of the Wild: Civilisation and its Discontents in a Serbian Town*. Amsterdam: Amsterdam University Press.

Van Waas, L. and De Chickera, A. (2017) 'Unpacking Statelessness'. In: T. Bloom, K. Tonkiss and P. Cole (eds.) *Understanding Statelessness*. London and New York: Routledge, pp. 53–69.

Vatican News (2019) 'Pope: Real Second Class Citizens are Those who Discard Others', *Vatican News*, 9 May. Available at: www.vaticannews.va/en/pope/news/2019–05/pope-francis-roma-sinti-prayer-meeting.html (accessed: 22 September 2020).

Venice Commission (2008) *European Commission for Democracy through Law (Venice Commission) Report on Dual Voting for Persons Belonging to National Minorities*. Available at: www.venice.coe.int/webforms/documents/default.aspx?pdffile=CDL-AD(2008)013-e (accessed: 22 September 2020).

Vermeersch, P. (2003) 'EU Enlargement and Minority Rights Policies in Central Europe: Explaining Policy Shifts in the Czech Republic, Hungary and Poland', *Journal on Ethnopolitics and Minority Issues in Europe*, 1(1): 1–31.

—— (2005) 'Marginality, Advocacy, and the Ambiguities of Multiculturalism: Notes on Romani Activism in Central Europe', *Identities: Global Studies in Culture and Power*, 12(4): 451–78.

—— (2006) *The Romani Movement: Minority Politics and Ethnic Mobilization in Contemporary Central Europe*. Oxford: Berghahn Books.

—— (2012) 'Reframing the Roma: EU Initiatives and the Politics of Reinterpretation', *Journal of Ethnic and Migration Studies*, 38(8): 1195–212.

—— (2014) 'The Romani Perspective: Experiences and Acts of Citizenship Across Europe'. In E. F. Isin and P. Nyers (eds.) *Routledge Handbook of Global Citizenship Studies*. London and New York: Routledge, pp. 477–86.

—— (2017) 'The Plight of Eastern Europe's Roma'. In A. Fagan and P. Kopecky (eds.) *The Routledge Handbook of East European Politics*. New York: Routledge, pp. 225–36.

Vidmar Horvat, K., Samardžija, M. and Sardelić, J. (2008) 'Balancing the Roma Voice: The Ambrus Drama and Media Construction of Intercultural Dialogue in Slovenia'. In K. Vidmar Horvat (ed.) *The Future of Intercultural Dialogue in Europe: Views from the In-Between*. Ljubljana: Filozofska Fakulteta, pp. 153–72.

Vidra, Z. and Fox, J. (2014) 'Mainstreaming of Racist Anti-Roma Discourses in the Media in Hungary', *Journal of Immigrant & Refugee Studies*, 12(4): 437–55.

Vlasić, B. (2019) 'Božinović je u pravu, Romi su se sami diskvalificirali iz života', *Jutarnji*, 5 June. Available at: www.jutarnji.hr/komentari/bozinovic-je-u-pravu-romi-su-se-sami-diskvalificirali-iz-zivota/8966792/ (accessed: 22 September 2020).

Vlieks C. (2017) 'Context of Statelessness: The Concepts "Statelessness *in situ*" and "Statelessness in Migratory Context"'. In T. Bloom, K. Tonkiss and P. Cole (eds.) *Understanding Statelessness*. London and New York: Routledge, pp. 35–52.

Vrăbiescu, I. and Kalir, B. (2018) 'Care-Full Failure: How Auxiliary Assistance to Poor Roma Migrant Women in Spain Compounds Marginalization', *Social Identities*, 24(4): 520–2.

Walter, M. (2014) 'Indigeneity and Citizenship in Australia'. In E. F. Isin and P. Nyers (eds.) *Routledge Handbook of Global Citizenship Studies*. London and New York: Routledge, pp. 557–67.

Washington Football Team (2020) 'Statement from the Washington Football Team', 3 July. Available at: www.washingtonfootball.com/news/washington-redskins-retiring-name-logo-following-review (accessed: 7 December 2020).

Watson, N. (2011) 'The Northern Territory Emergency Response: Has it Really Improved the Lives of Aboriginal Women and Children?' *Australian Feminist Law Journal*, 35(1): 147–63.

Weissbrodt, D. (2008). *The Human Rights of Non-Citizens*. Oxford: Oxford University Press.

Wekker, G. (2016) *White Innocence: Paradoxes of Colonialism and Race.* Durham, NC, and London: Duke University Press.

Wheeler, S. and Thomas, P. A. (2000) 'Socio-Legal Studies'. In D. Hayton (ed.) *Law's Future(s).* Oxford: Hart, pp. 267–80.

Wild, R. and Anderson, P. (2007) *Little Children are Sacred: Report of the Northern Territory Board of Inquiry into the Protection of Aboriginal Children from Sexual Abuse 2007.* Available at: https://web.archive.org/web/20070703014641/http://www.nt.gov.au/dcm/inquirysaac/pdf/bipacsa_final_report.pdf (accessed: 22 September 2020).

Willems, W. (1997) *In Search of the True Gypsy: From Enlightenment to Final Solution.* New York: Routledge.

Yildiz, C. and De Genova, N. (2018) 'Un/Free mobility: Roma Migrants in the European Union', *Social Identities*, 24(4): 425–41. DOI: https://doi.org/10.1080/13504630.2017.1335819.

Young, I. M. (1989) 'Polity and Group Difference: A Critique of the Ideal of Universal Citizenship', *Ethics*, 99(2): 250–74.

Yuval-Davis, N. (1997) *Gender and Nation.* London: Sage.

—— (2011) *The Politics of Belonging: Intersectional Contestations.* London: Sage.

Yuval-Davis, N., Wemyss, G. and Cassidy, K. (2017) 'Everyday Bordering, Belonging and the Reorientation of British Immigration Legislation', *Sociology*, 52(2): 228–44. DOI: https://doi.org/10.1177/0038038517702599.

Index

EU authorised representative for GPSR:
Easy Access System Europe, Mustamäe tee 50,
10621 Tallinn, Estonia
gpsr.requests@easproject.com

www.ingramcontent.com/pod-product-compliance
Lightning Source LLC
Chambersburg PA
CBHW070844300326
41935CB00039B/1445